THE.
Music Producer's
HANDBOOK

Second Edition

To access online media visit:
www.halleonard.com/mylibrary

Enter Code:

5457-7143-9827-6632

THE Music Producer's HANDBOOK

music **PRO** guides

THE
Music Producer's
HANDBOOK

Second Edition

Bobby Owsinski

Hal Leonard Books
An Imprint of Hal Leonard Corporation

Second edition published in 2016 by Hal Leonard Books

An Imprint of Hal Leonard Corporation
7777 West Bluemound Road
Milwaukee, WI 53213

Trade Book Division Editorial Offices
33 Plymouth St., Montclair, NJ 07042

First edition published in 2010 by Hal Leonard Books

All illustrations by Bobby Owsinski except the following: 7-3 from Snark Tuners; 10-10 from Hear Technologies; 10-11 from Vic Firth Company; 10-12 from Beyerdynamic Inc. USA

Printed in the United States of America

Book design by John J. Flannery

Library of Congress Cataloging-in-Publication Data

Names: Owsinski, Bobby.
Title: The music producer's handbook / Bobby Owsinski.
Description: Second edition. | Milwaukee, WI : Hal Leonard Books, 2016. |
 Includes bibliographical references and index.
Identifiers: LCCN 2015048785 | ISBN 9781495045226 (pbk.)
Subjects: LCSH: Sound recordings–Production and direction. | Popular
 music–Production and direction.
Classification: LCC ML3790 .O969 2016 | DDC 781.49023–dc23
LC record available at http://lccn.loc.gov/2015048785

ISBN 978-1-4950-4522-6

www.halleonardbooks.com

CONTENTS

INTRODUCTION xiii
Meet the Producers..xvi
Bobby Owsinski Bibliography...xvii
Bobby Owsinski's Lynda.com Video Courses xx
Bobby Owsinski's Online Coaching Courses xxi
Bobby Owsinski's Social Media Connections...........................xxi

PART 1. MUSIC PRODUCTION..1

Chapter 1. THE HISTORY OF MUSIC PRODUCTION 3
The Early Label Era 3
The Mature Music Era..4
The Independent Era..4
Game-Changing Producers 5
    The Pioneers..6
    The Trailblazers 8
    The Innovators 10
    The Trendsetters 10
    The Hybrids 12

Chapter 2. WHAT IS A MUSIC PRODUCER? 15
Different Types of Music Production 17
How to Become a Producer 18
    The Musician/Producer 18
    The Engineer/Producer..20
    The DJ/Producer 20
    And the Other Way 21
    You Still Need a Client 21
What Are the Responsibilities?...22
Who Do You Work for: Artist or Label? 23

Chapter 3. THE DUTIES OF A MUSIC PRODUCER 25

Project Management 26

    Managing Time 26

    Managing Rentals 28

    Managing People 31

Creative 31

Financial 31

Political 31

Chapter 4. THE BUSINESS OF MUSIC PRODUCTION 33

What's My Deal? 33

    The Basic Deal 33

    The Deal of the Past 34

    Who's Paying 35

The New Music Economy 36

    Payments from Digital Music 37

    The Producer's Piece Gets Smaller 39

When a Label Isn't Involved 40

Chapter 5. ASSEMBLING THE BUDGET 43

When a Label Is Involved 43

    Typical Label Budgets 45

    A Label Budget Example 45

An Indie Band Budget 49

Using Union Musicians 52

    Additional Fees 53

    Hiring Union Musicians 54

    Union Versus Non-Union Players 55

The Recording Fund 55

A Final Word on Budget 57

Chapter 6. IT'S ALL IN THE SONG 59

Let's Discuss Your Songs 59

    Dynamics on Records 63

Arrangements Are the Key 64

    Arrangement Elements 64

    Sonic Arrangements 69

    Clash of the Guitar Players 69

Rules for Arrangements 71

Chapter 7. MUSIC MECHANICS 73

Dynamics 73

How to Learn to Play Dynamically 75

Don't Confuse Volume Level with Intensity 76

Builds 77

Play Together and Listen to Each Other 77

Timing Is Everything 78

Song Starts and Stops 78

Accents 79

The Groove and the Pocket 79

How to Find the Pocket 80

Attacks and Releases 81

Turnarounds 82

Tempo 82

Faster Does Not Create More Excitement 83

A Click Can Help 83

Play in Tune 84

Developing Studio Ears and Eyes 86

Studio Eyes 86

Chapter 8. PREPRODUCTION: THE MOST IMPORTANT STEP 87

Getting to Know You 87

Selecting the Songs 88

Preproduction Rehearsals 89

You Gotta Hear Yourself 89

Practice in the Round 90

A Few Rehearsal Tips 90

Preproduction Demos 90

How Long Should Preproduction Take? 91

It's the Little Things That Count 93

Chapter 9. PREPARING FOR THE SESSION 95

Initial Decisions 95

Selecting a Studio 99

The Assistant Engineer 101

Chapter 10. BASIC TRACKS: WHERE THE MAGIC IS MADE 103

What Are Basic Tracks? 104

Setup Day 105

How Long Are the Sessions? 105
Getting Sounds 106
   Choose the Best Instruments 106
   Different Gear for Different Jobs 108
   Well-Maintained Equipment Required 108
   Is Vintage Gear Necessary? 109
Recording the Drums: The Song's Heartbeat 116
   The Keys to a Great-Sounding Drum Kit 117
   Drum Tuning Tips 117
The Headphone Mix 118
   Personal Headphone Mixes 118
   Recording Without Headphones 119
To Click or Not to Click 120
   Making the Click Cut Through the Mix 120
   Preventing Click Bleed 121
   When a Click Won't Work 122
Leakage Is Your Friend 122
The Scratch Vocal 123
Don't Forget to Record a Tuning Note 124
Don't Forget to Record a Count-Off 124
Whether to Use Session Musicians or the Band 125
Listening to Playbacks 125
Session Breaks 126
   Dinner Breaks 126
How Do You Know When You're Finished Recording? 126

Chapter 11. OVERDUBS 129
The Recording Plan 129
Make It Better, Not Different 130
Time to Experiment 131
When Artistic Block Hits 131
Limit the Attendees 133
Recording in the Control Room 133
   Vocals in the Control Room 134
Overdubbing Techniques 134
   Use the Big Part of the Studio 134
   Vocal Doubling 135
   Vocal Stacking 136

Instrument Doubling or Stacking...136
Vocal Comping...136
Tips for Comping 137
Track Editing 139
Timing Mistakes...139
Editing Time 140

Chapter 12. WORKING WITH YOUR TEAM...143
Be a Professional 143
The Importance of Diplomacy 145
Steps in Resolving a Conflict..145
Getting the Best out of Musicians 146
Getting the Best out of Singers 148
The Three Ps: Pitch, Pocket, and Passion 149
Background Vocals Need Attention Too 151
Harmony Vocals Take More Time 152
Working with the Engineer 153
Working with the Artist 154

Chapter 13. SELF-PRODUCTION..157
Overcoming the Self-Production Blues 157
Two Key Production Concepts...158
Small Studio Production 161
Pros and Cons of Mixing on Headphones 164

Chapter 14. MIXING: WHERE IT'S MAKE IT OR BREAK IT 167
The Mechanics of Mixing 167
Hearing the Final Product 168
Tall, Deep, and Wide 168
The Keys to a Great Mix 171
Find the Direction of the Song 171
Develop the Groove and Build It Like a House 172
Find the Most Important Element and Emphasize It................................172
The Master Mix...173
Competitive Level..173
Mixing with Mastering in Mind 174
Mixing in the Box..176
The Mixing Engineer's Style..176

How Much Should Mixing Cost?...177
How Long Should Mixing Take?..177
Alternative Mixes...179

Chapter 15. MASTERING: THE FINISHING TOUCH..181
What Is Mastering?...181
Why Is Mastering So Important?..182
    The Reason Why a Pro Makes It Sound So Good...183
    Experience Is the Key...184
    The Mastering Engineer's Sound..184
    The Mastering Engineer as a Security Blanket..185
How Long Should Mastering Take?..185
How Much Should Mastering Cost?..185
Preparation for Mastering..186
Competitive Level, Take Two...188
Hypercompression: Don't Go There!..188
Should You Use a Pro or Master at Home?..190
Mastering for Different Delivery Formats...191
    The Source File...191
Creating Files for Streaming Services...192
    Submitting to Online Stores and Services...193
Exporting for iTunes...194
    Submitting to the iTunes Store...194
    The "Mastered for iTunes" Format..195

Chapter 16. EDM, POP, AND HIP-HOP PRODUCTION..197
How EDM Is Changing Music..197
    Coming from a Different Place..199
    A Look at the New Song Structure..199
    The Modern Pop Formula..200
Fifteen Tips for Developing Your Own Sound...201

Chapter 17. PRODUCTION CHECKLISTS..205
Producer Checklist...205
    Getting Paid...205
    Assembling the Budget...206
Preproduction..207
    Questions for the Artist or Band...207
    Song Analysis...207

Song Arrangements 207

Rehearsal Guide 208

Preparing for the Session 208

Selecting a Studio 208

Production 209

Basic Tracks 209

Music Troubleshooting 210

Overdubs 211

Vocal Recordings 212

Mixing 213

Mastering 214

PART 2. INTERVIEWS 215

Mark Bright.. 217

Joe Chiccarelli 227

Richard Feldman... 235

Gareth Jones 243

Mark Plati 251

Carmen Rizzo 257

StoneBridge 265

GLOSSARY... 271

INDEX... 275

INTRODUCTION

For as long as I can remember, I've wanted to be a record producer. Back in my gigging days in the 1970s, I was fascinated by records and pretty baffled as to why the music on them sounded so good, since my bands at the time couldn't always capture the essence that a hit record had. You couldn't always hear into the nuances of a well-produced production back then, especially given the audio quality of the record and cassette players of the era.

Only after a Dokorder 4-track tape recorder became part of my musical arsenal did I begin to appreciate the mechanics of production, as I discovered techniques like doubling vocals, placing mics strategically, track bouncing to open up new tracks for overdubs, and stacking harmonies. But when my band finally signed with the Polygram subsidiary De-Lite and I got to work in a real 24-track studio with a real producer and engineer, I was hooked on recordmaking. We ended up making a thoroughly unremarkable record (one that I still refuse to play for people), but the experience led me to Berklee College of Music to bolster my musical chops in preparation for a production career.

Berklee had a pro studio with an MCI console (which was a hot piece of hardware at the time), and I spent as much time as I could learning everything I could about it, including some of the more esoteric and obscure functions that only get used once or twice in a recording lifetime. Before I knew it, I was Berklee's newest instructor, thanks to my prior recording experience and the knowledge I had gained from studying everything I could on the subject since my early teens (which wasn't all that much at the time, but it was more than anyone else in the school had).

From that point on, my whole life was built around that studio day and night, and I saw just about every kind of session you could think of, involving every kind of music. But after overhearing the fateful words of a frustrated instructor in the teacher's lounge ("This place is for rookies and has-beens!"), I abruptly came to the realization that Berklee was not the real world, so off to Los Angeles I went. Why L.A.? It was warmer than New York, London, or Nashville—the only other recordmaking centers that were an option.

Living in L.A. started me on a 20-year run of producing music for just about every kind of outlet you could think of: from mouthwash commercials to long-forgotten television shows to B and C movies, and to bands and artists in all shapes, sizes, and genres.

Many of these sessions took place in some of the best studios money could buy, and many were in some of the worst. Some of the work was for major entertainment companies and labels like ABC, Columbia Records, Warner Brothers, and Fox, while other work was for smaller entities long since gone or gobbled up by a conglomerate. Still other jobs were done totally on spec or even produced with money out of my own pocket (unfortunately, as is usually the case, none of those were ever hits).

For a few years I worked as a staff producer for the now-defunct Shattered Music, which lead me to produce a series of acclaimed blues records by ex–Rolling Stone Mick Taylor, Duane Allman protégé Gerry Groom, "The Legend" Joe Houston, guitar-slinger L.A. Jones, and even the famed bluesman Willie Dixon (I produced his last published song). You don't make too much money making blues records, but I learned a lot about being in the here and now, since most blues players don't much care for multiple takes. ("Why should I try it again? I already did it once!")

In later years I became one of the first producer-engineers to delve into 5.1 surround sound, working on DVDs for a whole slew of major artists including Jimi Hendrix (posthumously, of course), The Who, Iron Maiden, Neil Young, Christopher Cross, Willie Nelson, the Ramones, and many more. Producing the music on the DVDs also opened up doors for other content as I expanded into producing interviews for the DVD extras, which eventually opened up a new opportunity as executive producer on the television shows *Desert Island Music* and *Guitar Universe*.

Although television is fun, my passion is still music, so I'm now back behind the glass again, and I'm happy to say that as of the writing of this book, an album I produced and mixed sits at #2 on the *Billboard* Blues chart (Adrianna Marie and Her Bluescutters' "Double Crossing Blues"), and a single that I recorded and mixed for the band SNEW reached #5 on the iTunes Rock charts.

The point of my brief personal history lesson is that a producer is always learning new skills, and those skills are transferable across different types of productions, genres of music, and even parts of the entertainment business. Good producers are always organized, in control, and decisive in their actions. They're able to help realize the vision for the artist, A&R person, studio or network head, or just about anyone else who requires their services. They must be a leader, a diplomat, a therapist, an artist, and a craftsperson all in one.

Which brings me to the difference between an art and a craft. Here's a little rule that I've always lived by:

> **Art is something you do for yourself.**
> **A craft is something you do for everyone else.**

Unless you're the artist and are producing yourself (not an easy task, but something we'll cover later in this book), always remember that what a producer does is totally for the sake of the artist. The producer's job is to help realize the musician's artistic vision, and that's a craft. The art of production comes in the way you do it!

There have been other books written about production, and many of them are really good. Some focus on one aspect of the profession more than others, and so does this one, to some degree (although I tried to keep it pretty well balanced).

One thing that a beginning music producer comes up against is the "Why doesn't this sound right?" problem. Musically things don't seem to gel, or they're not as tight as they need to be before or during recording. What's the problem? That's what I've tried to zero in on in this book. I want to give you the ability to solve all those musical problems that inevitably arise with any production, regardless of how skilled the players are.

Just to be clear, determining why a song or a section of a song isn't cutting it is a skill that almost every successful music producer develops to some degree. The only difference is that the ones who are the most successful don't have time to write about it, and most everyone else hasn't thought about it enough to articulate it.

That's one of the things I feel I'm good at, though. After writing 22 other books (see the bibliography at the end of the chapter) about music, recording, and technology, I like to think that I can explain a difficult, sometimes nebulous topic with enough clarity that anyone interested can grasp it. Hopefully this book will do just that. Either way, email me at bobby@bobbyowsinski.com to let me know what you think. You might also want to follow my daily music production blog (at bobbyowsinski.blogspot.com) as well.

MEET THE PRODUCERS

As with most of my books, this book is made possible by its interviews with pros who are a lot smarter and wiser than I am. Here's a list of contributors to *The Music Producer's Handbook*, all of whose wisdom we could not have done without. The full interviews included at the end of the book are as entertaining and enjoyable as they are insightful.

Mark Bright. Enjoying a hit record with his very first production of Blackhawk in 1994, Mark Bright has gone on to become one of the architects of the modern contemporary country sound, with production credits on hugely successful albums by superstar acts Rascal Flatts, Carrie Underwood, and Reba McEntire.

Richard Feldman. Although featured in my *Music 4.0* book for his chops as a music publisher with his Artist First Music as well as being a past president of the American Independent Music Publishers association, Richard Feldman has an equally rich history in reggae music production, with credits of amazing reggae music stars like Andrew Tosh, Joe Higgs, Junior Reid, the Congos, I Threes, and the Wailing Souls. He also won a Grammy award for his 2005 production of the legendary Toots and the Maytals' *True Love*. While his non-Jamaican credits are formidable, producing artists like Keith Richards, Ben Harper, Willie Nelson, No Doubt, Eric Clapton, Bonnie Raitt, and many more, it's the reggae connection that truly makes Richard unique.

Gareth Jones. Starting his career as an engineer and mixer, Gareth Jones soon made the transition up the ladder as a coproducer with superstar band Depeche Mode. While producing such eclectic acts as Erasure, Can, Madness, Devo, Tackhead, and Nick Cave and the Bad Seeds, among many others, Jones's high-tech, no-nonsense production approach has won him acclaim and admiration from all corners of the industry.

Carmen Rizzo. Two-time Grammy Award nominee, electronic musician, and underground darling Carmen Rizzo has parlayed his technical and computer acumen into numerous credits as a producer, mixer, remixer, musician, and cowriter for a wide range of influential artists including Seal, Coldplay, Alanis Morissette, Paul Oakenfold, BT, Tiesto,

Jem, Esthero, Ryuichi Sakamoto, Cirque du Soleil, KD Lang, and Pete Townshend of The Who. Based in Los Angeles, Rizzo knows the electronic-music realm as well as anyone, and was kind enough to impart his considerable insight about the world of production for this book.

Mark Plati. Based in New York City, the versatile Mark Plati learned production the old-fashioned way, starting first as a musician and songwriter, and then later as an engineer. With a long list of diverse credits that range from a host of eclectic unsigned acts to David Bowie, The Cure, Robbie Williams, and Natalie Imbruglia, among many others.

StoneBridge. Noted for his hit remixes for Sophie Ellis-Bextor, Ayumi Hamasaki, Britney Spears, and Ne-Yo, StoneBridge has been nominated for a Grammy Award and has received the prestigious BMI Songwriter of the Year award for his contribution to Jason Derulo's "Don't Wanna Go Home." Stone also has a weekly show on Sirius XM/BPM called *#bpmMix*, and tours worldwide as a DJ with recent shows in Las Vegas, New York, Sydney, Jakarta, Stockholm, and Dubai.

Not everyone is cut out to be a producer, because it's just as much about temperament, personality, diplomacy, organization, and fiscal responsibility as it is about the music and technicalities. While this book can't provide those intangible elements that only you can furnish, it can indeed be a guide to help any size and type of project you produce be a success. Good luck!

BOBBY OWSINSKI BIBLIOGRAPHY

The Mixing Engineer's Handbook, 3rd Edition (ISBN 128542087X, Thomson Course Technology): The premier book on audio mixing techniques provides all the information needed to take your mixing skills to the next level, along with advice from the world's best mixing engineers.

The Recording Engineer's Handbook, 3rd Edition (ISBN 1285442016, Course Technology PTR): Revealing the microphone and recording techniques used by some of the most renowned recording engineers, you'll find everything you need to know to lay down great tracks in any recording situation, in any musical genre, and in any studio.

The Mastering Engineer's Handbook, 3rd Edition (ISBN 1305116682, Course Technology PTR): Everything you always wanted to know about mastering, from doing it yourself to using a major facility, utilizing insights from the world's top mastering engineers.

The Drum Recording Handbook, 2nd edition with DVD [with Dennis Moody] (ISBN 1495045242, Hal Leonard): Uncovers the secret of making amazing drum recordings in your own recording studio even with the inexpensive gear. It's all in the technique, and this book/DVD will show you how.

How to Make Your Band Sound Great with DVD (ISBN 1423441907, Hal Leonard): This band improvement book and DVD shows your band how to play to its fullest potential. It doesn't matter what kind of music you play, what your skill level is, or if you play covers or your own music, this book will make you tight, it will make you more dynamic, it will improve your show, and it will improve your recordings.

The Studio Musician's Handbook with DVD [with Paul Ill] (ISBN 1423463412, Hal Leonard): Everything you wanted to know about the world of the studio musician including how to become a studio musician, who hires you, how much you get paid, the gear you must have, the proper session etiquette required to make a session run smoothly, and how to apply these skills in every type of recording session regardless if it's in your home studio or at Abbey Road.

Music 4.1: A Survival Guide to Making Music in the Internet Age, 4th Edition (ISBN 978-1495045219, Hal Leonard): The paradigm has shifted and everything you knew about the music business has completely changed. Who are the new players in the music business? Why are traditional record labels, television, and radio no longer factors in an artist's success? How do you market and distribute your music in the new music world—and how do you make money? This book answers these questions and more in its comprehensive look at the new music business.

The Musician's Video Handbook with DVD (ISBN 978-1423484448, Hal Leonard): Describes how the average musician can easily make any of the various types of videos now required by a musical artist either for promotion or final product. The book will also demonstrate the tricks and tips used by the pros to make it look professionally done, even with inexpensive gear and not much of a budget.

Mixing and Mastering with T-RackS: The Official Guide (ISBN 978-1435457591, Course Technology PTR): Learn how to harness the potential of T-RackS as well as the tips and tricks of using its processor modules to help bring your mixes to life, and then master them so they're competitive with any major label release.

The Touring Musician's Handbook with DVD (ISBN 978-1423492368, Hal Leonard): Answers all the questions regarding becoming a touring musician, regardless of whether you're a sideman, solo performer, or member of a band. As a bonus, individual touring musician guides for guitar, bass, drums, vocals, keys, horns, and strings, as well as interviews with famous and influential touring players are also included.

The Ultimate Guitar Tone Handbook with DVD [with Rich Tozolli] (ISBN 978-0739075357, Alfred Publishing): The definitive book for discovering that great guitar sound and making sure it records well. The book outlines all the factors that make electric and acoustic guitars, amplifiers, and speaker cabinets sound the way they do, as well as the classic and modern recording and production techniques that capture great tone.

The Studio Builder's Handbook with DVD [with Dennis Moody] (ISBN 978-0739077030, Alfred Publishing): While you might think that it costs thousands of dollars and the services of an acoustic designer to improve your studio, *The Studio Builder's Handbook* will strip away the mystery of what makes a great-sounding studio and show how you can make a huge difference in your room for as little as $150.

Abbey Road to Ziggy Stardust [with Ken Scott] (ISBN 978-0739078587, Alfred Publishing): The memoir of legendary producer/engineer Ken Scott, who holds a unique place in music history as one of only five engineers to have recorded The Beatles, and produce and/or engineer on six David Bowie records, among many others. Funny, poignant, and oh so honest, Ken pulls no punches as he tells it as he saw it, as corroborated by a host of famous and not-so famous guests who were there as well.

Audio Mixing Boot Camp with DVD (ISBN 978-0739082393, Alfred Publishing): If you're creating your first mix and don't know where to begin, or your mixes aren't as good as you'd like them to be, *Audio Mixing Boot Camp* is here to help. Built around a series of hands-on mixing exercises designed to show you how to listen and work like a pro, the book reveals the tips, tricks, and secrets to all the different facets of mixing, including instrument and vocal balance, panning, compression, EQ, reverb, delay, and making your mix as interesting as possible.

Audio Recording Basic Training with DVD (ISBN 978-0739086001, Alfred Publishing): If you're new to recording and don't know where to begin, or your recordings aren't as good as you'd like them to be, *Audio Recording Basic Training* is a great place to begin. Built around a series of hands-on recording exercises designed to show you how to listen and work like a recording pro, the book reveals the tips, tricks, and secrets to all the different facets of recording—including miking a drum kit, recording vocals, and miking just about any kind of electric or acoustic instrument.

You can get more info and read excerpts from each book by visiting the excerpts section of bobbyowsinski.com.

BOBBY OWSINSKI'S LYNDA.COM VIDEO COURSES

The Audio Mixing Bootcamp Video Course: Over eight hours of movies outlining the various steps, tips, and tricks of mixing like the pros.

Audio Recording Techniques: Discover the industry secrets to recording crisp, rich vocals and instrument tracks, as renowned audio engineer Bobby Owsinski walks through the process of miking and tracking a complete song using A-list session musicians in a top-of-the-line studio.

Mastering for iTunes: Best practices for mastering music and audio destined for sale on Apple iTunes with their new Mastered for iTunes high-resolution audio program.

Audio Mastering Techniques: Explore essential mastering concepts and techniques used by experienced audio engineers to create a cohesive album from a set of mixed tracks.

BOBBY OWSINSKI'S ONLINE COACHING COURSES

101 Mixing Tricks. Big studio tricks for the small studio at 101mixing-tricks.com.

Music Prosperity Breakthrough. Take your music career to the next level at musicprosperitybreakthrough.com.

BOBBY OWSINSKI'S SOCIAL MEDIA CONNECTIONS

Music production blog: bobbyowsinski.blogspot.com

Music industry blog: music3point0.blogspot.com

Inner Circle podcast: bobbyoinnercircle.com

Facebook: facebook.com/bobby.owsinski

Forbes blog: forbes.com/sites/bobbyowsinski/

YouTube: youtube.com/user/polymedia

LinkedIn: linkedin.com/in/bobbyo

Twitter: @bobbyowsinski

Website: bobbyowsinski.com

PART 1

MUSIC PRODUCTION

CHAPTER 1
THE HISTORY OF MUSIC PRODUCTION

Although the position of producer seems like a modern aspect of the record business, the job has been around from the beginning of recorded music. Through the years, the profession has become more refined in terms of responsibilities, but the job has become more complex as well. To illustrate the evolution of the music producer, it's best to break the profession into three distinct eras: the early label era, the mature music era, and the independent era.

THE EARLY LABEL ERA

Although recorded music goes back as far as 1857, it wasn't turned into a business until around 1900. Because of the primitive nature of the recording equipment, the recordist acted as more of an archivist than a producer in that he (it was almost always a man) was just trying to capture the music onto a medium suitable for reproduction. The composers, arrangers, and bandleaders of the day had final say with regard to the direction and style of the music, just as many do today.

Several pioneers of the era, including Ralph Peer and Lester Melrose (more on them in a bit), began to record less popular forms of music in an effort to target specific audiences. The "producers" of this period were part talent scout, part entrepreneur, and part technician, sometimes going on location and holding massive auditions until they found the music that they thought was unique. They were also some of the people who eventually gave the music industry and record-label executives a bad name by stealing copyrights, not paying royalties, and stereotyping groups of people by using terms like "hillbilly" and "race music."

THE MATURE MUSIC ERA

As the music industry matured, record labels began to employ men (once again, they were almost always men) specifically to discover talent, then shepherd that talent through the recording process. These individuals were known as artist and repertoire (or A&R) men, and they were the first vestiges of the producer that we know today.

Unlike the A&R men of today, who are mostly talent scouts and product managers, A&R people of the mature music era were usually well schooled in music, being talented composers and arrangers themselves. They were in charge of everything from signing an artist to finding songs to overseeing the recording, just as today's producers do.

As magnetic tape became the production media of choice, producers soon had more control over their productions. Now it was easy to have multiple takes, and as 2-, 3-, and 4-track machines became available, the ability to separate instruments brought a whole new palate of possibilities. For the first time, the producer's role became as technically creative as it was musical.

Still, producers of the era were little more than label employees, sometimes not even receiving a bonus despite being directly responsible for the success of a label's artists, and the company's bottom line as well. This was often in spite of a producer being responsible for earning a label sometimes massive amounts of income (as was the case between EMI and George Martin with The Beatles).

THE INDEPENDENT ERA

As the technical possibilities continued to soar, so did a quiet rebellion on the business side of production. Even though independent record producers had existed going back to the '50s with Sam Phillips (of Elvis Presley, Johnny Cash, and Jerry Lee Lewis fame), Phil Spector, Creed Taylor, and Joe Meek, they all had their own record labels, and it was lot easier to be in control as a producer if you were the label owner, too.

The true revolution began when George Martin left music giant EMI to go independent in 1969. Until then, producers were little more than salaried staff with no participation in the profits they had such a big part in developing. After having to fight for a small bonus when The Beatles had made EMI literally a billion dollars, Sir George decided to use his considerable leverage to obtain a piece of the action by leaving his EMI staff position and going his own way. Soon many other successful producers followed, finally starting to cash in on large advances as well as a piece of their best-selling artist's pie.

But fortunes turned, as they so frequently do. After a while, record labels began to see producer independence as a bargain, because they were able to wipe out the overhead of a salaried position by turning the tables so that hiring the producer became the artist's expense instead of the label's. This meant that the label could afford to have the best production talent in the world, yet in the end it wouldn't cost them a dime as long as the record sold.

As time went on, the producer took more creative control, becoming everything from a coach to a guidance counselor to a psychiatrist to a Svengali. Some producers such as Holland, Dozier, and Holland at Motown and Stock, Aitken, and Waterman used a factory approach, where the artists were interchangeable and subordinate to the song. Some, like Phil Spector and Brian Wilson, had a grandiose vision for their material that only they could imagine until it had been completed. Some, like Ted Templeman, Tony Brown and Dann Huff, Moby, Dr. Dre, David Guetta, and Max Martin changed the direction of a style of music. And others, like Quincy Jones, saved the music industry from itself and started the longest run of prosperity it would ever see.

GAME-CHANGING PRODUCERS

All along the way through the history of music production, there have been many producers that could be called "game changers." I call them that because through either their creative vision or the necessity of the situation, they were able to take a genre of music (and sometimes all music) in a new direction, create a different sound, or even sometimes create a level of social change. Here's a brief overview about each of these game changers, listed chronologically by when each was working as a producer.

The Pioneers

Ralph Peer. A groundbreaking record producer to be sure, Peer produced Mamie Smith and Her Jazz Hounds' multimillion-selling "Crazy Blues" in 1920 for OKeh Records, which was reputed to be the first recording made specifically for the African-American market. He is also credited with producing the first recording of an Appalachian folk song recorded by the record industry, Fiddlin' John Carson's version of "The Little Old Log Cabin in the Lane," in 1923. Peer then went on to record both Jimmie Rodgers and the Carter Family in Bristol, Tennessee, in a series of recording sessions that became known as the "Big Bang of Country Music."

Lester Melrose. One of the first producers of blues records, Melrose was a freelance A&R man and producer who met with success in 1925 with his hits by Tampa Red and Thomas A. Dorsey. He is considered by some to be the father of Chicago-style blues, with most of his recordings made by a small group of session players who gave the music a sound that was a mixture of black blues and vaudeville styles, and material with newer swing rhythms. Melrose's chief contribution was to establish a sound with full band arrangements, ensemble playing, a rhythm section similar to what would become a hallmark of the electric blues of the late 1940s, and the small group sound that would become dominant in rock 'n' roll. Among the artists Melrose produced were Sonny Boy Williamson, Memphis Minnie, Big Joe Williams, Bukka White, Champion Jack Dupree, and Big Boy Crudup.

Milt Gabler. Perhaps the first version of the what we currently think of as a record producer, Gabler produced many of the giants of jazz in the '30s for his Commodore Records. These included Billie Holiday (whose recording "Strange Fruit" was named the Song of the Century by *Time* magazine), Joe Venuti and Eddie Lang, and Bessie Smith. In the '40s Gabler worked with some of the era's biggest musical stars, including Lionel Hampton, the Andrews Sisters, Louis Armstrong, and Ella Fitzgerald. But perhaps Gabler's most significant contribution to music came in 1954, with his two-take recording of Bill Haley and His Comets' "Rock Around the Clock," the song that launched the era of rock 'n' roll.

Leonard Chess. His record label, Chess Records, pioneered the electric-blues genre with releases by Muddy Waters, Sunnyland Slim, Willie Dixon, Jimmy Rogers, Bo Diddley, Chuck Berry, and many more. Chess had a documentary style of production (recording equipment was primitive in '50s), essentially capturing whatever performance he was given, but his keen ear for talent has influenced generations of musicians and producers since.

Sam Phillips. From his Sun Studio in Memphis, Phillips practically invented rock 'n' roll with his recordings by Elvis Presley, Carl Perkins, Johnny Cash, Roy Orbison, and Jerry Lee Lewis. The signature slapback echo he used on all his recordings became the sound of '50s pop.

Mitch Miller. During the '50s and early '60s, Miller was head of A&R and producer for the powerful Columbia Records, and oversaw the recording careers of Tony Bennett, Rosemary Clooney, Frankie Laine, Johnny Mathis, Patti Page, Marty Robbins, and Frank Sinatra, among others. During Miller's era, he produced by the theory that it was the man in the recording booth (more than of the artist, the accompaniment, or the material) that determined whether a record was a hit or a flop. Miller also conceived of the idea of the "pop-record sound," which was an aural texture that could be created in the studio then replicated in live performance, instead of the other way around—a direction that would become the norm in the future.

Chet Atkins and Owen Bradley. The chief architects of the "Nashville sound" of the '50s and early '60s, Atkins and Bradley changed the way consumers thought about country music by stripping away the folkier elements like banjo and fiddle in lieu of lush string sections and smooth background vocals. The two virtually created the genre that we've come to know as "easy listening." During his time as head of RCA Records' Nashville operations, Atkins (a popular artist in his own right) propelled an entire generation of country stars to fame, including Dottie West, Waylon Jennings, Bobby Bare, Porter Wagoner, Dolly Parton, and Eddy Arnold. Bradley produced such household names as Patsy Cline, Brenda Lee, Loretta Lynn, and Conway Twitty.

Creed Taylor. Probably the most prolific jazz producer in history, Taylor created three record labels (Impulse Records, CTI Records, and Kudu Records) and was an influential producer for the still-popular Verve Records. He is widely acknowledged for bringing major bossa nova artists such as Antonio Carlos Jobim, João and Astrud Gilberto, and Walter Wanderley from Brazil, as well as overseeing John Coltrane's landmark *A Love Supreme* and albums by jazz greats Stan Getz, Charlie Byrd, Freddie Hubbard, George Benson, Herbie Hancock, and Charles Mingus, among others.

Jerry Wexler. A partner (along with Ahmet and Nesuhi Ertegün) in the famed Atlantic Records, Wexler was known for his development of black artists during a time when race was an extremely divisive issue in America. He developed an influential stable of seminal artists that included Aretha Franklin, Wilson Pickett, Dusty Springfield, Ray Charles, the Drifters, and later Led Zeppelin, Bob Dylan, and George Michael.

The Trailblazers

Joe Meek. As Britain's first independent record producer, electronics genius Meek pioneered the use of many now-commonly-used studio tools and effects such as compression, reverb, echo, and sampling. He became famous for producing hits such as the Honeycombs' "Have I the Right?" and the Tornados' instrumental "Telstar," the first #1 record in the United States by a British group.

Phil Spector. The originator of the "Wall of Sound" production technique and a pioneer of the girl-group sound of the '60s with The Ronettes and The Crystals, Spector set the trend of producer as songwriter and label owner. The 1965 song "You've Lost That Lovin' Feelin'," produced and cowritten by Spector for the Righteous Brothers, is listed by BMI as the song with the most U.S. airplay in the 20th century. Spector also lent his trademark sound to The Beatles on "Let It Be," as well as on solo records by Beatles George Harrison and John Lennon.

Shel Talmy. An American producer working in England in the '60s and early '70s, Talmy's major contribution was bringing heavy and distorted riff-based guitar (a sound that's emulated to this day) to the previously clean British sound. Talmy produced hits such as "I Can't Explain" for The Who, and the seminal "You Really Got Me" and "All Day and All of the Night" for the Kinks.

Sir George Martin. Known as the "Fifth Beatle," Sir George changed the face of music production in several ways: first, by becoming a true collaborator with the band by expounding on their ideas and taking them to another musical level, and second, thanks to his considerable leverage caused by the success of The Beatles, by becoming the first truly successful independent producer, a trend in the business that all others would soon follow. The Beatles went on to sell more than 1 billion units worldwide to date, the biggest-selling musical act ever, and by a large margin.

Teo Macero. A producer for Columbia Records, Macero built Miles Davis albums such as *Bitches Brew*, *In a Silent Way*, and *Get Up With It* by using tape editing to turn themes and improvisations into songs. The electric-jazz albums he helped Davis create, especially *Bitches Brew*, remain the best-selling and most highly regarded albums by a jazz artist more than forty years after their creation, and have influenced musicians of all musical genres. Macero strongly believed that the finished versions of Davis's albums, with all their intricate splices and sequencing done on tape with a razor blade (those were the days long before digital editing) were, in fact, the work of art. As a result, he opposed the current practice of releasing boxed sets that include all the material recorded in the studio, including alternate and unreleased takes.

Holland-Dozier-Holland. H-D-H was Motown Records' leading song-writing/production team of the early to mid-1960s' "Golden Age" and was one of the first real production teams in the industry. Utilizing an excellent group of session musicians known as the Funk Brothers, Brian Holland, Eddie Holland, and Lamont Dozier took advantage of one of the first musical assembly lines, and wrote and produced more than 25 Top 10 hits, including "(Love Is Like a) Heat Wave" and "Nowhere to Run" by Martha and the Vandellas, "Can I Get a Witness" and "How Sweet It Is (to Be Loved by You)" by Marvin Gaye, "(I Know) I'm Losing You" by the Temptations, "Baby I Need Your Loving" by the Four Tops, and "Baby Love" by The Supremes.

The Innovators

Ted Templeman. A staff producer for Warner Bros. Records in the '70s, Templeman's collaboration with Van Halen was responsible for a significant historical shift in rock music, ushering in what is thought of as the modern era of heavy metal/hard rock. He also had a long-standing production relationship with one of the most successful bands of the '70s and '80s, the Doobie Brothers.

Kenny Gamble and Leon Huff. Gamble and Huff developed the "Philadelphia soul sound" that was so popular in the '70s, a sound that featured slick arrangements, lush strings, and the disco flavor of the rhythm section. Some of the artists they worked with on their Philadelphia International label included Harold Melvin and the Blue Notes, Teddy Pendergrass, the O'Jays, Patti LaBelle, Lou Rawls, the Jacksons, Billy Paul, and Archie Bell and the Drells. Notable productions include "Me and Mrs. Jones" by Billy Paul, "Love Train" and "Backstabbers" by the O'Jays, and "If You Don't Know Me by Now" by Harold Melvin and the Blue Notes, among many others.

Lee "Scratch" Perry. One of the originators of dub, Perry's influence through his recordings of Bob Marley and the Wailers, Junior Byles, Junior Murvin, the Heptones, the Congos, and Max Romeo helped spread reggae around the world. All the more amazing was that most all of his recordings were done on a semipro 8-track tape recorder and with marginal audio gear.

Adrian Sherwood. If Lee "Scratch" Perry is the creator of dub, Adrian Sherwood can be credited with bringing it to the masses. It is generally acknowledged that Sherwood has produced truly innovative, groundbreaking U.K. roots music since the late '70s, even when the music was no longer considered fashionable.

The Trendsetters

Quincy Jones. Quincy Jones has had a life full of successes as a writer, arranger, film composer, and trumpet player, but as a producer, nothing tops his run of success with Michael Jackson. Between *Off the Wall*, *Thriller*, and *Bad*, Jackson's records have sold more than 150 million copies, but a little-known fact is how *Thriller* might have saved the record business from a terrible recession and helped propel the industry to heights unforeseen and undreamed. Forgotten is the fact the by the end of the '70s, the record business was in a steep decline and the quality of records had slipped badly as artists had become fat and complacent. On the very first day of recording *Thriller*, Q announced, "We're here to make people want to go to record stores again." And did they ever, with *Thriller* alone going on to sell nearly 110 million copies worldwide.

Jimmy Jam and Terry Lewis. With their own band the Time and clients like Janet Jackson, Usher, Mary J. Blige, Boyz II Men, and Mariah Carey, Jam and Lewis more than anyone shaped the sound of modern R&B, especially with their use of the Roland TR-808 drum machine (a sound that was copied in many musical genres throughout the '80s).

Trevor Horn. Known as one of the innovators of modern production through his use of samples and computers at the start of the '80s, Horn's production career in the U.K. included a string of impressive hits in the '80s and '90s. His hit releases were from ABC, Malcolm McLaren, his own band the Buggles, Yes, Frankie Goes to Hollywood, Art of Noise, 10cc, Pet Shop Boys, Simple Minds, Cher, Bryan Ferry, and Seal.

Stock-Aitken-Waterman. Mike Stock, Matt Aitken, and Pete Waterman, collectively once known as Stock-Aitken-Waterman, or SAW, were generally despised for developing a song production-line concept in the '80s that was adept at producing successful pop music. Ironically, that's why they should also be celebrated. SAW was responsible for creating hits for Rick Astley, Dead or Alive, Bananarama, and Kylie Minogue, among others.

Tony Brown. By changing the direction of country music from easy listening to a more upbeat, rock-influenced style, Brown ushered in what was to become the "new country" with his work with country superstars such as Vince Gill, Reba McEntire, George Strait, Trisha Yearwood, and Wynonna, as well as with favorites like Steve Earle, Patty Loveless, Lyle Lovett, Nanci Griffith, and the Mavericks.

Rick Rubin. Given credit for merging rap and heavy metal, Rubin's biggest trademark is a more in-your-face sound that's devoid of overdubs such as string sections and background vocals (and with very few effects). He has produced a host of acts, including Johnny Cash, Neil Diamond, the Beastie Boys, Metallica, Tom Petty, and the Red Hot Chili Peppers. Rubin is another producer/label owner, with his Def Jam and, later, American Recordings.

Moby. Richard Melville Hall, aka Moby, was one of the leading electronic dance music producers of the early '90s, helping bring the musical genre to a wider audience both in Europe and the United States. Moby coupled rapid disco beats with heavy-sounding, distorted guitars; punk rhythms; and detailed productions that drew from pop, dance, and movie soundtracks.

Brian Eno. A pioneer of out-of-the-box thinking and production techniques thanks to his *Oblique Strategies* cards (see Chapter 10 for a complete description), Eno is one of the originators of ambient music and an early champion of world music. His production credits include U2, David Bowie, Talking Heads, Devo, and Laurie Anderson.

Dann Huff. Taking "new country" yet another step toward rock by utilizing rock production values to their fullest, Huff makes rock records that happen to contain fiddle and steel guitar. He has produced #1 albums for mainstream country crossover acts Faith Hill, Martina McBride, Keith Urban, and Rascal Flatts.

Dr. Dre. Andre Young (aka Dr. Dre) is credited with creating and popularizing West Coast gangsta funk (G-funk), a style of hip-hop characterized by the use of slow funk groove samples and layered synthesizers. Dre was a member of the seminal N.W.A. rap group and has produced hits for Snoop, Eminem, Mary J. Blige, and his own releases on his Death Row and Aftermath labels.

The Hybrids

The late '00s have given way to a new kind of producer, one who mainly programs the tracks and then either adds or collaborates with a vocalist later. The hybrid producer doesn't need outside musicians, and doesn't even have to be one himself (although many are excellent players), as the song is built from the ground up inside a digital audio workstation (DAW).

There are two producers who have done more to change music during this time period than anyone else.

Max Martin. Swedish producer Max Martin (real name Martin Karl Sandberg) began his reign on the charts with Ace of Base's "Beautiful Life," and ended the decade with numerous hits for the Backstreet Boys, NSYNC, and Britney Spears (her "Baby One More Time" was his first *Billboard* #1). Since then, Martin has gone on a remarkable run of 54 Top 10 hits with superstars like Katy Perry, Taylor Swift, Kelly Clarkson, Spears, and Maroon 5. He is responsible for more hits than Phil Spector, Michael Jackson or The Beatles.

David Guetta. Electronic dance music (EDM) has slowly crept not only into the U.S. Top 40 but into American music in general, and no one is more responsible than French DJ and producer David Guetta. A huge hitmaker in Europe first, Guetta has perfected the art of creating a danceable backing track and then adding a popular vocalist on top to create a hit, and has done so with Kid Cudi, Kelly Rowland, Ludacris, Usher, Rihanna, and most notably, Nicki Minaj. Guetta also had a huge hit as a producer with the Black Eyed Peas' "I Gotta Feeling," which topped the charts in 17 countries.

CHAPTER 2
WHAT IS A MUSIC PRODUCER?

As anyone who has ever produced any sort of entertainment project knows, one of the first questions you might get from a non-music person is, "What exactly do you do?" or, "What's a producer?" That's totally understandable, since producers in music, television, and film take on many roles (some honorary and some deep in the trenches of the creative tasks at hand) yet are mostly out of the public eye.

A music producer, in the most basic sense, is different from his or her similarly named film and television counterparts (in which a "line producer" and a "coordinating producer" constitute separate and specific jobs), because the producer on a music project has many job descriptions rolled into one.

He's the creative director. Just like the director on a movie has the overall vision for that movie and is the boss on the set, so is the producer in the studio. The producer not only sees the big picture in terms of how all the songs of the album will fit together into a cohesive package, but can also control the day-to-day minutiae of how a part is played or even what notes are in the part.

He's a diplomat. The producer's number one job is to bring harmony to the creative process so that everyone can create at his or her highest level. Although some producers have used terror as a method to get what they want, most successful producers make everyone feel comfortable about contributing and make the environment conducive to creativity.

He's the decision maker. A good producer will be the final decision maker in any creative argument (especially one between band members). Even if the producer defers to the artist's creative vision (which most producers will do), it's still his decision whether to defer or not.

He's the go-between. The producer keeps the pressure of the outside world away from the artist or band during recording. In some cases, he may speak for the artist with studio musicians, and will generally shield the artist from anything she might deem uncomfortable.

He's the financier. The producer is responsible for the budget. He makes the deals with the studio, engineer, mixer, mastering studio, rental shop, studio musicians, arrangers, songwriters, food deliverers, and anything else that might need to be negotiated for or paid. In some cases, he'll also administer union contracts and submit cue sheets.

He's the casting director. A good producer will choose the right group of musicians or vocalists who will get the feel that the artist is looking for, which might change from song to song. He might even help choose material for the artist that best showcases her musical attributes.

He's a project manager. A good producer knows just what needs to be accomplished in a given amount of time and for a given budget. His job is to turn in the project on time and on or under budget, and he must manage each project accordingly.

He "drives the bus." No matter how or to what degree a producer is involved, he's the one that sets the direction for the project. He determines what the artist's vision is and helps her achieve it, or he may even help her find it with a vision of his own. Either way, he's the leader that everyone will follow.

He's the one who is responsible. In the eyes of both record label executives (when a label is involved) and the artist, the success of the project is the direct responsibility of the producer. Although the public will judge the artist on the project, how it ultimately turns out falls squarely on the producer's shoulders.

DIFFERENT TYPES OF MUSIC PRODUCTION

Traditional music producers fall into two categories: active and passive. Active producers are involved in all of the day-to-day decisions, both creative and financial, as outlined above. Passive producers are more laid back and leave the day-to-day creative decisions to others (the artist, engineer, arranger, project coordinator, and so on), usually making a comment only when the project threatens to get off track, or to break a decision stalemate.

While the passive producer gets a lot of derision for not being as hands-on, his contributions are as real and useful as that of an active producer. Sometimes it's easy for a hands-on producer to lose track of the overall vision because of having to take care of so many day-to-day decisions, while a passive producer can see the forest for the trees.

Producer George Martin (The Beatles) and Linda Perry (Pink, Christina Aguilera, James Blunt) are good examples of active producers who oversee every stage of the recording process, from playing on the record down to arranging the music and overseeing every overdub. Richard Perry (Rod Stewart, Tina Turner, Pointer Sisters, Barbra Streisand) and Rick Rubin (Red Hot Chili Peppers, Jay-Z, Tom Petty) are examples of producers who are more passive, leaving the hands-on part of making the record to people more skilled in specific areas, but being sure to steer the ship back on course if they feel it's going astray.

Then there are the hybrid producers like Red One (Lady Gaga, Nicki Minaj, Pitbull) or Max Martin (Taylor Swift, Britney Spears, Maroon 5) who have the ultimate control in that they create the tracks and then collaborate with the artist on the final product, many times without ever seeing an additional musician during the recording.

While you'll see more references in this book to active than passive producers, that doesn't diminish the role of someone who is less hands-on. A producer has a vision for the artist, and while he may not know exactly how to attain it, he knows enough to hire others that do. Without that vision, the ship would be rudderless in the big musical ocean.

HOW TO BECOME A PRODUCER

I don't remember who I heard it from, but the following question and its answer are really true. They go like this:

"How do you know when you're a producer?"

"When you have a client."

That means that as long as someone believes you can do it, then you've joined the production ranks. While the process of becoming a producer can sometimes follow an improbable path, today there are usually three career tracks that take you there: being a musician, an engineer, or a DJ (see Figure 2-1).

The Ways To Become A Producer

Musician

Engineer

DJ

Other
(Financier, Club Owner, Radio Personality, etc)

Figure 2-1: The Ways to Become a Producer

The Musician/Producer

The way a musician becomes a producer is by spending a lot of time in the studio and learning what works and what doesn't, either by trial and error, through a mentorship with a successful producer, or by constant observation as a session musician or as an artist or band member making a record. If you're a musician who has risen to that level as a player, it's a good bet that your musical taste and sensitivity are already highly developed and the jump into production will be short.

Of these three ways, the mentorship is usually the fastest way to reach your goal by virtue of the fact that you are learning from someone who's successful on some level, and you can follow many different projects from beginning to end. The diversity of the projects you work on is important, since the production approach can vary greatly from artist to artist and musical genre to genre. A mentorship also has the advantage of the possibility of being handed a project once your mentor feels you're ready, or if he's so busy that you get to be the day-to-day producer while he stays on as executive producer.

The next fastest way to learn how to produce is by observation as a session musician. While you usually can't follow a project from start to finish, you get a chance to work with a number of different producers and artists, so you can absorb different styles and techniques. This usually takes longer than a mentorship, and it's harder to break in as a producer since you're thought of only as a musician for hire.

Being an artist or playing in a band that works with a great producer is another way that you can learn the ropes. The advantage here is that if you have enough success to be able to record several albums, you'll have the advantage of working with different producers or even the same one several times. Another advantage is that you'll get to follow the project and interact with the producer all the way through it.

Being a songwriter usually means that you've developed pretty good production skills along the way, since you've wanted to present your song demos in the best light. Many songwriters hear the final version of their song in their head and won't rest until it's recorded that way. Phil Spector, Mutt Lange, and Brian Wilson are some classic examples of songwriters who are mega-successful producers, while Pharrell Williams and Paul Epworth have had more recent success. Quincy Jones is an example of an arranger and writer who became maybe the most successful of all time based on the sales record of Michael Jackson alone.

The trial-and-error method takes the longest time by far, but it can lead to the most success. That's because if you spend enough time experimenting, you will not only determine what works, but you might also develop an unusual sound or direction in the process.

Once upon a time, it was nearly impossible to learn this way (unless you were really rich or lucky) because the cost of making a record was so high. Now virtually everyone can have a studio in their home for so little money that learning this way is more possible than ever.

The problem is that if you're not in a big media center or have no access to people who can help you when you have a question, it can take what seems like forever to learn. Hopefully, this book will provide some basics to cut that learning curve down a bit.

The Engineer/Producer

Engineering has been a long-standing farm system for producers for many of the same reasons listed for musicians, producing all sorts of successes dating back to Glyn Johns (The Who), Phil Ramone (Billy Joel), Hugh Padgham (The Police), and Jimmy Iovine (Bruce Springsteen, Patti Smith), to today with Charlie Hugall (Florence and the Machine, Ed Sheeran) and Graham Marsh (CeeLo Green), among many others.

Engineering is the perfect educational environment for becoming a producer for several reasons. First, an engineer is able to see many different projects through from beginning to end, which enables him to participate in all aspects of the project. Second, an engineer works with a multitude of artists, producers, musicians, and bands and can glean something from them all. It's that depth of information and experience that is most valuable. Lastly, an engineer can frequently become the preferred guy of a successful producer, which becomes an unofficial mentorship and can later lead to referrals.

While engineering can be a career stepping stone to producing, it can take a long time and there's no guarantee that your break will happen, especially if you're not working with "name" clients and producers. Also, most of the engineers who cross over to production have some type of musical training, with many of them being accomplished players. That experience gives them both the technical and the musical skills required to make the jump.

The DJ/Producer

In recent years a new type of producer has become prominent thanks to the ascendance of electronic music—the DJ/producer. The desire for many DJs to create their own beats began their trek towards production, leading to either collaborating with an artist/vocalist or hiring one to sing on their tracks.

On one hand, the DJ/producer has it easier than the other producer types in that he doesn't have to contend with getting performances from musicians or worrying about capturing the sounds during a session in the studio. Thanks to loop and sample libraries, great-sounding basic sonic building blocks are readily available. That said, the competition is fierce and the DJ must bring something special to the table to stand out from the crowd.

Since the method for releasing electronic-based material is far different from that in the normal record label world, the opportunity for growth can be easily stifled with little help from the outside available.

That said, more and more DJs have a strong music and engineering background that allows them to jump ahead of those that don't.

And the Other Way

There is another way to become a producer, and that's to declare yourself one, find an artist, and pay production costs out of your own pocket. Rich entrepreneurs, athletes, and drug dealers try this way, and usually fail. Artist managers and attorneys try it, thinking they know something because they're in the business, but usually fail. Concert promoters, club owners, and radio personalities try it and usually fail.

They fail because producing music takes more than just liking music or having disposable income. We'll cover the skills and techniques later in this book, but know that being successful takes a lot more time and hard work than most people realize or are willing to put in.

You Still Need a Client

Regardless of your experience, capabilities, and ambition, most producers still need an artist or client who trusts you with their project enough to let you produce it. The client is what makes you a producer in the first place, although your talent and experience will make you a success at it. So how do you get a client?

The time-honored way to break into production is to discover a young artist looking for a break. If you've been coming up through the ranks by working in the various capacities above, you can probably ask for a favor for some musical, arranging, and studio help to get a short project recorded (if you don't have a way to do it yourself). Or you can pay for it out of your own pocket. Either way, you can be on your way at that point, or not.

An artist or a band member who meets with some music business success usually has a pretty good head start into the production world by virtue of that success. If you find an artist you want to produce while riding that success, a record label is usually inclined to let you do it, figuring that your notoriety might rub off on the new artist. Sometimes they'll let you do it just to keep you happy.

Success on any level will tend to rub off on you and make it easier to find a project to produce. A songwriter, musician, engineer, or other in the business is much more likely to get a referral for production work if they were connected to a hit (the bigger the hit, the easier it becomes). It's a sad fact that it happens this way, and it sometimes bestows undeserved opportunities on the undeserving, but that's the way the business works.

WHAT ARE THE RESPONSIBILITIES?

The producer has a number of responsibilities, all of which we'll go over in more detail in upcoming chapters. But to summarize, they include the following:

Financial. The producer is responsible for the budget and is charged to stay within that budget to finish the project. Sometimes the producer is asked to determine what the project will cost ahead of time, before the money is allotted. Although he may not sign the checks for the expenses personally (the record label, artist management, or project financier might do that), he's usually required to sign off on all invoices and purchase orders.

Political. The producer must keep the peace between all parties in order to make the mood conducive to creating. This means trying to alleviate any tension between band members, the artist and the label, the artist and management, and the artist and anyone else who might cause undo strife (session musicians, rental companies, management, a boyfriend, a girlfriend, a wife, a husband, or the pizza delivery guy). It's a tough job, but someone's got to do it.

Creative. The producer is responsible for making the project the best that it can be musically. This means picking the best material and making sure that the material is arranged well, the technical and musical standards are high, and the product will satisfy the artist's current fan base and attract new fans—no small job in itself.

Project management. The producer must bring the project in on time. This means that a great number of mini-events and moving parts must be coordinated throughout the project, from booking studio time on days off to arranging rental gear to keeping song files from leaking before the release date. Because there's so much to think about, many successful producers employ dedicated assistants or project coordinators to handle the many small tasks and general busywork.

WHO DO YOU WORK FOR: ARTIST OR LABEL?

If you're producing yourself or your band and you're not signed to a record label, then this section won't apply to you. If you've taken the next step beyond that, then an important question inevitably arises — who does the producer work for: the artist or the record label?

The answer is both, but not necessarily. If that's too vague an answer, remember that where your allegiance lies is an age-old producer question. I personally believe that the answer is simple — your loyalty should lie with who hires you.

Once upon a time, it was the record label that paired the artist with the producer, in which case the producer became the steward of the project for the label. This model is still used with record-company signings of an untested artist (known in industry parlance as a "baby artist" or a "baby band"). Even though the artist ultimately paid for the producer's services (more on that later), the producer was hired by the label, and if he ever hoped to be hired again, then the primary level of client satisfaction needed to come from primarily the label.

These days, the decision as to who to select to produce a project is usually a mutual one between the artist and the label, with the artist making the primary request and the label approving, if they've worked with them before. In that case, it's an even tougher decision as to who to please first, and a good producer toes the fine line between commerce (his future work) and art. Ultimately, if the artist isn't pleased with the work, then you probably won't work with him again anyway. And after all, it's his or her art, not yours or the label's, so unless you are specifically brought on by the label, art takes precedence.

We're back to the diplomacy thing again, trying to make everyone happy.

Actually, during these days of Music 4.0, in which an artist deals directly with his fans, it's become increasingly the case that the producer works solely for the artist, since many times a label isn't even involved with financing the record. The artist hires you to facilitate his vision in whatever way possible. That might mean simply giving your opinion when asked, or it might mean handling everything down to writing chord charts and lead sheets for the musicians — but his vision must be upheld.

CHAPTER 3
THE DUTIES OF A MUSIC PRODUCER

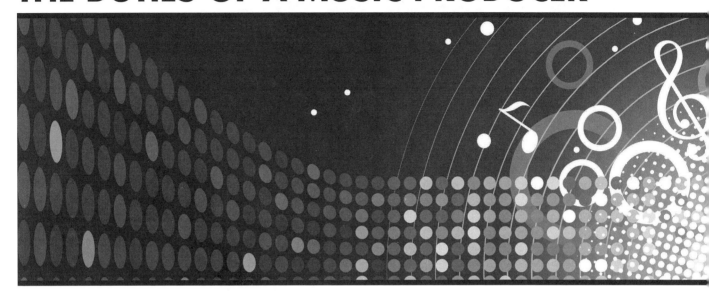

Production used to start and stop with the client, because that's whose vision you were realizing and executing, but more often than not these days, the client is you. While we'll cover self-production in a later chapter, for now let's consider the producer's traditional role as facilitator of someone else's music on behalf of a client.

The client can be an artist or band on a record, a songwriter on a demo, an ad agency for a commercial, or a record label wanting to capture an artist in a certain way. Regardless of whom you work for and with, music production can be broken down into a few areas of execution that are the expected duties of most music producers.

There are four elements involved in music production (in almost any production, really) that a producer must be familiar with. Usually a producer is a master of at least one of the four, but most producers are expert in all four: the creative, the financial, the project management, and the political elements.

The creative element is what everyone usually wants to know about, and so most of the rest of the book is dedicated to it. The financial element is important and nuanced enough that it deserves its own chapter, as does the political element, which leaves us with project management.

PROJECT MANAGEMENT

Project management is the one element that usually slips beneath the radar of most budding producers, but it can easily break you if you don't pay attention to it. Project management consists of planning, organizing, and managing the resources necessary to complete the project, be it just one song, a cue or jingle, or a full ten-song album.

Most projects, even those of superstar acts, have a timeline that must be followed, since the days of open-ended recording sessions are pretty much over thanks to marketing campaigns and tours that are developed before the record is even completed (and sometimes started). This means that all the time elements of your project have to be planned out well in advance, with a little leeway built in as needed.

Managing Time

Managing both project time and people time is one of the more difficult jobs of a producer, since it involves a lot of educated guessing. You never really know exactly how much time any one segment will take, but you do have a general idea if you've done your production homework.

So how do you figure out how much time you'll need? Just like any project in any company, you make a timeline that includes specific milestones, while leaving a little leeway in case the unforeseen happens.

- **Take stock of the situation.** Let's say that the record label wants to have the project delivered to them by October 1, and you're asked to participate in the project on May 15. There's no way that you can determine just how long each project segment will take until you evaluate the songs, listen to the demos, listen to any previous recordings, hear the artist or band at a gig or in rehearsal, and generally get a good feel for what's possible and how much will need to be fixed or tweaked. This evaluation period might take a week or two, but it could be compressed into as little as a day if necessary, depending on your experience in these situations and the quality of the songs and players.
- **Approximate how long each project segment will take.** After you evaluate the artist's or band's songs and get a feel for the arrangements and how well the artists play them, you can determine how much preproduction time it will take to get everything into shape. You might determine that you'll need a month of preproduction because the arrangements are weak, or maybe just a few days for some song

tweaks. If you don't have that kind of time or the artist is resistant to more rehearsal, then you'll have to allot more time for basic tracking, maybe an extra day for each song, instead of the two or three songs per day that you might expect if everything is finely tuned.

During preproduction, you'll also get a feel for what kind of overdubs you'll be doing and what kind of time for experimentation you'll need. Unless most of what you're recording during tracking is a keeper, you should plan on spending at least a day for each instrument to do all the overdubs. This means that you'll record all bass fixes for all the songs one day, one day for guitars, one for lead vocals, and so on. If you have more time and your budget permits, you would stretch that out to a day to record the lead vocal for each song (ten songs in ten days), a day of guitar fixes from the basic tracks, a day for guitar overdubs, a day for guitar solos, a day for background vocals for each song, a day for percussion for all songs, and so on. Ultimately, overdub time will be determined by the number of overdubs that you have in mind, their difficulty, and the skill sets of the players and singers. Having better players means being able to do faster overdubs.

- **Develop your milestones.** First, work backward from your delivery or completion date. You now plug in the time allotted for mastering, mixing, overdubbing, tracking, and preproduction. From there you can put in your milestones for completion. For instance:

Preproduction start:	May 21
Preproduction complete:	June 7
Tracking start:	June 10
Tracking complete:	June 17
Bass fixes:	June 20
Guitar fixes:	June 21
Guitar overdubs:	June 22–29
Guitar solos:	June 30
Keyboard overdubs start:	August 1
Keyboard overdubs complete:	August 7

Lead vocals start:	August 8
Lead vocals complete:	August 18
Background vocals start:	August 20
Background vocals complete:	September 1
Percussion overdubs:	September 3
Extra:	September 5–10
Mixing start:	September 11
Mixing complete:	September 26
Listening session:	September 28
Mastering:	September 30
Delivery:	October 1

Notice the extra days in between preproduction and tracking, tracking and fixes, lead vocals and background vocals, and background vocals and percussion, plus the extra days built into the schedule. This is to make sure that there's plenty of leeway should something take longer than anticipated or unforeseen circumstances arise.

Managing Rentals

A fairly large project usually requires numerous rentals of both long and short term. The trickiest long-term rental is always the studio if you have to rent one, since if you don't complete what's needed on time, then you'll have to move somewhere else if the studio has committed to another project after your booking has run out. This can be a royal pain, since it means tearing everything down and setting up again, losing some time and momentum (and therefore, your sound) in the process.

Of course in these days where everyone has their own personal studio, many times just the basic tracks are done in a larger studio, mainly for recording drums, and all overdubs are done in a much less expensive (or free) private studio. That said, if the budget exists to do so, many artists, producers, and engineers prefer to be in a commercial studio because the environment is more structured and disciplined, and the sounds are usually better as well.

Studio time is broken into five categories:

- **Preproduction.** This stage is the time to work out material before hitting the high-priced studio. It can be in a garage, a bedroom, or a rehearsal room and can last from as little as a day to a couple of months (see Chapter 7 for more on preproduction). Having a long preproduction schedule usually occurs when working with artists or bands that write their own songs and that are relatively early in their careers, since their songs and arrangements may require a fair amount of tweaking at that point.

  Artists and bands that are further along in their careers and have recorded before usually have a greater sense of arrangement and have become sophisticated enough musically that they don't need as much preproduction. There's no preproduction for commercials or movie and television scores because the composer/arranger has things pretty well worked out and the musicians are skilled enough to learn or perform the music on the spot.

- **Tracking.** Sometimes called "basic tracks," tracking usually consists of recording just the rhythm tracks, although in certain situations it can mean the entire band. The basic tracks can consist of only the drums, only bass and drums, or only drums, bass, guitar and/or keyboards, and can last anywhere from a single day to months, if there's no preproduction (see Chapter 10 for more on tracking).

- **Overdubs.** Overdubs consist of recording at least the lead vocals and/or any kind of solos and lead lines that the song requires, but it can also mean overdubbing layers of guitars, keyboards, horns, strings, percussion, and background vocals. The overdub phase can last anywhere from a day to months or even years (in extremely rare cases).

  Overdubs may take place in the same studio as the tracking, but in these days of smaller budgets, it's now common to go to a smaller, less expensive facility or a free one owned by the producer, engineer, or band member. Overdubbing is also the most difficult portion of a project to gauge how much time is actually required, since it can vary widely (see Chapter 11 for more on overdubs).

- **Mixing**. It used to be pretty easy to determine how much time was required for mixing in the schedule. Allotting a day to a day and a half per song was pretty standard, especially if you used an A-list mixing engineer.

Today with more and more mixing being done "in-the-box" in a DAW, you can throw those numbers out the window. Many mixers find it tough to allocate exactly how much time they spend on a mix since it's now possible to work on several at the same time because it's so easy to bring back a mix exactly from where you left it. While that seems as though it should lead to faster fixes, more time is spent mixing than ever—a result of trying to make every last tweak possible.

It's still best to figure a couple of days per mix if you're mixing in a studio with an analog-style console (see Chapter 14 for more on mixing), but remember that the tradeoff is great sound versus not being able to recall your mix exactly if you need changes, plus a greater cost as well.

- **Mastering.** The mastering phase is the easiest to gauge, because it usually takes only a half to a full single day to complete an entire album, regardless of the number of songs. In rare cases (and with big budgets), mastering can turn into a multiple-day affair or even involve using a couple of different mastering houses, but that isn't the norm.

Short Term Rentals

Short-term rentals can include everything from keyboards, guitar amps, and microphones to reverbs and outboard gear while tracking. In fact, just about anything you can think of can be rented these days.

Rentals usually go by a daily, weekly, or monthly rate. The weekly rate is based on a four- or five-day week, depending upon whom you rent from. This means that if the rental is $100 per day, you pay only $400 for the full week (if based on a four-day week). The monthly rate is usually based on a three-week month, which means that if your rate were based on a $400-per-week rental, it would cost $1,200 for the month instead of $1,600 (see Table 3.1).

TABLE 3.1: EQUIPMENT RENTAL RATES			
Description	Daily	Weekly	Monthly
Neumann U-67 mic	$100	$400	$1,200
Lexicon 960L reverb	$150	$600	$1,800
Neve 1073 mic preamp	$70	$280	$840

Managing People

A producer has to manage not only project time but also the time of the people he's working with. For instance, if the engineer that he prefers to use can't be available for the tracking dates, he has to either reschedule to accommodate the engineer or find a replacement for him. If the lead singer is unavailable for several of the planned lead-vocal overdub days, the producer has to reschedule them and put something else in their place to stay on schedule. If studio musicians are to be hired, he has to find out when the best people for the project are available, and work around their schedules.

This adds yet another layer of complexity to scheduling and project management, but it comes with the territory of being a producer.

Many producers that work on A-list projects employ project coordinators that take care of most of the mundane work of scheduling, leaving the producer to work on just the creative aspects of the project. For the rest of us, that's not an option, as the scheduling is just another part of the job.

CREATIVE

The creative elements that a producer is required to bring to the project can be few or many, but usually many. He must bring taste, musical expertise, and a keen ear for what works and what doesn't. In fact, this aspect is so broad that I spend eleven chapters on it in this book (see Chapters 6 through 16).

FINANCIAL

One of the main jobs of a producer is financial, and this is broken into two categories: the producer's deal and the project budget. There are many ways that a producer can get paid and many nuances to those ways. Handling the project budget also requires a deft hand in making sure there's enough money allotted to complete the project to everyone's satisfaction. Like the creative aspect of production, the financial aspect is detailed enough to require several chapters (see Chapters 4 and 5).

POLITICAL

Unless you're dealing with a singer-songwriter in his or her own studio, every project is filled with multiple, diverse personalities. Some of these people are levelheaded, reasonable, and professional, while others (hopefully not many) are childish, diva-like, and headstrong, always wanting their own way.

As the producer, one of your main jobs is get everyone to work in as much harmony as possible, mediating any arguments and channeling any resentment or hard feelings into a great performance. This job alone could be full-time, and is one in which trained professionals make a lot of money, but it just comes with the territory of being a producer. (See Chapters 10 and 11 for more about the diplomacy aspects of production.)

CHAPTER 4
THE BUSINESS OF MUSIC PRODUCTION

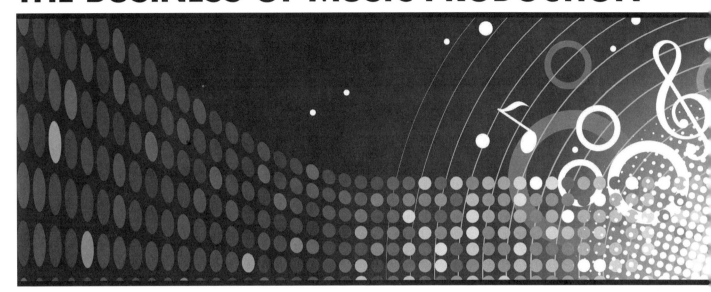

Like it or not, music production is a business on just about every level, and taking care of the business end is an essential element of a producer's day-to-day operations. Therefore, let's take a look at the essential business elements and some typical deals, as well as the question that eventually comes to the forefront of every producer's mind: "How do I get paid?"

This chapter is going to cover producing a project either for a label or an artist that hires you. Self-produced projects are different because the artist is actually the producer (or the other way around)—any production fees or royalties are built into the artist agreement with the label.

WHAT'S MY DEAL?

Over the years, the deal that a producer can cut for him or herself has varied greatly, depending upon the health of the industry and the times we were in. In order to understand how we got to the production deal of today, we have to look to the past first.

The Basic Deal

As stated earlier in this book, during the '50s through the end of the '60s, most producers were employed directly by the record label and were paid a salary that might contain a year-end bonus option and little more, despite how well the records sold. In fact, George Martin's productions with The Beatles sold hundreds of millions of units and made around a billion dollars for EMI in the '60s, and he never saw a piece of the action. In fact, he was even passed over for a bonus one year despite a succession of #1 worldwide hits.

Martin eventually took the bold move to become an independent producer in order to take financial advantage of the cash cow he had spearheaded. In doing so, he blazed a trail for all producers thereafter. Most producers today are independent, or not a salaried staff member of a record label, as a result.

But Sir George wasn't the first producer to make money on the basis of an artist's success. Snuff Garrett, a producer and A&R man for the old Liberty Records of the '50s and '60s, is credited with getting the first producer's royalty, even though he still remained a salaried employee of the label. After much success with artists such as Cher, Sonny and Cher, Bobby Vee, and Bobby Vinton, Garrett convinced the owner of the label to pay him one cent on every record sold, which—considering that the records were selling by the millions then—gave him a pretty nice override.

The Deal of the Past

A typical producer's deal on a major-label release is based on a percentage of sales (called points), which amounts to a royalty payment, and an advance against that royalty payment.

The typical deal calls for the producer to get three points (or 3 percent) of the wholesale price of the record. A hot producer might get 4 points, and a superstar producer might get as many as 5, but 3 is the norm. This means that if a CD is wholesaling for $10 (just to make it easy to compute), the producer gets $.30 from every unit sold, if he or she is getting 3 points (see Figure 4-1). This figure can be deceiving though, as we'll soon see.

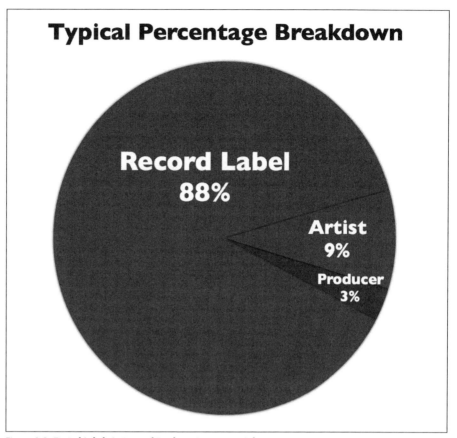

Figure 4-1: Typical Label, Artist, and Producer Percentage Splits

As for an advance against later royalties from the project, a new producer used to get $2,000 to $4,000 per song, while a superstar producer with a superstar act might receive as much as $25K, or even more, per song.

While this sounds like a lot of dough (and it is), there are numerous games that are played to take what seems to be a windfall and diminish it substantially.

Who's Paying?

In order to determine how much you can make, you have to understand that it is ultimately the artist who is paying you. That means if the artist is getting 12 points, you're getting 3 of those 12. Before you can get paid, the artist has to recoup any of his or her advances received or production costs before you see a dime.

Let's say that the record label gave the artist a $100,000 recording fund to make the album, which will hypothetically only be distributed as a CD, for the purpose of this example. A fund is a lump sum that is given to the artist, who must then deliver a completed record for that amount. The advantage of a fund is that if the project comes in under budget, the artist gets to keep the excess. The fund amount of $100K is considered an advance, and it must be paid back before you or the artist see any additional funds. Here's how that works out:

> $100,000 advance/$1.20 per record
> (12% of a theoretical $10 wholesale) =
> 83,334 CDs

That means you won't see another dime until unit 83,335 CDs have been sold, which is highly unlikely given the state of CD sales these days.

The good part about this for you (as compared to what happens for an artist) is that you can usually put in the contract that you are to get paid all the way back to CD sale number one once the record recoups. This means the following:

$$
\begin{array}{r}
83,335.00 \\
\underline{\$.30 \quad (3\% \text{ royalty})} \\
\$25,000.50 \quad (\text{royalty payment})
\end{array}
$$

You'll get a check for the above amount, minus your advance (which we'll say is $10,000):

$$
\begin{array}{rl}
\$25,000.50 & (3\% \text{ royalty}) \\
\underline{-\$10,000.00} & (\text{advance}) \\
\$15,000.50 & (\text{royalty payment})
\end{array}
$$

The band doesn't have this same deal—so take notice, because if you're not careful, neither will you. The band receives a royalty for any record sold after unit 83,334. If your contract states that that's how you get paid (instead of from record one after recoupment), you just lost 25 grand.

THE NEW MUSIC ECONOMY

With the Music 4.0 stage of the music business, in which the artist doesn't need a label because he or she can market directly to their fan base (see my book *Music 4.1: A Survival Guide for Making Music in the Internet Age* for more information), the old business model doesn't work anymore. It's just as likely that the artist's songs will mainly be found on a variety of streaming services, which have a very low payout for the artist and even less for you.

Payments from Digital Music

Digital music royalty payments can be an enormously involved subject, so we'll just look at some very basic examples, starting with digital downloads. The typical download costs anywhere from $0.69 to $1.29, but we'll use $0.99 for our example.

The iTunes Music Store (which is now part of Apple Music) pays about 70 percent of the sale back to the record label. That means that for every download, the label receives 70 cents (see Figure 4-2) and pays a percentage of that to the artist. If the artist has a 12 point deal, that means that they make about 8.4 cents on every sale (70 cents x 12 percent = 8.4 cents).

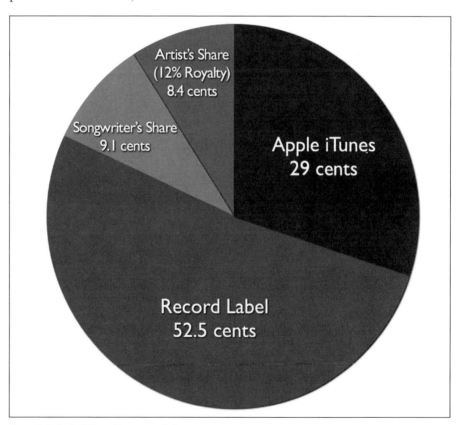

Figure 4-2: Typical iTunes Percentage Splits

Now let's look at our same example as above where the artist received a $100,000 advance.

$100,000 advance / 8.4 cents per download =
1,190,476 downloads to recoup the advance

That means that you won't see penny number one until download number 1,190,477. Pretty harsh, right?

It gets worse with streaming. Streaming royalty rates are all over the place. Non-interactive services like Pandora (which are like listening to a radio broadcast) pay a lot less than an interactive site (where you can choose which song you want to hear), plus each pays a different rate for the free and premium tiers. To make it even more confusing, each country pays a slightly different royalty rate because they charge the consumer different prices.

That said, Spotify pays an average of $0.007 (7/10ths of a cent) per stream, so let's use that as an example.

$100,000 advance / $0.007 average per stream =
142,857,714 streams to recoup the advance

That means that you won't see your first payment until stream number 142,857,714!

It gets worse if you look at Pandora, which pays about $0.0019 per stream on average.

$100,000 advance / $0.0019 average per stream =
52,631,578 streams to recoup the advance

These figures look pretty grim, but they're not as bad as they look. For one thing, a million streams doesn't mean the same thing as they used to mean with sales of CDs or even downloads. A million streams barely registers on the music industry's radar, while it begins to take notice at 10 million, and 50 million is considered a minor hit. Major hit records routinely rack up hundreds of million of streams.

Secondly, today's artists receive a combination of payments from all of the above sources and from streaming services all over the world. This makes for an accounting nightmare (with lots of places for accounting hanky-panky to take place), but a true hit will have no problem making those numbers.

The Producer's Piece Gets Smaller

As you can see, you can't count on royalties anymore unless the song or album blows up and you have a giant hit on your hands. Advances have shrunk, and where once a working producer could make a good living even without having a hit, that road is now tougher than ever. As a result, producers now try to get as much money as possible up front, or take some piece of the action, such as a piece of the publishing of the songs worked on.

Producers have always tried to control a piece, if not all, of the artist's publishing, and it's only been since the '80s or so that artists' attorneys have tried to fight to keep it from them. If you recall, in Chapter 1 we covered the early years of record production, which were particularly brutal on songwriters and artists. Producers, label owners, and industry execs who knew the ropes and how the money was made did everything they could to grab what rightfully belonged to the artist and gave the industry a black eye and a bad name as a result. It's not surprising that when a producer brings up publishing ownership that the artist immediately wants to run for the hills.

But the state of the business has changed a great deal since then. Physical sales are at an all-time low (down by more than 80 percent since the year 2000 alone—see Figure 4-3), and so when a #1 record on the charts can be expected to sell only 50,000 units (as is frequently the case), the producer can't hope to ever be properly compensated for the time and expertise it takes to make what today is considered a hit.

Add to the above fact that advances and recording budgets are at an all-time low. Whereas a typical budget for a medium-selling act might have been $250,000 at one time, you might be lucky to

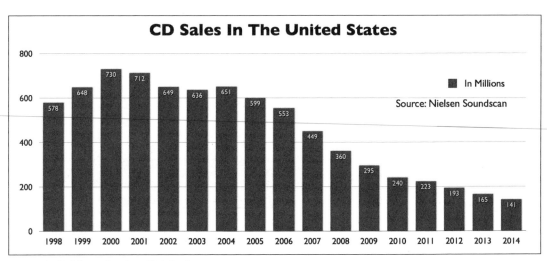

Figure 4-3: CD Sales Decline Since Their Peak

get $50,000 in today's financial climate. While a producer's advance might have been $10K per song previously, now you might be lucky to get $10K for the entire project of a young artist. The money from producing a label act just isn't there for a producer anymore.

While an act might still be making good money touring and selling their own branded merchandise, that's no consolation for the producer, who never sees a dime from any of those items.

That's why publishing has become such a big deal, especially with a new act. The publishing business is still the one area of the music business that is still somewhat healthy.

So what does a producer ask for? With a new act that can't afford a large advance, a producer might ask for 5 percent of the writer's portion of the publishing for the songs that the producer works on. This way, there's at least some possibility of getting paid down the road if the song has any success or airplay. Keep in mind that this will probably be acceptable only to a "baby" band or artist, since an act with some success will be able to pay a higher advance to compensate, instead of giving away the publishing.

WHEN A LABEL ISN'T INVOLVED

What if the members of a local band ask you to produce them? What do you charge if they're not attached to a label? There are a number of approaches you can take, although none will have you retiring to the Bahamas any time soon. You can do the following:

- **Charge a flat project fee.** How much should that be? So much depends on the type of project, how many overdubs you'll need, the artist's or band's competency, the artist's or band's income level, and the number of songs they want to record. A jazz or blues band that has 20 songs will usually take a lot less time to produce than a pop band with eight songs will, because of the layering that's normally required with pop music. Plus, if the band has a marginal player or two, that can almost double the time spent just trying to get their parts to match the skill level of other players (unless you can persuade the rest of the band to use a session player instead).

  A flat fee is the least desirable way to get paid, because projects have a tendency to run a lot longer than anticipated and will drag on and on when the artist realizes that you get paid the same, regardless of the time spent. If the flat fee is the easiest or only way to get the gig, then that's what you'll have to do. Otherwise, avoid it if you can, unless you're very well compensated.

- **Charge a per-song fee.** This approach is better than the flat project fee, but not by much. The per-song rate has all the same problem areas as the flat-fee approach, with the exception that it can sometimes cause the artist to scale back from recording 15 songs to 10 (even though it means less money in your pocketbook). You won't have to worry about the artist wanting to record an extra song at the last minute or suddenly wanting to complete a track originally deemed too weak after basic tracking. With a per-song rate, if any additional songs are recorded, then you have to get paid.

- **Get paid on spec.** This approach is the one that most fledgling producers use when starting their careers. The deal is that if the artist or band "makes it" (meaning they get signed by a major label and get an advance), then you'll get paid your project fee, points on the project (a percentage of the royalties), or both. The chances of that happening are always long, no matter how much you believe in the act, so be prepared to spend your time working for free. The one good thing here is that you'll be gaining experience.

If you're going to work on contingency, you'll need to get two things from the artist or band. The first thing is to strike a larger deal than what your normal rate would bring because you need to be more highly compensated to make it worth your while, since you'll be working on spec. That could be anywhere from 20, to 50, even 100 percent more—whatever you can negotiate. You can justify the higher rate by saying, "I'm providing a lot of valuable time and expertise that you're not paying me for right now. Maybe it'll take a long time to see this money, or maybe I'll never see it. That's worth an extra premium."

The second thing to get is an agreement stating the terms of how much and under what circumstances you'll get paid. While you should go to an attorney to get this drawn up, that can cost money you either might not have or don't want to spend on a project that may never pay off.

Even if the agreement is only a single paragraph long, be sure to get it in writing because people tend to forget or remember differently over time, and it pays to have something on paper.

At the very least, write down which songs you've worked on (or are going to work on), the dollar amounts agreed upon, the time frame in which you'll be paid (for example, "30 days after signing a major- or indie-label agreement"), and how you'll get paid (for instance, "in full by cashier's check"), just so no one forgets. This agreement may not be legally binding and may have plenty of holes that a high-priced lawyer could drive a truck through, but if the people you're dealing with are on the up-and-up, you'll at least have a piece of paper to remind everyone of your contribution to their success and how you all agreed you'd be compensated.

- **Charge an hourly rate.** As long as you know you'll get paid, this arrangement is the safest way to go. When, for example, you inevitably spend that extra week on overdubs or mixing, you'll get paid for the time you put in. The hourly rate keeps people focused and stops them from adding those extra five overdubs "just to see what they sound like," or from trying ten more takes when you all agreed that the third take was great.

- **A combination of the above.** Many times payment can consist of a little bit of money or a little bit of spec, some items at a flat rate and some at hourly, or some combination. Try not to get too complicated. A simple deal works best for everyone, especially when it comes to getting paid. Just realize that there are a lot of options available.

There are a lot of good books on the subject of how to structure a deal for yourself that are more comprehensive then what was just laid out above. Even if you decide that the reading material is too dry or boring to tackle, get an attorney if you're sure that the money you'll earn will cover the cost. At the very least, always get it in writing.

CHAPTER 5
ASSEMBLING THE BUDGET

andling the budget for a recording project can be one of the most challenging aspects of being a producer. Regardless of who's paying for the project, it's up to you to not only create the budget but also spend the finances wisely.

WHEN A LABEL IS INVOLVED

If a label will be paying the bill for recording, most likely they'll say, "We need you to bring in this project for xxx dollars." That makes your life a bit easier, since that will give you a major parameter to work with, so you'll just try to fit everything into the financial box that you've been given. Most likely, though, your project will start with the words, "What do you think it will cost . . .?" Those words suddenly take the project to another level of difficulty, since you'll need to gather up a lot more information before the question can be answered.

Assuming that you're already familiar with the artist and her material, here's what you'll need to find out:

- **How many songs?** The more songs, the more time you'll need to complete the project. The more time you need, the more money it will cost.

- **How will the project be released?** If the final release will include CD or vinyl formats, you'll have to figure additional mastering costs. If the release is intended only for online distribution, that will also impact your budget, because the revenue generated might not be enough to recoup the costs.

- **Will the costs of manufacturing be included in the budget?** A neophyte artist, band, or record label sometimes includes the entire cost of CD or vinyl manufacturing in the recording budget,. More established or experienced entities recognize that manufacturing is a burden that shouldn't be charged to the artist. Regardless, including the manufacturing costs in the budget can put a serious ding in the amount of money you have for recording, so it's best to get the answer to this up front.

- **Are mastering costs part of the budget?** Sometimes mastering is seen as the first part of manufacturing and is not charged to the production budget. Make sure that you find out if you're responsible for mastering expenses, even though they shouldn't be part of your budget.

- **What kind of sound or direction are you looking for?** The answer to this question will determine whether the band members will play together in the studio or the parts will be layered, and whether studio musicians will need to be hired, a large tracking room will be required, and exotic musical instruments or recording gear must be rented, all of which will impact the budget.

- **What kind of facilities are you comfortable recording in?** This determines the environment and the type of studio that the project might require. Some artists don't care how lowbrow the studio or even if it's a small home studio owned by a band member or the producer, as long as the final product is what they're looking for. Other artists have to be in a top-notch facility that caters to their every whim in order to perform well. Yet other artists have a certain facility that they're particularly comfortable working in. The answer to this question may impact your final budget more than anything.

- **Does the budget include my fee?** This question is somewhat moot if you're going to be working on spec, but if not, its answer can have a large impact on your budget. Regardless of who's paying the bill, you've got to know how much you ultimately have to work with to be able to successfully produce the product.

- **Are you sure you don't have a budget in mind?** Most artists, bands, neophyte labels, and financiers have a figure in mind before they even speak with you, but are afraid to tell you because they don't want to look as inexperienced as they are. It's best you learn what that figure is as soon as possible so you don't do a lot of budget-development work only to find out that the artist had only a fraction of the amount to spend in the first place—or, even worse, to find that you left money on the table that could have been used for production.

Typical Label Budgets

Budgets vary wildly depending on the previous success (or lack of success) of the artist; the strength, size, and priority of the record label; the cash available to the person writing the check; and even where you're recording. Still, it helps to know what's considered to be a budget norm for the type of project you want to do so that you don't have to reinvent the wheel.

There was a time in the music business before online music became prevalent where a newly signed baby artist might get between $150K and $250K to record their first album. Artists further up the success ladder received larger budgets well beyond that. Although it's still true that the more success you have, the larger your budget will be, the days of large standard budgets are long gone, with the norm now somewhere between $50K (or even less) and $80K for a baby act.

For most of you reading this book, $50K may seem like a lot of money, but it's really difficult to make a great record in a first-class studio with a great engineer for that amount. As a result, most producers of label acts have resorted to many of the tricks you'll find covered in this book, like spending more time in preproduction or tracking in a large studio for a limited amount of time with a great engineer, and then doing overdubs in a home studio with an assistant engineer.

That said, unless you're signed to a label, you probably won't have $50K available for your project. Take heart, because it's still possible to do something great for hardly any money. Whatever your budget, you can make things work with a little planning.

A Label Budget Example

Here's a typical $50,000 budget for a band that just signed with a subsidiary of a major label (see Table 5.1). They want to record an eight-song album that will be released on CD and online. The first thing to do is to schedule ten days for rehearsal:

- One day to listen to all the material that the band has, and then pick the best possible songs to record
- One day of rehearsal for each song chosen
- An additional day to work up some alternative songs in case one of the eight just doesn't fly in the studio

Next, schedule five days for tracking, assuming that you can complete two tracks a day, with a half day for setup and another half day for leeway in case one of the songs just won't come together.

For overdubs, figure about two days per song, for a total of 16 days. Break that into four days for lead vocals (two vocals per day), two days for background vocals, a day for miscellaneous overdubs (percussion and a horn section), four days for guitar overdubs, four days for keyboard overdubs, and an extra day in case it's needed.

For mixing, plan on each song taking about a day to mix by a competent engineer in his home studio (eight days), with another four days for a series of tweaks or remixes as necessary. Finally, you'll want to master at a high-level mastering facility that will give you a deal (about half off), because you're not using the top guy and using off-hour time.

For overdubs, let's pretend you're bringing in a four-piece horn section, three of whom are getting paid a union rate of $398 for a three-hour session, with the leader being paid double. Also say that you're going to bring in a top of the line percussionist to fill out the track at a double scale of $795.

The percussionist asks you to pay the cartage fee of $125 for his vast array of percussion gear. The union requires that you pay 12 percent of the session pay rate into a pension fund, and an additional $24 per player into a health and welfare fund.

Finally, say you hire a background vocal section consisting of three female singers. They are non-union and charge $150 each for the session.

The producer's $5,000 advance comes out of the budget, as well as $500 for the label's hottest artist to come play a guest guitar solo on a song. One of the songs has a sample of a minor hit from the

'80s, and the publisher gives you a super deal so that you can get the license to use it for only $1,000.

With five people in the band, a road manager, a recording engineer and an assistant, and a producer and maybe a production assistant, there are ten people that have to be fed every day. Figuring a lowball figure of $10 per person per day for a total of 42 days (all the production days), the total comes out to $4,200 just for food. Of course, all ten people will not be in studio on all of the days, which makes this part of the budget stretch a little.

A Neumann U-67 large-diaphragm condenser mic fits the lead singer's voice perfectly, so you rent it and a couple of Neve 1073 mic amps for the five days of tracking and five days of overdubs. You also need to buy at least three hard drives: one for daily use, and the others for backup.

You've managed to get a pretty good engineer for basic tracking who's charging only $500 a day since business is slow. He's throwing in his rack of microphone preamps and compressors, but asking that you pay the $200 cartage fee. You're using an up-and-coming engineer to help engineer the overdubs for $250 a day. Finally, a pretty good mixer is giving you a bargain at $500 per day for his services and $250 for the use of his studio.

The budget you're working with has provisions for travel and auto expenses in case they're required, although there are none on this project. You also figure in a 10 percent contingency in case of any unforeseen expenses, like needing an extra day of tracking, overdubs, or mixing.

TABLE 5.1: BUDGET FOR A BABY BAND SIGNED TO A LABEL				
Budget Item	Number of People	Number of Days	Cost per Day	Total
Studio				
Rehearsal		10	$75	$750
Tracking		5	$750	$3,750
Overdubs		16	$250	$4,000
Mixing		12	$250	$3,000
Mastering		1	$1,000	$1,000
TOTAL STUDIO EXPENSES				$12,500

Musicians				
Single scale	3	1	$398 (NY local)	$1,194
Double scale	1	1	$790	$790
Leader	1	1	$795	$795
Doubles				
Cartage			$125	$125
Background singers	3	1	$150 (non-union)	$450
American Federation of Musicians Union (12% + $24)	5	1	$63	$454
TOTAL MUSICIAN EXPENSES				$3,808
Advances				
Producers			$5,000	$5,000
Guest artist			$500	$500
License fees for sampling			$1,000	$1,000
TOTAL ADVANCES				$6,500
Rentals		15	$250	$3,750
Miscellaneous				
Food	10	42	$10	$4,200
Hard drives		3	$100	$300
TOTAL MISCELLANEOUS EXPENSES				$8,250
Labor				
Engineer (tracking)	1	5	$500	$2,500
Engineer (overdubs)	1	16	$250	$4,000

Engineer (mixing)	1	12	$500	$6,000
Cartage			$200	$200
Production assistant	1	30	$60	$1,800
Production coordinator				
TOTAL LABOR EXPENSES				$14,500
General miscellaneous				
Travel and living				
Auto				
TOTAL GENERAL MISCELLANEOUS EXPENSES				
TOTAL				$45,558
10% Contingency				$4,556
GRAND TOTAL				$50,012

AN INDIE BAND BUDGET

Table 5.2 shows much the same circumstances, only with a band that wishes to release their music via all the online digital services plus an eight-song CD, but this time the band isn't signed to a label and is financing the project with a combination of their own money and money from some investors. Everything has to be done on as tight a budget as possible.

In this case, the ten days of rehearsal are done in the garage of one of the band members for no cost. Five days of tracking is done in the best studio in the area, which costs $350 a day. All 16 days of overdubs are done in the home studio of one of the band members. The best engineer in the area agrees to mix the record for a flat fee per song "all in" (meaning all the costs are included, including the charge for his studio), and mastering is done at a mid-level mastering house.

There's not enough money for a horn section, so it's done with samples from a keyboard, but three female background singers are brought in, and they charge $50 each for the session.

The producer is a friend of the band and the leader of the biggest band in the area, and the band members agree to pay him a $500 advance so he won't feel as though he's working for free, with another $4,500 and four points promised if the project gets signed and the band sees an advance from the label.

There are no rentals except for a Hammond B-3, where the owner charges $150 for two days of use, including cartage. There's no cash allocated for food, and everyone survives on his or her own lunch money, just as they always do. A main project hard drive is purchased along with a couple of extra drives as backup.

The tracking engineer charges $250 a day (a good rate for the locality), but different members of the band and the producer all engineer the overdubs, so there's no cost there. The same engineer who tracked the project will mix it, again for $250 a day, but the number of tweaks or remixes is limited to only an additional couple of days past the initial eight. The engineer doesn't bring his own gear, so there's no need to pay any cartage fees.

The project comes in at $7,000 exactly, and the 10 percent contingency brings it to just $7,700, a price that's still high, but reachable, for the band and their investors.

TABLE 5.2: BUDGET FOR A SELF-FINANCED PROJECT				
Budget Item	Number of People	Number of Days	Cost per Day	Total
Studio				
Rehearsal		10	$0	$0
Tracking		5	$350	$1,750
Overdubs		16	$0	$0
Mixing		12	$0	$0
Mastering		1	$750	$750
TOTAL STUDIO EXPENSES				$2,500
Musicians				
Single scale			$398	$0
Double scale			$795	$0
Leader			$795	$0
Doubles				

Cartage				
Background singers	3	1	$50	$150
American Federation of Musicians Union (11% + $22)			$63	$0
TOTAL MUSICIANS EXPENSES				$150
Advances				
Producers			$500	$500
Guest artist				
License fees for sampling				
TOTAL ADVANCES				$500
Rentals		2	$75	$150
Miscellaneous				
Food	10	42		$0
Hard drives		3	$100	$300
TOTAL MISCELLANEOUS EXPENSES				$450
Labor				
Engineer (tracking)	1	5	$250	$1,250
Engineer (overdubs)	1	16		$0
Engineer (mixing)	1	8	$250	$2,000
Cartage				
Production assistant				$0
Production coordinator				$0
TOTAL LABOR EXPENSES				$3,250

General miscellaneous				
Travel and living				
Auto				
TOTAL GENERAL MISCELLANEOUS EXPENSES				
TOTAL				$7,000
10% Contingency				$700
GRAND TOTAL				$7,700

USING UNION MUSICIANS

As you saw in Table 5.1, it costs a lot more money to hire musicians who work under the American Federation of Musicians (AFM) union rules than to hire ones who don't.

Not only is the pay generally higher for union musicians than it is for non-union players (and they work shorter sessions as well), but you also have additional costs that go beyond what the player gets directly, which I'll cover in a bit. What's more, union rates can be somewhat of a maze, because different scales cover different situations and the rates are renegotiated every few years.

Generally, the union pay scales for recording are based on three-hour sessions and are broken down as follows:

- **Basic session scale.** This is the scale used to pay musicians to record a typical medium- or big-budget master recording for a major record label. It's the highest-paying scale and has the most perks.
- **Premium rate scale.** If a session is booked on weekdays after midnight, on Saturdays after 1 p.m., or on Sundays, the premium rate scale kicks in at 150 percent of the basic session scale.
- **Demo scale.** With this type of scale, the demo can only be used to secure a master record deal and can't be sold commercially. This rate is the least expensive (to the producer) of all the scales. Demo scale is a relic from a time when having a demo was a necessity to take your project to a higher level in the business. Even though this pay scale is still on the books, it is now outdated because demos are so easy to make and any recording is so easy to release commercially.
- **Limited-pressing scale.** This scale is another relic of the past, thanks to digital music. It allows the producer or label to make

and sell up to 10,000 copies of anything the musicians play on. The limited-pressing scale pays a bit more than the demo scale.

- **Low-budget scale.** The low-budget scale was originally created to help small indie record labels that never had the large recording budgets typical of a major-label product. The key here is that the budget needs to be below $99,000 total (that means including all costs including mixing, engineers, food, etc.), but the label can sell as many copies of the product as they want.

- **Music video scale.** This is almost the same as the basic session scale except for a slightly lesser rate.

- **Jingle scale.** The jingle scale is a little different in that most jingle (music for commercials) sessions are so short that everything is based on a single hour of recording with 20-minute increments. The number of jingles that can be recorded in that time period is limited to three (or three minutes of music total), or else you must pay the musicians for another session. The musicians also get paid for every 13-week run that the commercial stays on the air, although that doesn't come out of your budget. In addition, the musicians get paid if the producer takes the music bed that was recorded and creates an additional commercial (called a "dub fee") or a new commercial (called a "conversion fee").

- **Motion picture and television film scales.** This is a dizzying array of different scales that cover different types of films and budgets.

Additional Fees

There are other fees that must be paid under certain circumstances on a union date.

- The leader is always entitled to twice the scale rate, regardless of which kind of session or what rate scale you're using.

- If a musician doubles on a second instrument during the session, he or she will make an additional 20 to 30 percent (depending on the type of session and scale) and an extra 15 to 20 percent for each additional instrument played after that.

- In some cases, a musician may even get an additional payment for cartage of large instruments. For example, $12 for cello, baritone sax, bass sax, contrabass clarinet, tuba, drums, marimba, chimes, accordion, Cordovox, and each amplifier, and $30 for harp, keyboard, tympani, vibraphone, and bass.

- In addition to the hourly scale amount, the producer will contribute another 12 percent or so to the musician's union pension fund, an additional 3 percent to his or her health and welfare fund, and in some cases, 4 percent more to a vacation fund.

As stated before, the scales and rates are subject to change every few years, so it's best to check with your union local to find out exactly what those rates are today. This section is just a thumbnail of the details, so be sure to check for all the particulars that might apply to your specific session well in advance of the downbeat, and make sure that the session leader or contractor (whoever files the paperwork) is on the same page as you are.

Here's a list of the major media centers' union locals and websites:

New York City Local 802, local802afm.org
Los Angles Local 47, promusic47.org
Nashville Local 257, afm257.org
Chicago Local 10-208, cfm10208.com

Hiring Union Musicians

The best way to ensure that you get the players you want, stay within the confines of the union, and have all the paperwork filed, is to hire a union contractor who will put the appropriate players together for you. If you need a horn or string section, a single call to a contractor will get you the players you need, instead of having to assemble the section yourself (which can be hit or miss as to the quality of players if you're not familiar with them).

The contractor acts as a go-between for musicians and producers, and is required to be present at all times during the session when his contracted musicians are recording.

Contractors come in two varieties: union and independent. Both are usually musicians themselves who supervise and provide additional services for a session. A contractor can help musicians and singers prepare by supplying them with the necessary information for the session and making sure that they and their specified instruments and equipment arrive at the event or session on time. A contractor coordinates the event, coaches, conducts, computes session fees, and submits the proper union forms to the employer and union office.

It is not uncommon for contractors to specialize in a specific area of the business, such as jingles, orchestral dates, or film and television sessions. For a contractor, it's all about relationships. His or her reputation is founded on the experience level and quality of the musicians they make available, so it makes sense for you to cultivate relationships with the local contractors.

Union Versus Non-Union Players

Any time you do a project with a record label, film studio, or production company that is a union signatory, you must use union players and pay union rates as per their contract with the union. Officially, this means that if a new band has signed to a major label, they'll have to join the union and be paid union wages to perform on their own album.

There are numerous ways around this (like the recording fund discussed in the next section), and so this rarely happens, but you get the idea as to how this can impact your budget if you're not aware of what you're getting into.

Even if your project is non-union, you may still have to pay union rates to string, horn, and vocal sections, especially if they're top-notch, or else they just won't make themselves available. Of course, that applies more to the major media centers than it does anywhere else.

That being said, most union musicians will take a non-union gig when times are slow and money is tight. Once again, their fee might be based on an hourly, a daily, or a by-the-song/project rate, but if they're available and you've got the money, chances are they'll be set up in the studio waiting for your downbeat.

Right now, even some of the best musicians in New York, Nashville, and Los Angeles can be had for $100 as long as there's no hassle, no cartage involved, and you can work around the player's schedule. Many will give you a big discount if you work at their home studios or just send them the project files so they can work on it when they have the time. No matter how you do it, you can always find bargains for getting great players as long as you make the session easy for them to do.

THE RECORDING FUND

Once upon a time, the recording budget was totally controlled by the record label. This system worked pretty well in the early days, when a staff producer used the in-house studio to produce the record. As independent studios and producers sprung up during the '80s, however, the record label would pay the production bills through a series of purchase orders (which was essentially an agreement to purchase goods or services at a set price, so you didn't get any unexpected bills down the road) and invoices from the studio, players, tape suppliers, and anyone else having anything to do with production.

Everyone hated this system. Vendors hated it because it would take so long to get paid (at least 90 days). Labels hated it because of the increased paperwork and administration involved. Producers hated it because they were usually caught between screaming vendors who demanded payment, and the label's accounting department, which could pay only after the purchase order was signed by the ninth person (no joke) up the executive ladder. Eventually, the "recording fund" solved all that.

When payment is made by using a recording fund, the entire recording budget is paid to the band or artist in one lump sum. At that point it then becomes the musicians' responsibility to pay all the expenses pertaining to making the record. The band can use the money any way it sees fit, but it has to deliver a quality product by a specific date as outlined in an amendment to their recording contract. If the project comes in under budget, the band gets to keep the excess. If the budget runs a little over (up to about ten percent), the label will pay that also, but if the costs ran higher than that, it comes out of the band's pocket.

The fund was a great idea for the labels, because they no longer had to worry about the hassle of paying every vendor involved with the production, which saved money on accounting costs. If an experienced producer was hired, a label could be reasonably sure that the project would come in on time and on budget.

For most artists and bands, having the budget money in their bank account suddenly made them a lot more cost-conscious, always a good thing. It also gave the band members the opportunity to buy their own recording gear, so they didn't have to worry about spending money on studio time. The fund could also be a godsend for the producer, who could now make sure that a vendor got paid either on the spot or in a short period of time if a manager or business manager was cutting the check.

Although a recording fund might be a revelation for a label artist, it's the normal way of doing business for every artist or band that isn't signed. Even legacy superstar acts like Prince, Rush, and The Stones pay their own recording costs these days. Although it still might take a while to get paid via the business management from a superstar act, it's still a lot faster than waiting for the label's accounting department (most are now paying at 120 days or more).

A FINAL WORD ON BUDGET

Whether your budget is $750 or $750,000, don't look at it only as a financial abstraction. A budget is your road map. A budget is your plan. It's how you get smoothly from a concept to the finished product.

With a well-thought-through budget and timeline, you will always stay on schedule when there's nothing unforeseen, and you'll easily adapt when the unforeseen arises. Don't take your budget lightly.

CHAPTER 6
IT'S ALL IN THE SONG

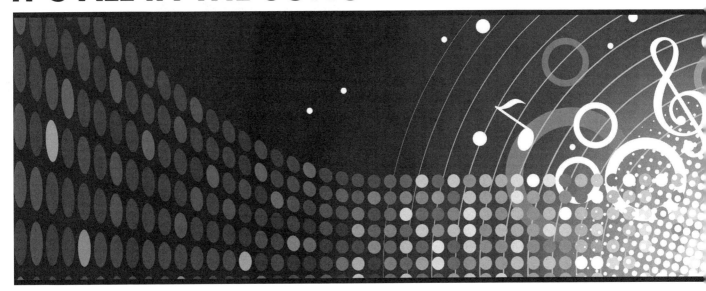

t the heart of every music production is its basic building block—the song. It's the key element, because if you don't have a great song or songs, you won't have a great record. You can have the most brilliant players provide excellent performances, and you can do a masterful production job, but if the songs aren't there, not much of the audience is going to care beyond the first listen. Indeed, music history is littered with artists, bands, and records that had everything going for them except the most important thing: the songs.

That's why I'm spending an entire chapter analyzing song structure. In the end, no one can predict what will be a hit or what might touch your audience's heart or feet, but certain elements have tended to work in popular music of all types since the beginning of recorded music. It helps to know what works before you try something else.

LET'S DISCUSS YOUR SONGS

While this book is not a songwriting handbook, I'd like to point out a number of common problems that stick out when an artist or band inexperienced at songwriting or arranging first play their songs to me. Keep in mind that I'm talking about songs from all genres of music.

No matter what it is, from rock to country to goth to rockabilly to alien space music, you want the song to be interesting to your particular audience, so beware of any of the following elements if they apply to any song or songs that you are planning to record.

- **Too long.** One thing I hear a lot are songs with sections that are way too long. Two-minute intros, three-minute guitar solos, and five-minute outros are almost always boring. The idea should be to keep everything interesting and to the point. You are always better off having a section be too short rather than too long. The only exception is if you can make a long section interesting, which takes a lot of arranging skill, and even then still might not keep the audience's attention.

  One really long outro that does work, for example, is the outro to Lynyrd Skynyrd's classic "Free Bird," because of the slight arrangement changes, kicks, and accents every 16 bars. A great band, great performance, and great arrangement hold the listener's attention to the very end—and that's your goal, after all.

- **No focus.** Beginning songwriters often have songs that lack focus, which means that the songs meander from chord to chord with no apparent structure and no clear distinction between sections. This is often the result of not honing a song enough and thinking it's finished way before it really is. Sometimes there's a song in the unfinished form if you peel the layers back and dig a bit, but usually the only way to fix it is to go back to the drawing board for a major rewrite.

- **Weak chorus.** In many songs written by neophyte writers, it's difficult to tell when the verse stops and the chorus starts—they're basically the same. An interesting chorus has something different from the verse. It may be just a little different, like adding background vocals or another instrument, or an accent or anticipation to the same chord changes and melody (like Mark Ronson/Bruno Mars' "Uptown Funk," with its synthesizer and horns; Stevie Ray Vaughn's "Crossfire," with its horn hits and guitar fill; and Michael Jackson's "Don't Stop 'Til You Get Enough," with its string pad and horn fill).

  The chorus could also be a lot different from the verses as well, with a different set of chord changes or melody combined with the arrangement changes previously mentioned. "Vertigo" by U2, "This Kiss" by Faith Hill, or the Eagles' classic "Hotel California" fall into this class. Either way, something has to change in the chorus to lift the energy and keep the song memorable.

- **No bridge.** Another common songwriting mistake is neglecting to include a bridge in a song. A bridge is an interlude that connects two parts of a song, building a harmonic connection between those parts by increasing or decreasing the tension. Normally, the verse is played at least twice before a bridge is introduced. The bridge may then replace the third verse or precede it. In the latter case, the bridge delays an expected chorus.

The chorus after the bridge is usually the last one and is often repeated in order to stress that the song is nearing its end. When you expect to hear a verse or a chorus but hear something that's musically and lyrically different from both the verse and chorus, it's most likely the bridge (Katy Perry's "Firework" comes to mind).

A bridge is important because it provides a basic quality found in all art forms: tension and release (in music, going from loud to quiet or quiet to loud; in painting, going from dark to light colors; in photography, moving visually from light to shadows, and so on). Using tension and release keeps things interesting. The bridge is sometimes the peak of the song, the point at which it's at its loudest and most intense (check out the bridge of the Foo Fighters' "Rope"). Or the bridge could be a song's quietest and least intense point (The Who's "Baba O'Riley," when Pete Townsend sings "It's only teenage wasteland").

Almost every great song has a bridge, but there are the occasional exceptions. Songs that are based on a straight 12-bar blues pattern frequently don't have bridges, but they might use dynamics or a specific arrangement to provide the tension and release. An example would be the ZZ Top classic "Tush." There's no bridge in the song, but the snare fill by itself after the last verse into the outro guitar solo supplies the release. Another would be the Guess Who/Lenny Kravitz song "American Woman," where there are just four bars of a different guitar rhythm and a stop.

And then there are the songs that can get by without a bridge by virtue of how they're arranged or how long each section is. Fleetwood Mac's "Dreams" has only two verses and three choruses, but listen to how everything builds so that the peak of the song is the last chorus.

- **Poor arrangement.** Even with great songwriters, this mistake is the most common one I hear. Usually this means that the guitar or keyboard will play the same lick, chords, or rhythm throughout the entire song. That can work perfectly well and might even be a great arrangement choice if another instrument plays a counter-line or rhythm, but normally it just means that the arrangement will be boring. You've got to make sure that the song stays interesting, and that means the addition of lines and fills. An example of a song in which a structure like this does work is "American Woman" (again).

- **No intro/outro hook.** If we're talking about modern popular music (not jazz or classical), most songs have an instrumental line, or hook, that you'll hear at the beginning of the song, maybe again in the chorus, and any time the intro repeats in the song. Great examples of hooks are the opening guitar riff in The Stones' "Satisfaction," the whistle on Maroon 5's "Moves Like Jagger," or the opening piano part in Coldplay's "Clocks." Developing a song's intro/outro hooks is one of the major challenges that a producer faces.

- **No song dynamics.** Once again, one of the secrets to creating an interesting song is to use tension and release. Regarding dynamics, tension and release is expressed by the music getting loud, and then soft (or vice versa). Grading the volume level on a scale of 1 to 10 (10 being the loudest), the typical song will look something like this:

TABLE 6.1: SONG DYNAMICS			
Song Section	Dynamic Level	Song Section	Dynamic Level
Intro	8	Prechorus	7
Verse	5	Chorus	9
Prechorus	7	Bridge	10
Chorus	9	Chorus	9
Intro	8	Chorus	9
Verse	6	Outro	9

Notice how the song breathes in volume from loud to soft, to louder to softer, to louder to really loud. Notice how the intensity builds. That's tension and release. Even if the song doesn't use this song structure, you always have to consider the volume envelope of the song before recording it. Ultimately, the sound and the arrangement will both be a lot better right out of the box (see Chapter 7 for more on dynamics).

Dynamics on Records

While playing dynamically by varying the playing intensity works during recording (especially if you're all recording live), another way to change dynamics on a record is by adding and subtracting instruments to the mix. A typical arrangement might look something like the following:

INTRO
Drums (drummer playing
   on ride cymbal)
Bass
Rhythm guitar
Organ
Lead guitar playing a line
Verse
Drums (drummer playing
   on hi-hat)
Bass
Rhythm guitar
Vocal

PRECHORUS
Drums (drummer playing
   on hi-hat)
Bass
Rhythm guitar
Organ
Vocal
Harmony vocal

CHORUS
Drums (drummer playing
   on ride cymbal)
Bass
Rhythm guitar
Organ
Vocal
Lead guitar line against vocals

2ND INTRO
Drums (drummer playing
   on ride cymbal)
Bass
Rhythm guitar
Organ
Lead guitar line from intro

2ND VERSE
Drums (drummer playing on hi-hat)
Bass
Rhythm guitar
Organ
Vocal
Lead guitar playing answer riffs in
   the holes between vocal phrases

2ND PRECHORUS
Drums (drummer playing on hi-hat)
Bass
Rhythm guitar
Organ
Vocal
Harmony vocal

2ND CHORUS
Drums (drummer playing
   on ride cymbal)
Bass
Rhythm guitar
Organ
Vocal
Background vocals
Lead guitar line against vocals

BRIDGE
Drums (drummer playing
    on ride cymbal)
Bass
Rhythm guitar
Organ
Piano
Vocal
Tambourine

CHORUS
Drums (drummer playing
    on ride cymbal)
Bass
Rhythm guitar
Organ
Piano

Vocal
Background vocals
Lead guitar line against vocals
Tambourine

CHORUS
Drums (drummer playing on ride
    cymbal)
Bass
Rhythm guitar
Organ
Piano
Vocal
Background vocals
Lead guitar line against vocals
Tambourine
Lead guitar solo fills

Notice how something different happens in every section of the song. An instrument is either added or subtracted or played a little differently, as with the drums alternating between the hi-hat and ride cymbals. This arrangement not only makes the song sound naturally dynamic, but it also makes it sound a lot more interesting as well. Compare the above outline to many of the big hit songs from the past 40 years or so, and you'll find they all use some variation of the above. If it's worked so well before, it will work for you, too.

ARRANGEMENTS ARE THE KEY

One of the first things a producer does during preproduction is to dig deep into the song to check out the arrangement and the song's structure. Even if a song is written well and has catchy hooks, the arrangement is what really makes it cook.

How you arrange the song is the key to how it will ultimately sound. The song can be played with great precision and dynamics, but it will never catch fire sonically unless all the instruments and vocals complement each other in such a way that the sum of the band's parts sound bigger and better together than as individual instruments and voices. Here are some things to consider:

Arrangement Elements

Some songwriters have the arrangements worked out in their heads for each band member to play, but for most songwriters (even the most accomplished), that skill has to be developed, or else handed off to a specialist. In order to understand how an arrangement influences a song, you must first understand the mechanics of a well-written arrangement.

Most well-conceived arrangements are limited with regard to the number of elements that occur at the same time. An element can be a single instrument (like a lead guitar or a vocal), or it can be a group of instruments (like the bass and drums, a doubled guitar line, a group of backing vocals, and so on).

Generally, a group of instruments playing exactly the same rhythm is considered an element. For example, a doubled lead guitar or doubled vocal is a single element, as is a lead vocal with two additional harmonies. Two lead guitars playing two different parts are two elements, however. A lead guitar playing a single note line and a rhythm guitar playing chords are two separate elements as well.

Here are the typical arrangement elements that make up most modern music:

- **Foundation.** The foundation is the rhythm section, and usually consists of the bass and drums, but can also include a rhythm guitar and/or keys if they're playing the same rhythmic figure as the rhythm section. Occasionally, as in the case of power trios, the foundation element will be drums only, since the bass usually has to play a different rhythm figure to fill out the sound, and must become its own element.
- **Pad.** A pad is a long, sustained note or chord. In the days before synthesizers, a Hammond organ provided the best pad, and was joined later by the Fender Rhodes electric piano. Synthesizers now provide the majority of pads, but a real string section or a guitar power chord can also suffice.
- **Rhythm.** Rhythm is any instrument that plays counter to the foundation element. This can be a double-time shaker or tambourine, a rhythm guitar strumming on the backbeat, or congas playing a Latin feel. The rhythm element is used to add motion and excitement to the track.
- **Lead.** A lead vocal, lead instrument, or solo.
- **Fills.** Fills generally occur in the spaces between lead lines, or they can be a signature line. You can think of a fill element as an answer to the lead element.

That's not to say that each individual instrument is a separate element, however. On Bruno Mars' "Grenade," the instruments are used in a traditional fashion found in most pop and rock songs.

BRUNO MARS, "GRENADE"	
Foundation	Bass, drums
Pad	Organ
Rhythm	Arpeggiated electric piano line in the verse, the double time feel of the drums in the chorus and outro, percussion
Lead	Lead vocal
Fills	Background vocals and the occasional percussion sound effect

First of all, the song has standard yet effective dynamics, with less intense verses compared to the big-sounding choruses. An interesting difference from most songs is that the drums play a tom pattern to add motion to the song rather than the snare, although a small-sounding snare (which actually fits the song perfectly) enters in the second verse. Using the drums in this way is not only unusual, but really interesting as well.

"Grenade" also uses a variety of fills to keep the listener constantly engaged, with percussion, vocals, piano, and synthesizers all sharing that duty. Finally, the background vocals add to both the motion and the tension of the song as well. This song was a huge international hit and the production is a big reason why.

In Pharrell Williams' big hit "Happy," there are bass and drums, guitar, piano, lead vocal, background vocals, and claps. This is how they break out.

PHARRELL WILLIAMS, "HAPPY"	
Foundation	Drums, electric piano
Pad	Background vocals and electric piano in chorus
Rhythm	Bass, claps in the chorus
Lead	Lead vocal
Fills	Background vocal answers, and guitar fills in the holes

Usually the bass is a big part of the foundation element of a song, but in "Happy" it serves almost as a counterpoint to drums (although it's buried in the mix and difficult to hear). Likewise, the electric piano can sometimes serve only as a pad and it does in the chorus, but otherwise it's a big part of the foundation of the song, which is unusual.

"Poker Face" was a huge hit for Lady Gaga, and a close listen to the song tells you exactly why; it has everything we've come to expect from a megahit. Although the song form may be pretty basic, it's expertly arranged to continually keep the interest high, since there's always forward motion and dynamics.

LADY GAGA, "POKER FACE"	
Foundation	Kick drum
Pad	String lines during chorus
Rhythm	Synthesizer, claps
Lead	Lead vocal
Fills	Background vocals

"Poker Face" takes a page from electronic dance music and focuses the foundation around the kick drum. There's no real bass instrument in the song, so the kick takes up that sonic space, along with a number of synthesizers.

What's especially interesting is that both the bridge and interlude/choruses at the end of the song are primarily choruses with either new parts or a combination of new and previously heard parts. It's a great way to keep things familiar yet different.

Rascal Flatts' "What Hurts the Most" is an example of the "new" country music, which closely resembles layered pop music except traditional country instruments (steel, banjo, fiddle) are added.

RASCAL FLATTS, "WHAT HURTS THE MOST"	
Foundation	Bass, drums
Pad	Steel and guitar in chorus
Rhythm	Acoustic guitar in verses, banjo and shaker in chorus
Lead	Fiddle in intro, lead vocal, lead guitar in solo
Fills	Steel answer to fiddle in intro, harmony answer to vocal at the beginning of the outro

The arrangement for "What Hurts the Most" is unusual because it has no fills in the intro or outro (and only in one spot for each). The bass is very loud in the mix and takes up a lot of space as a result.

What's especially cool is all the sections of the song that repeat but are slightly different the second or third time through. A good example is the line in the last bar of the first half of the intro, which is first played on acoustic guitar, then doubled with the fiddle the second time through. On the third pass there's a steel fill.

Another great example is the last chorus, where the song stops and the melody changes, and then the background vocals enter right afterwards.

Also listen to how the second verse develops with the entrance of fiddle and electric guitar. Then in the second chorus the steel and banjo enter.

FOO FIGHTERS, "ROPE"	
Foundation	Bass, drums
Pad	Guitar power chords in the chorus
Rhythm	Rhythm guitars in the verse
Lead	Lead vocal, interlude guitar, drum solo, wah guitar solo
Fills	Guitar on the riff turnaround

This song has more than the the usual number of arrangement pieces occurring, which makes it different from most other rock songs. First of all, there are a couple of rhythm guitars playing tremolo parts (the intro), and then both guitar players are strumming rhythm guitar during the verse and choruses instead of predetermined parts like other songs from the genre. A third guitar plays the heart of the riff, then enters only at the syncopated verse turnarounds.

The bass is free-floating and creates a nice tension against the chords in spots that's very cool, as is the drum solo in the bridge. (When's the last time you heard one of those?) Interestingly, some of the cool bass lines that Nate Mandel plays are in the first verse rather then the second, where you'd typically change things up to sound different or develop the song.

Another interesting thing is that the second verse doesn't change much from the first, so the song doesn't develop at that point, but this isn't something you'll necessarily notice when listening to the song.

Yet another interesting part is the bridge, which features a drum fill/solo on the first half, which then introduces a wah guitar solo on the second half.

Sonic Arrangements

When two instruments with essentially the same bandwidth frequency (like guitars) play at the same volume at the same time, the result is a fight for attention. Think of it this way; you don't usually hear a lead vocal and a guitar solo at the same time, do you? That's because the human ear isn't able to decide which to listen to, and becomes confused and fatigued as a result.

So how do you get around two instruments "fighting" one another? First and foremost is to have a well-written arrangement that keeps the various instruments out of each other's way right from the beginning. The best writers and arrangers have an innate feel for what type of arrangement will work, and the result is an arrangement that automatically comes together without much help—but they're the lucky ones. Most of the rest of us have to use our experience along with some trial and error to make everything work together.

Clash of the Guitar Players

Most bands have more than one guitar player and most songs have more than one guitar part, so it's important to learn how to refine the guitar sounds so the recording sounds big and fat instead of loud, thin, and confused. In order to accomplish this, you have to make sure that the songs are arranged so that the guitars stay out of each other's way. If you listen closely to just about any recording by a popular artist, you'll see that this is just what's happened in the studio already. If you can hear within the song (which isn't always easy with certain types of music or low-quality audio delivery formats like MP3s), this is what you'll hear.

- **Each guitar is playing something completely different.** One guitar might be playing full chords, while the other is playing a line like the one in the Strokes' "Under the Cover of Darkness" or the Eagles' "Already Gone."
- **Each guitar is playing in different registers or voicings.** If one guitar is playing an A chord on the 2nd fret, the second guitar would be playing it on the 5th fret. If one guitar is playing a line on the 5th and 6th strings, the second guitar would be playing the same thing, only up an octave on the 1st and 2nd strings. The signature intro line of Lenny Kravitz's "Are You Gonna Go My Way" is a perfect example.
- **Each guitar is playing a different rhythm.** If one guitar is playing long, sustained chords, called "power chords" (or in studio parlance, "footballs," because they're whole notes that look like footballs when transcribed), the second one is playing a faster rhythm like quarter or eighth notes—again like the intro to "Already Gone."
- **Each guitar has a different sound.** It's really common for a guitar player who's a neophyte in the recording studio to have loads of ideas for guitar parts but also want to play them all on the same guitar with the same amplifier setup. This is usually a recipe for a sonic jumbled mess, but the fix is an easy one: use a different guitar, amplifier, or both for each different part. This is the reason that studio guitar players come with a wide array of guitars and amps—different sounds make the arrangement more interesting, and the guitar parts fit together better. Usually a minimum of two different styles of guitars (a single-coil, like a Strat, and a humbucker, like a Les Paul) make multiple guitar parts fit better together. Having two different styles of amps (a Fender and a Marshall, for example) provides another level of difference. Add another guitar style or two (a Tele, a Gretsch, or a Rickenbacker) or amp (a Vox AC-30, a tweed Fender, a Boogie), and you can add any number of guitar parts but still keep them interesting and have them heard (within the right arrangement, of course). See Figure 6-1 for an example.

Figure 6-1: An Example of an Excellent Guitar Recording Array

You'll find that if you use these arrangement techniques, the guitars will lay in better with the track and better support the vocals and rhythm section, and make the song a lot more interesting to boot.

RULES FOR ARRANGEMENTS

There are a couple of easy-to-remember rules that make even the densest arrangement manageable.

1. **Limit the number of arrangement elements.** Usually, no more than four elements should be playing at the same time. Sometimes three elements can work well. Very rarely will five simultaneous elements work.

2. **Everything in its own frequency range.** This rule is so important that it needs to be stressed: the arrangement will fit together better if every instrument sits in its own frequency range. For instance, if a synthesizer and rhythm guitar play the same thing in the same octave, they will usually clash. The solution would be to either

change the sound of one of the instruments so each fills a different frequency range, have one play in a different octave, or have them play at different times but not together.

We could spend this entire book on modern arranging, but if you follow these two simple rules, you'll find that you'll have an arrangement that lays together well.

CHAPTER 7
MUSIC MECHANICS

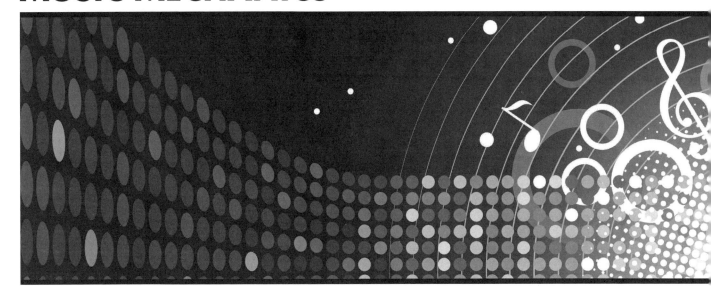

No matter what your background or experience is, as a producer, it's likely you'll be confronted with the same question on many of your projects—"Why doesn't this song (or part in the song) sound right?"

Maybe it'll feel great on one run-through, and not as good on the next. Maybe it sounds great except for one section. Maybe it never sounded great, but you think the song has something special and it's worth spending time to work it out.

There are certain mechanics that determine how tight the music is, how it feels, and how "big" it sounds. These mechanics work for any kind of music, from marching band to deep house to reggaeton to speed metal—the principles are all the same. If something doesn't sound right, it's a pretty good bet that one or more of the following principles are being overlooked.

DYNAMICS

Playing with dynamics means playing with less intensity (i.e. not playing as hard or as loud) in certain places in a song, and with more intensity (playing harder) in other places. Some bands are oblivious to dynamics and play at the same volume and intensity throughout an entire song, which can get boring for the listener very quickly.

Generally speaking, here's how you use dynamics effectively.

- When the song begins, the band plays fairly loudly, about 7 or 8 on a scale of 1 to 10 (10 being the loudest).
- When the vocal or lead instrument (if the group is instrumental) comes in at the verse, the band drops down to about 4 or 5.
- When the chorus comes in, the volume level comes back up to a 7 or 8.
- When the second verse begins, the band drops down to a 5 or 6 (notice it's a little louder than the first verse, but not as loud as the chorus).
- When the second chorus begins, the band comes back up to a 7 or 8.
- When the bridge (or whatever section is the peak of the song) starts, the band comes all the way up to 9 or 10.
- For the outro of the song, the band drops down to 7 or 8 (see Figure 7-1).
- If the song has a breakdown, the level might come down as low as a 1 or 2.

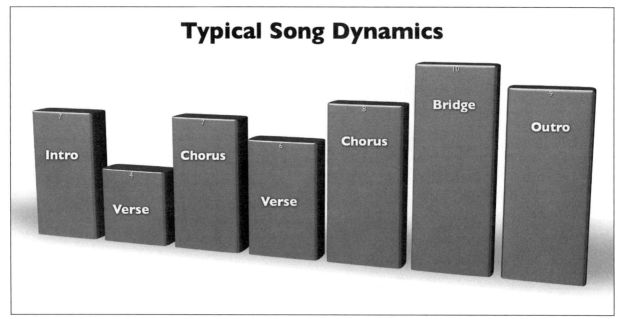

Figure 7-1: Typical Song Dynamics

While the level of intensity (and, as a result, the volume level) may change from the numbers indicated above, depending on what finally feels the best, that's basically how dynamics are created. If the band plays a song dynamically, the song breathes volume-wise, and will be a lot more interesting as a result.

THE SECRET TO PLAYING DYNAMICALLY

When you play loudly, play as loudly as you can.

When you play softly, play as softly as you can.

Learn to play at a third intermediate volume.

There are a few byproducts from playing dynamically, too. The vocals can be heard more easily because there's more space and there are fewer loud instruments for the vocalist to fight against (easier on the singer's throat as well). Songs become more fun to play because true interaction exists between all the players to make the dynamics work, and as a result, the band automatically sounds tighter.

For a really great example of dynamics, listen to "Smells Like Team Spirit" by Nirvana. The verses are at about a 5, the prechorus at 7, and the chorus roars at 10.

How to Learn to Play Dynamically

Most bands learn to play dynamically if just one player is dynamics-aware and the others follow that person's lead (it helps if that one aware person is the drummer).

If a band is together for a long enough time and plays enough gigs, dynamics will seem to magically seep into the group's playing once it begins to get some self-awareness of just what it takes to get a crowd going.

You can't spend years waiting for these things to happen by themselves, though (after all, you're making a record), so just use the following method:

- When the band is going over a song, treat the dynamics as an integral part of the song and spend as much time learning them as you would learning the chord changes and the groove. As shown above, map out each section of the song on a loudness scale of 1 to 10, with 10 being the loudest.
- The following step is the most important: *make sure that all band members agree on how loud or soft each dynamic number is.* In other words, be sure that the drummer's level 8, for example, is the same as the rhythm guitar player's, and that the bass player's level 2 is the same as the lead guitarist's. After that's commonly agreed upon, rehearse the dynamics of a song until they're second nature, and then watch the audience take notice.

Don't Confuse Volume Level with Intensity

A common complaint from a band that's being taught dynamics is that the song just doesn't drive as much when they play a section quietly. That's because it's easy to confuse volume level with intensity.

TO PLAY AT THE SAME INTENSITY AT A LOWER LEVEL

Make sure the attacks and releases are the same.

Make sure the tempo is the same.

Make sure each player plays with the same dynamic level from section to section.

Most beginner bands tend to get sloppier the softer or less intensely they play. They begin to play the individual beats at slightly different levels and even have slight tempo variations between beats. As a result, playing softly sounds wimpy.

Another thing that happens is that the band gets so used to playing at one level (usually loud), that anything compared to that level sounds so different that it's perceived as less exciting. The same thing happens when you drive your car at 80 mph for a long time. When you bring it back to 65 mph, it feels as though you're going very slowly, even though you're still going pretty darn fast.

And finally, the internal dynamics of each individual player go out the window. Instead of playing crisply yet quietly with the same attack and releases (covered later in the chapter) as at the higher volume level, the attack and releases get relaxed and so the playing becomes less precise.

The real trick is learning to play with the same intensity at lower levels. Make sure that the tempo is even, the groove stays the same as at the higher volume, and the attacks and releases are crisp, and you should sound powerful at any volume level.

Builds

Another part of playing dynamically is to pay attention to builds. Builds usually occur during turnarounds (for example, the two or four bars between the verse and chorus), but they sometimes occur at the beginning or ending of a song, too.

For a good example, you'll find a build at the beginning of each section of Rush's "The Spirit of Radio." Once again, all band members have to play the build the same way, starting from the same low volume and going to the same high volume.

Builds are easy to overlook, and many times a band will think that it's performing one well if it just plays the rhythm of the build cleanly. It's called a "build" for a reason though, since just playing it cleanly doesn't mean much unless there's an actual volume difference between each note.

PLAY TOGETHER AND LISTEN TO EACH OTHER

One of the fundamental errors that band members frequently make is not listening closely to the rest of the band. It's easy to focus just on your own performance, but in order to play well together, what really counts is listening closely to each other as the band plays. *This is the single most important action that a musician can take when playing with other musicians, and is essential for playing well in the studio.*

So what do you listen for? You listen to how the other musicians are playing or singing a phrase or part. How loudly are they playing? What are their dynamics like? How do they start and end each phrase? Where are they placing their accents? How are they playing the accents? Are they playing ahead of the beat or behind it? Does their tempo speed up when they play louder or slow down as they get softer?

All these items require as much of your attention as possible. The more you listen to each other and how each of you play and sing, the tighter you become. It's that simple.

That being said, it does require some work. During rehearsal, if you notice that a phrase or part isn't being played the same way (or if a player doesn't seem in sync), stop the song immediately and ask each player, "How are you playing that?" Then determine which way sounds best, and rehearse just that phrase or part until everyone's playing it together.

THINGS TO LISTEN FOR WHEN PLAYING WITH OTHERS

How loudly are they playing?

What are their dynamics?

How do they start and end each phrase?

Where are they playing the accents?

How are they playing the accents?

Are they playing ahead of the beat or behind it?

Do they speed up when they play softer or louder?

TIMING IS EVERYTHING

A big part of playing together well is developing good timing. Playing in time means that each player must play to the pulse of the song. But while an individual player may be doing that well, if the entire band isn't following a song's pulse in exactly the same way, it sounds sloppy.

There are three parts to timing: song starts and stops, the groove, and attacks and releases. Let's look at each one.

Song Starts and Stops

You could call song starts and stops "beginnings and endings" except for the fact that there are sometimes stops and starts in the middle of a song. The trick here is to make sure that everyone starts and stops the song at the same time.

Practicing starts and stops cannot be left for later or treated with an "It will be better in the studio" attitude. Rehearse each start and stop until everyone is locked in and knows each one like the back of their hand! If things still don't sound right after five or six tries, go back to the reliable "How are you playing it?" question.

As is the case with most things that don't lock in tight, there's probably at least one player who may be playing things slightly differently from the rest.

Even if one of the instruments begins the song with a pickup or fill (as with U2's "Get on Your Boots"), everyone still has to play the start of the song the same way after the fill. Regardless of how the song starts or ends, everyone has to play it the same way—no exceptions.

Accents

Once again, any time there is an accent in the song, everyone has to play it the same way. This means with the same feel, timing, and phrasing. If it just doesn't seem to sound right, make sure that everyone is playing it the same way.

The Groove and the Pocket

All good music—regardless of whether it's rock, jazz, classical, rap, or some new space music that we haven't heard yet—has a strong groove. You always hear about "the groove," but what is it?

> **The "groove" is the pulse of the song and how the instruments dynamically breathe with it.**

To your audience, the groove is an enjoyable rhythm that makes even the people that can't dance want to get up and shake their booty. And while the concept of "the groove" is very subjective, the idea is well understood by experienced musicians at a practical, intuitive level. Musicians who play funk and Latin tunes refer to the groove as the sense of being "in the pocket," while jazz players refer to the groove as the sense that a song is really "cooking" or "swinging."

A common misconception about groove is that it must have perfect time, but *a groove is created by tension against even time.* That means that it doesn't have to be perfect, just even, and all performances don't have to have the same amount of evenness. In fact, it makes the groove feel stiff if the performances are too perfect.

This is why quantizing all the song elements and lining up every hit in a workstation when you're recording frequently takes the life out of a song. Its time becomes too perfect because there's no tension. The song has lost its groove.

Just about every hit song has a great groove, and that's why it's a hit. If you want to study what a groove really is, go to the masters: James Brown, Sly Stone, Michael Jackson, George Clinton, and Prince. Every song is the essence of what a groove feels like.

Groove is often thought of as coming from the rhythm section, especially the drums, but that's not necessarily always the case. In The Police's "Every Breath You Take," for instance, the rhythm guitar establishes the groove. In most songs by The Supremes, Temptations, and Four Tops, from Motown's golden age, the groove was established by James Jamerson's bass.

How to Find the Pocket

The phrase "in the pocket" is used to describe something or someone playing in such a way that the groove is very solid and has a great feel. When a drummer keeps good time, makes the groove feel really good, and maintains it for an extended period of time while never wavering, it is often referred to as a "deep pocket." It should be noted that it's impossible to have a pocket without also having a groove.

Historically speaking, the term "pocket" originated in the middle of the previous century, when a strong backbeat (the snare drum striking on beats 2 and 4) became predominant in popular music. When the backbeat is slightly delayed creating a laid–back, or relaxed, feel, the drummer is playing in the pocket.

Today, the term "in the pocket" has broadened a bit. If, for example, two musicians (usually the bass player and the drummer) are feeling the downbeats together and hitting beat 1 (the downbeat) at the exact same time, they are said to be in the pocket.

Whether you're playing ahead (in front) of the beat, behind (on the back of) the beat, or on top (in the middle) of the beat, as long as two musicians (for instance, the bassist and the drummer) feel the downbeat at the same time, they'll be playing in the pocket.

The Three Places a Beat Can Land

In terms of bass and drums locking to create a cohesive part, there are three main areas of focus. You have to know where your drummer is most comfortable in terms of the beat.

Does your drummer play "straight," playing meaning that he or she plays right on top of the beat (which can sound like disco music or a quantized drum machine)? Is he or she laid back, sitting in that area way on the back of the beat (the way Phil Rudd does on AC/DC's "Back in Black," like John Bonham on anything by Led Zeppelin, or like Clyde Stubblefield on James Brown's "Cold Sweat" or "Funky Drummer")? Or does your drummer's playing have the urgency of a musician who plays on top of the beat (like Stewart Copeland of The Police)?

This is crucial to know, because the bass and drums have to function as a unit. They don't have to play everything precisely the same way, but they have to know and understand the way the other thinks and feels.

Getting the rhythm section to groove with the rest of the band is much more difficult than you might think, since guitarists don't always listen to the drummer, a keyboardist may have metronomic time yet have a difficult time coordinating his or her left hand with the bass player, and vocalists often forget that there's a band playing behind them. *The key is for everyone in the band to listen to one another*!

Many people feel that the question is not so much what the pocket is as much as how you know when you're in it; I guarantee that you'll know it when you feel it, because the music feels as though it's playing itself. It feels as though everything has merged together, with all the rhythmic parts being played by one instrument. Whichever definition you choose to go with or use, having a pocket is always good thing!

Attacks and Releases

Attacks and releases (sometimes called "articulations") are some of the most overlooked yet important elements in playing together. Attacks and releases usually refer to a phrase that you're either playing or singing. The attack part is easy: everyone starts to play or sing at exactly the same time in the same way. The releases, however, are often overlooked.

A release is how you end a phrase, and that's as important as how you begin a phrase. Once again, everyone has to end the phrase at exactly the same time in exactly the same way. Listen to the Eagles' "Hotel California" for examples of attack, release, and phrasing of both guitar and vocals.

Getting the attacks and releases to fall together is essential to making a good record (thanks to editing in the DAW, you hardly ever hear an attack or a release that's off anymore), because if they're off in any way, the part just won't sound tight.

TURNAROUNDS

Another often-overlooked portion of a song that needs to be tight is the turnaround between sections, like the one or two bars between the verse and chorus, chorus and verse, verse and outro, chorus and bridge, and so on. This part requires a lot of focus because it's played a little differently from the rest of the section.

For the drummer, it's usually a tom or snare roll into the next section, but unless it's a build, most players inexperienced in recording will usually just randomly play something over the roll. This doesn't work, because a turnaround requires a precise line that has to be played in order to stay tight with the drums. As an example of how it's done well, listen to the bar before each new section of Lynyrd Skynyrd's classic hit "Sweet Home Alabama."

Most neophyte bands (and even some experienced ones) don't think about the turnarounds too much, and so it's your job to make them aware. Make sure that every player has an exact part to play and that all parts work together and sound tight (a good idea for the rest of the song as well).

TEMPO

Every song needs the perfect tempo to groove. One of the things you discover early on when making records is that something as small as a single beat per minute (bpm) can make a big difference in how a song feels. Just a little too slow, and the song seems to drag; a little too fast, and it feels uncomfortable or becomes difficult to play. Therefore, it's really important that you establish the song's ideal bpm before you record it.

Determining a song's best bpm is pretty easy if the band is learning a cover song (and the tempo is already established), but when band members are working out one of their own songs, finding that perfect tempo can be a challenge.

I've found that the best way is for the writer of the song to play it by him or herself, and then establish the tempo that feels right. After you determine the bpm that the writer has established (there are lots of mobile apps that do this, my favorite being Tap That), then the entire band should play the song at this tempo a few times.

Even if the song feels just fine, it's still best to move the song's tempo up a couple of bpm, and then down a couple, just to see how it feels. You might find that just going a little bit slower or faster from that initial point can make a big difference. If the song is difficult to perform, backing it down a few bpm might make it easier to play, whereas playing it faster might give the song more urgency.

Faster Does Not Create More Excitement

It's really important that you don't get sucked into the "faster is more exciting" syndrome. Typically, the only things you get from playing a song faster than its established tempo are sloppy playing, lack of dynamics, and no groove.

Playing a song at its correct tempo (especially something that is already slow, like a ballad) is especially difficult, because it requires a lot of concentration to play slowly with precision and also stay in the pocket. Once again, the best way to overcome any anxiety about losing the excitement is to relax, exaggerate the dynamics, and concentrate on the starts and stops and the attacks and releases.

A Click Can Help

The age-old argument about playing to a click will never go away, but it's easier to do now than ever before because most players (especially drummers) learn to use one so early in their career. Some musicians play better to a click than others, and that's just a fact. The most widely used session drummers work so much because they make playing to a click sound as though they're playing to their own inner beat, and that's the big trick.

> *I realized that I really could play to a click and make it breathe at the same time, and that really is an important thing for drummers to learn. If you play to a click, don't be so focused on the click that you lose sight of the fact that you're actually playing a song.*
> —Session drummer Brian MacLeod

While you're recording, I'd recommend using a click if at all possible. Doing so will make the jobs of the producer, engineer, programmer, editor, and anyone doing overdubs a lot easier in many ways. It will even make your mix better, because it will be easier to time delays and reverbs.

That being said, if the band sounds too stiff while playing to a click, then use it only to get a feel for the tempo for, say, the first 16 bars, and then turn it off. Sometimes just having it for the intro of a song can do wonders in keeping the tempo locked.

Also remember that it's not uncommon to increase the tempo by a bpm during the chorus to push the band a little. This requires that the tempo be premapped in the DAW, but this trick successfully mimics what a player might naturally do without a click and is used all the time in recordmaking.

PLAY IN TUNE

If you're making a record, it's important that every instrument be in tune. Being out of tune is one of the most serious offenses that can occur during a recording session, yet it's also one of the easiest to control.

Young musicians with stringed instruments (horn players, too) sometimes overlook this critical aspect of playing, partially because they're either unsure exactly how precise they need to be or their ear is undeveloped. Once upon a time before cheap electronic tuners were abundant, everybody was a little out of tune. If you don't believe me, just listen to a few records from back in the '50s and '60s.

By the '70s most recording musicians discovered the Conn Strobotuner (see Figure 7-2), an electronic tuning device developed primarily for tuning pianos. Using a Strobotuner was an expensive ($350 in 1970s money) way to get in tune, but it made all the difference in the world.

This fueled the demand for an inexpensive version, which resulted in the models that you can purchase for as little as ten bucks today (see Figure 7-3). Since tuners can cost so little and do so much (far more than their predecessors could), there's no excuse for any musician not to own at least one, and to know how to use it.

But just having one position on the instrument in tune isn't enough. It's absolutely imperative that the instrument be properly intonated, which means that the instrument plays in tune in any octave up and down its playable register (up and down the neck, for guitar and bass players). Good intonation on guitars and basses can be tricky to achieve, at best. Just like on a piano, an instrument is never completely in tune all the way up or down the neck. A relatively new intonation system called the Feiten Tuning System, developed by session guitar player

Figure 7-2: A Conn Strobotuner

Figure 7-3: An Inexpensive Snark Tuner

Buzz Feiten, actually solves this problem, but requires a qualified pro to install it because it involves resetting the bridge and the nut.

The bottom line is that the closer everyone is to being perfectly in tune, the better the band will sound. Having an instrument that's in tune with itself is only half the battle, though. You're not really in tune until all instruments in the band (except for the drums, of course) are in tune with each other. You might think that just because each player uses a tuner that everyone will be in tune with each other. Not so fast—there are a couple of complications.

First of all, all tuners are slightly different, and even though it says one tuner might indicate that an E string is in tune, that particular  tuning can differ ever so slightly from another tuner's either because of the way it's being read, or because some of its internal settings have been accidentally adjusted to something other than the standard 440 Hz A note. The easy way around that is for everyone in the band to either use the same tuner or own the same brand and model.

But that's still not enough. Everyone who's going to use the tuner (guitar and bass players, horn players) should get together to make sure that they're all reading the meter the same way. That way there won't be any confusion as to what an E really sounds and looks like with that meter.

Finally, after everyone tunes, it's best to all play a couple of chords together just to make sure that nothing sounds sour. If it does, go back and look at how each player is using the tuner, and I bet you'll find that someone is reading it a little differently than everyone else.

A few times at rehearsal will probably tell everyone exactly what they need to know to make sure that their instrument will be in tune from that point on. In this day and age, with an abundance of available inexpensive and accurate electronic tuners, there's no excuse to ever be out of tune.

DEVELOPING STUDIO EARS AND EYES

What are "studio ears?" It's the ability to hear deep inside a track—to hear all the details, good and bad. At the beginning of a project, it's easy to hear major mistakes and flams, but it's difficult to hear the really small ones. Unless you're in the studio every day nonstop, it takes at least a few days to get them back. Things that sound perfectly acceptable during week one of recording will probably drive you crazy by week three.

How do you develop studio ears? For many producers, the best way is by editing the tracks after basics. Regardless of the musicians, there are always fixes in timing that are necessary to tighten things up.

As a producer, I'm a big one for working it out during preproduction, getting it close during recording, and fixing it during editing. This keeps musicians from feeling beat up from too many takes, as long as they're playing with feeling but just not laying perfectly together.

That means that I'll have at least several days per song fixing things up later, which is where my studio ears get bigger and bigger. Now a 10-millisecond flam, which is about as little as you can perceive, will drive me crazy until I fix it.

Studio Eyes

A bad habit that many engineers and producers fall into is "studio eyes," which means that you move tracks around on the timeline so they perfectly line up just because they look like they're not aligned, even though they may sound perfectly fine.

This is when your experience kicks in. You close your eyes and let your heart and brain take over. If it feels good, it is good!

CHAPTER 8
PREPRODUCTION: THE MOST IMPORTANT STEP

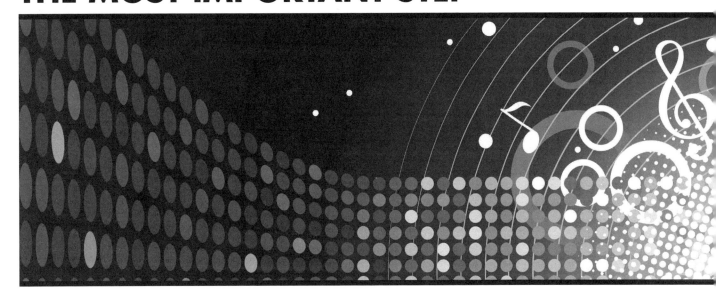

f you're working with real players, the most crucial time in the entire recording process is before you actually record, which is known as preproduction. Almost always, the more time you spend in preproduction, the smoother the recording will go. In preproduction, the songs are chosen, arrangements are worked out, and parts are learned so well that the only thing to concentrate on during recording is the execution of the performance.

GETTING TO KNOW YOU

Preproduction is often much more than the process of working out songs. For a producer working with a new artist or band, it's a time of getting to know each other. It's important for the producer to learn the likes and dislikes of the artists he or she is working with—be it food, music, or politics—in addition to their working habits and idiosyncrasies.

Knowing these things can help the producer determine how far to push a singer, or discover what gets the best performance out of the guitar player, or the signs that the drummer is getting tired, or the hot-button issues of the day to stay away from. If you're going to be working closely with an artist, even for a short time, the more you know about him or her, the better you can serve the project.

One of the most important aspects of getting to know an artist is learning what music she loves, was influenced by, and is listening to now. Back in the days of the vinyl record, one of the most effective ways of doing this was for the producer to go to the artist's house and have them throw a bunch of albums from their collection on the floor and then describe what they liked and didn't like about each one.

Today, it's more about looking at a favorite Spotify playlist, but the same thing is accomplished. Among the questions to ask might be the following:

- What do you like or dislike about the artist you're listening to?
- Do you like the sound of the recording?
- What recordings do you like the sound of?
- What are some of your favorite records? Why?
- What/who are your biggest influences? Why?
- If you have a body of work as a producer already, what does the artist like about you? Why?

You can add any number of questions to those above, but can you see where this is heading? This is the information that you need to help attain the artist's vision.

It gives you a common point of reference so that you can say, "Let's go for a sound like the lead guitar on The Cure's "Boys Don't Cry," and have the artist know exactly what you mean because you've found out in preproduction that's one of his favorite songs.

Or if the artist says to you, "Can we get the sound like on The Weeknd's "Can't Feel My Face," you'll know exactly what he's talking about.

SELECTING THE SONGS

Selecting the songs for the project is usually a function determined by how much preproduction time you have. If you don't have a deadline to worry about, you might work on songs that have strong hooks but are incomplete or have a weak arrangement or structure. If you don't have a lot of time, however, you might be looking to use only the songs that are in the most record-worthy shape—ones that you know will sound good, and that you can you can therefore easily record.

As you've read in Chapter 6, songwriting is a craft, and the more you do it, the better it gets as you learn what works and what doesn't. The more you record, the more attuned your ear becomes to what to listen for with arrangements, so an artist or band that's on their fourth album will have songs that sound much more together than an artist or band on record number one. Because of that experience, the songs will be in better shape, any changes can be made faster, and the pre-production time will be shorter.

It's always a good idea to work up at least one extra song in addition to the ones intended for recording. There are two reasons for this: first, if an intended song just isn't captured to everyone's expectations during basic tracking, you'll have an alternative available. Second, sometimes you may have a little extra time during the basics stage, so it's nice to be able to take advantage of that opportunity and use it wisely by working on another song.

PREPRODUCTION REHEARSALS

The preproduction rehearsal is the stage where much of the heavy lifting of the project takes place. This is when the songs get honed until they're deemed ready for recording. Here are a number of tips and tricks to get the most out of your preproduction time.

You Gotta Hear Yourself

For players to hear the nuances of their parts and determine how to integrate those parts with all the others in the band, they need to be able to hear themselves and everyone else equally well.

One of the problems that young bands have is that they tend to crank up the volume before they learn a song or work on any changes to its parts or arrangements. It's best to learn a song or change its parts at low level first so that everyone can hear each other's parts, and then play it at normal stage volume once things have been worked out. This will save you a lot of time later, when you have to go through the song player by player and part by part to find out why something isn't sounding right.

In fact, sometimes the best rehearsals are the ones that happen in someone's living room with only acoustic guitars and drum pads. These kinds of rehearsals can be surprisingly effective, since it's easy to hear what everyone's playing and especially easy to hear the vocals (it's great for working out harmonies). Of course, bands that have been gigging for a while find working this way a lot easier than do new players who've been together for a short time.

Practice in the Round

A really good rehearsal technique is to set up in the round so that everyone is facing one another, instead of setting up like the way you would on stage. This configuration allows each player to hear him or herself really well, as well as the rest of the band. It's also the way that almost everyone records, since it's so important to have eye contact when you're doing a take. When people play in the round, everyone has to control their volume a bit so they don't blow out their fellow band members, but that's not such a bad thing, is it?

A Few Rehearsal Tips

No matter what kind of music you're producing, the following rehearsal tips can help things go a bit smoother and enable you to get the most out of your preproduction time.

- When going over a song, stop as soon as there's a train wreck and work it out. Talk it over to see what everyone is playing, and then play just the problem part until everyone gets it. Sometimes the problem may be in the middle or at the end of a section, so if the band is able to play just that section, great. Most bands, however, find it easier to start four bars before or even at the beginning of the section to work it out. That's okay—whatever it takes to make things sound great!
- Find the part of the song that needs the most work and concentrate on that first. Slow the song down to a tempo that's easy for everyone to play, and then gradually bring it up to speed until everyone can play it cleanly.
- Sometimes it's best to start with the chorus, especially the out chorus, since it usually repeats. If a band is working on groove or tempo, the out chorus is the section of the song that's played the most, and probably has the song's hook, so it's easy to remember. Starting with the out chorus can give you confidence about playing the rest of the song.

PREPRODUCTION DEMOS

No matter how well preproduction rehearsals seem to go, it's important to make a preproduction demo recording, too. Why? You never really know how a part sounds until it's recorded.

Also, getting a band out of its safe and comfortable environment will make them play differently. Psychologically, it helps a band to know that when things sound different in a new environment (as they will when recording takes place) that it's not necessarily a negative thing.

The preproduction demo doesn't have to be expensive. In fact, the cheaper the better. Even someone's home studio will do, because you don't care about the track count or quality as much as discovering just what each instrument is playing. What you're trying to learn is how well everyone is playing together and whether the arrangements and song structures work.

Don't spend too much time recording the demo. A couple of passes of each song at the most is all that's necessary, unless there's a major train wreck. Performance mistakes are okay, as long as you can hear the complete form of the song.

Don't worry about overdubs or layering unless it's for a quick run-through to see if an idea works. Perfection is not the objective for the demo; obtaining information about the song structure, the arrangement, and the individual parts is.

After you listen to the recording, or even just listen to playbacks while recording, it should be apparent what needs to be fixed or improved (which should take place at another round of rehearsals). Listening will also help the players as they hear what they're playing against everyone else. It's not uncommon to hear comments like, "I didn't know you were playing it like that," during a playback.

The idea behind all of this is to get the parts down so that the real recording can be done efficiently and with no surprises, and so that the players can concentrate solely on their performances instead of having to learn new parts. Many times, by the time a player learns the new part in the studio, his performance has suffered so much it takes an additional session just to capture a great performance. Spending an ample amount of time in preproduction will hopefully eliminate that scenario.

HOW LONG SHOULD PREPRODUCTION TAKE?

The length of preproduction time has a major impact on your final recording, since it's ultimately determined by the songs that you pick to record. The more preproduction time available, the more time you have to work on songs that aren't all together. The less preproduction time available, the better off you'll be picking songs that are ready to go, even though they may not be the best.

You always hear about label acts that work out things in the studio, and you'll have to assume that no matter how well prepared you are, some of that will happen anyway. That said, the purpose of this book is to get you through a recording project efficiently and easily, assuming that you have a limited budget. It's always better to spend more time in preproduction than production: for one thing, it can be a lot cheaper if you're using a commercial studio, and for another, it's less stressful.

Below is a guideline that I like to use, but realize that each situation is unique, so these numbers might not be in the ballpark for your particular project. For a band that's never been in the studio before, allow time in the schedule for the following:

- At least two rehearsals of preproduction per song to be recorded.
- One session to record a demo.
- One rehearsal for each song for fixes as a result of the demo.

That means for a 10-song album you'd spend 22 rehearsals (10 songs plus an extra x 2 = 22 rehearsals), a day for the demo, and another 11 rehearsals for fixes—for a total of 34 rehearsals.

For a band of studio veterans who've made records before, allow time in the schedule for the following:

- One rehearsal of preproduction per song to be recorded.
- One session to record a demo.
- Half of a rehearsal for each song for fixes as a result of the demo.

That means for a 10-song album you'd spend 11 rehearsals (10 songs plus an extra = 11 rehearsals), a session for the demo, and another 6 rehearsals for fixes—for a total of 18 rehearsals.

Of course, many other factors come into play that could make you take these guidelines and throw them in the trash can. The band could be on its fifth album and everything might be so together than a lot less time is needed. Or maybe the band wants to record live for a really raw-sounding punk record with no overdubs, so again, a lot less time is needed.

Maybe it's a jazz or blues band, where there won't be much recorded beyond the basic 12-bar song structure with few overdubs and layering. Or perhaps the band has limited time for rehearsal because of touring or family commitments. All of these factors play into how much preproduction time you'll need or get.

IT'S THE LITTLE THINGS THAT COUNT

As we've been saying throughout this book, it's the little things, the nuances, that make a song sound great. We've talked about these things before, but let's list them again, because these are the things that you've got to have down.

- Everyone must know their parts inside out.
- The starts and stops in the song must all be played together.
- Everyone must be able to play the same part the same way every time (except if it's jazz or blues).
- Everyone must know the dynamics of the song.
- All rhythms must be in the pocket and the songs must groove.
- The turnaround between each song section must be defined.
- Attacks and releases for each part must be executed together.
- The sounds of each instrument must be layered so that nothing clashes frequency-wise.
- The tempo must be right for the song.
- The band must be in tune.
- All vocals must be in the best range for the singers.
- Background vocals must be defined and tight.

These are the things that you should be concentrating on during preproduction rehearsals.

CHAPTER 9
PREPARING FOR THE SESSION

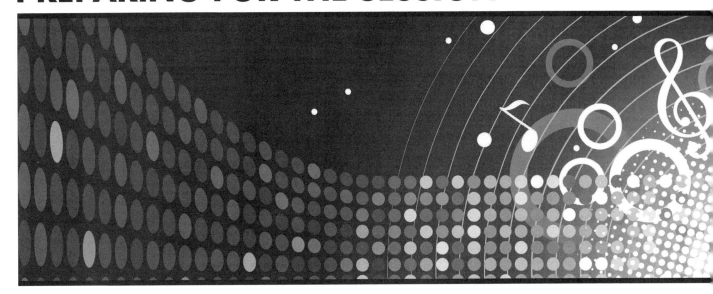

Everyone has a home studio these days, but many either can't fit all the players of a band or just don't have the gear needed for a good basic recording. If this is the case, many times it's worth spending the money to go to a commercial studio to record at least the drum tracks.

Preparing for that recording session does require some planning, and choosing between options may be something that only you, the producer, can do.

INITIAL DECISIONS

Before the first session begins, a host of decisions have to be made that range from the mundane to the important. Here's an overview of the many production considerations a producer is confronted with in a typical project.

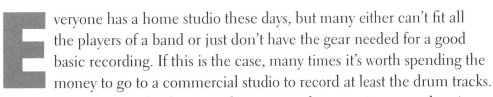

- **Who is the engineer (or engineers)?** Your choice of who engineers the project is critical, and, like many other aspects of production, this is not an element to cheap out on. A great engineer is your safety blanket. He'll make things sound great even with gear that's not up to snuff and provide useful technical advice, audio expertise, and even production suggestions when you need another opinion.

Many producers will use a top engineer for basics and mixing, and then use a less expensive one for overdubs (or engineer the overdubs themselves), in order to save some money. While this can work, the continuity of having the same engineer all the way through a project will keep the quality uniformly high and actually save time and money, since there's the possibility for confusion when projects are handed off between engineers.

- **Is any rental gear required?** Even the most well-equipped studio in the world probably still won't have something that you'll want or need for the session, be it an esoteric piece of audio or musical gear, or just something that's essential for you to get your desired sound. Make sure you plan ahead for when you'll need the rental, and then schedule around that. An example of this could be the rental of a grand piano or a Hammond organ. You'll want to use it as soon as it arrives, instead of paying rental time for it to just sit around.

- **What's the best time of day to record?** This question can actually be a loaded one. While most bands would rather start early in the day to stay fresh, many singers don't feel as though their throats open up until later in the day. While you might need only a guide vocal from the singer when the basics are being recorded, you certainly don't want the singer to be harmed or feel abused, and herein lies the dilemma. You don't want to start recording too late in the day, since you'll end up having everyone burn out early, and you might lose the advantage of a few hours of the studio's daily rate that you've paid for. While starting the session at 10 a.m. might not work, try to start no later than noon if possible. Many musicians want or need to get home at a reasonable hour to be with their families, and working too far into the night can upset your body clock if you're not used to it.

- **Are there any additional musicians required?** Once again, it's best to plan as far in advance as you can so you can schedule the other players as needed. The more players you need to have together at one time (like a string or horn section), the more time in advance you'll need in order to schedule them.

- **What format and sampling rate will you use?** While it's possible that you might still want to break out an analog tape machine to record your basics, chances are that at some point in the project you'll return to the comfort and flexibility of a DAW (most likely Pro Tools). Your choice of bit depth and sampling rate can be critical to the amount of hassle that you'll encounter down the road. Here's a chart that can help you make your choice.

TABLE 9.1: ADVANTAGES AND DISADVANTAGES OF RECORDING FORMATS	
Sampling Rate/Bit Depth	**Description**
192 kHz/24 bit	PROS: Sounds fabulous. Is as close to analog as you can easily get right now. CONS: Expensive. Takes a lot of disk space, and you might need extra A/D and D/A converters. Requires a lot of computer processing on a big session. Track availability may be cut in half, and many plug-ins don't work at this sample rate.
96 kHz/24 bit	PROS: With the right converters, this rate can sound a lot better than 48/24. Much better for archival purposes. CONS: Processing and track count may be cut in half in some DAWs. Some home studios aren't capable of 96/24. Might not be worth the hassle under normal circumstances.
48 kHz/24 bit	PROS: A good combination of audio quality with a minimum of hassle. CONS: May be a lower resolution than the common audio formats of the future.
44.1 kHz/24 bit	PROS: Native resolution for CD. CONS: A major disadvantage if video is involved, which operates at 48 kHz.

Here are some simple guidelines for choosing sampling rate/bit depth:

- If you want a good compromise between audio quality and hassle, choose 48 kHz/24 bit.
- If you're recording loud music like rock or rap, 48 kHz/24 bit could be a good choice. The higher sampling rate doesn't buy you enough discernible sound quality to make it worthwhile.
- You might wish you recorded at 96 kHz in the future when all formats are high-resolution and you want to rerelease older material.
- If you're recording music for film, the standard is 48 kHz/24 bit.
- If you're producing acoustic music like jazz, bluegrass, or classical for string quartet, 96 kHz/24 bit will provide a discernible improvement in audio quality.
- While 192 kHz/24 bit sounds great, use it only if your engineering team is comfortable in that domain and can guarantee you a hassle-free session. Not all DAW apps and convertors work well at this resolution.
- Don't mix sampling rates. While you might be tempted to use different sampling rates on different songs, do so only if your engineering team can assure you that it will be hassle-free. A 96k session might not be a big deal at one studio, but might be impossible if you have to move to another. Why limit your choices?
- What's the order of recording? Choosing the order of recording is one of the most strategic decisions that a producer can make. Most producers like to start off with something relatively easy so the band members get comfortable with the studio and gain confidence in their playing. One school of thought says that the most difficult song should be recorded right after that first easy one so that you tackle it while you're fresh and you have the ability to come back to it later if need be.
- What studio or studios will you be using? It's entirely possible that you'll be using more than one studio to record your project, as is the norm these days. Oftentimes you'll use a studio with a room large enough to record drums or the rhythm tracks, and then move on to a smaller and cheaper room or a home studio for the overdubs. Most mixing these days is done in the box, but you may want to go old school and mix on a console at a different studio as well. That means that you'll have to make sure that each studio can accommodate the recording resolution that you've chosen.

SELECTING A STUDIO

The studio or studios you choose may be critical to how well the project comes out as well as how much time it takes to complete. A studio affects a project in so many ways that it's almost impossible to determine what the most critical item is. Everything from the acoustics to the equipment to the vibe to the staff to the location are all factors to consider when making your final decision.

Let's look at each of these factors individually:

- **The location.** Location is important for some artists and not so much for others. Some might want the studio to be located as close to home as possible, while others might want to be as far away from possible distractions (like fans or family) as they can get. Sometimes, just a little extra drive time might take an artist out of her comfort zone. For example, an artist who lives in West L.A. or Santa Monica wouldn't even consider driving to a studio in Burbank or Glendale, even though it's less than 20 miles away. Sometimes even only driving to downtown Hollywood can be considered too far at less than 10 miles, so driving distance can be a factor.

- **The vibe.** Every studio has its own vibe, which stems from its location, decor, cosmetics, and staff. Some studios are high-tech and sterile, while some are funky yet comfortable. Some artists will perform better in a studio located in an industrial park that reminds them of their rehearsal facility (see Figure 9-1), while others respond better to something that's modern and ultra-slick (see Figure 9-2). Usually, the longer you stay in a facility, the more the vibe matters, so that factors in to your final selection as well.

Figure 9-1: Some Artists Perform Better in a Smaller Studio

Figure 9-2: Some Artists Prefer to Record in a High-Tech Studio

- **The staff.** Nothing can turn a client (that's you and your artist) off as much as a disengaged or an incompetent studio owner or staff, so be sure to check with other producers and get recommendations before booking a place. A great staff can easily make up for many shortcomings of the studio if the people are fun and accommodating, but you need a core competence in the basics of studio management first.

- **The deal.** You may want to book a great place that everyone wants to record in, but if you can't afford it, you might need to reconsider your choice. That said, a studio's advertised rate usually isn't its final price. Most studios will cut you a deal off the "book," or advertised rate, depending on several factors including, for example: how busy they are, how long you intend to stay, and whether you have a reputation as being a hassle-free client. Talk to the studio manager or owner; tell him what you need and how much you have to spend, and you might be surprised how accommodating he can be.

- **The studio size.** Are you going for full-band takes, or are the drums the only instrument you intend to record for basics? This factor will determine how large a recording room you'll need as well as the type of isolation that will be required for each instrument. If you plan on tracking an entire band at once, the size of the tracking room will be critical, since larger is definitely better. Unfortunately, most of the really old large studios are now a thing of the past, but most commercial studios can accommodate at least a rhythm section. If you're creating mostly electronic music with a few overdubs, then you're probably more concerned that the studio has enough room that you feel comfortable and has a small overdub area.

- **The acoustics.** Most commercial studios have a recording room that sounds reasonably good, but each studio will sound different depending on when it was built. Throughout the years, studio acoustics have gone back and forth in popularity between reflective, "live" sounding rooms and relatively dead rooms, and you want to be sure to book a room that will give the sound you're going for. Generally speaking, rock and live recording (like jazz) tend to work best in a livelier, more reflective room, while R&B and dance work better in a dead room, although these are broad generalizations and there are certainly plenty of exceptions. You'll find a lot more live rooms available though, as the dead-room era was mostly a byproduct of the late '70s disco era. Remember, it's a lot easier to deaden up a live room than it is to liven up a dead-sounding room.

- **The gear.** Sometimes the gear that a studio has is the determining factor in helping you decide which studio you'll use. Maybe the studio has an API console (or even just a rack of their mic preamps) and you like the way they sound on the rock band you're about to produce. Maybe the studio has a great collection of vintage keyboards or guitar amps. Maybe the studio has a great microphone locker. All of these things play into your selection of the right studio for the project.

It's always a good idea to pick the best studio you can afford when recording the basic tracks. As I said before, the basics are critical to the outcome of the final product, so this isn't the place to skimp. Overdubs might be a different story, as you'll see in Chapter 10.

The Assistant Engineer

If you've booked a commercial facility, chances are that you'll have an assistant engineer assigned to your session. Don't underestimate how important this individual can be to you, as the assistant is the key to making your life easier as you record. If the assistant is really good, he can provide the following:

- Intimate knowledge of the studio and its quirks, from finding the best-sounding places in the room to record, to the contents of the mic locker, to which mics are working well, and to what the idiosyncrasies of the console and patch bay are.
- A great working knowledge of the house Pro Tools system (or whatever DAW you choose to work with).
- The scoop on the best places to order take-out or get food delivered from, as well as knowledge of the best restaurants nearby.
- Information about any musical instruments and amps that the studio may have, as well as the rental services available.
- Information about any house computer systems and wireless network connections.
- Documentation of the session, from track sheets (yes, they're still used) to mic-placement charts and setup pictures to marking the console tape if there is one in the studio.
- A good pot of coffee!

Above all, a great assistant is transparent. When you really need him, he's there, and all other times, he's in the background but always paying attention to what's going on. If the assistant sees a problem, he tells the engineer at the appropriate time and it's the engineer's job to take care of it. A good assistant never displays a bad or negative attitude, and always leaves his or her ego at the door.

CHAPTER 10
BASIC TRACKS: WHERE THE MAGIC IS MADE

Basic tracks, or "basics," are the initial recordings of the rhythm section that are done prior to any overdubbing or "sweetening." Whether building a track by creating your own beats or using live instruments, basic tracks are the foundation for the music being recorded and for any other parts that come afterward. If there's something faulty in the foundation, it will either be impossible or very costly (in time and money) to fix things later. That's why it's essential to make each basic track the best it can be.

Regardless of whether you spend a little or a lot of time in preproduction, have a good handle on the songs or are just winging it, or are able to visualize the final outcome or not, recording basic tracks is where you either make the project or break it. Even if you had a great preproduction, you never really know how things will record or what unforeseen circumstances will pop up until you begin to record.

While the end product might be difficult to hear in your head with the stripped-down basic track (unless you're recording the entire band at the same time), it's still important to get a great vibe and feel for the song even if you can't "hear through it" (hear the end product in your head). I remember playing with a multitrack tape of Fleetwood Mac's huge '70s hit "Dreams" during a recording console demo, soloing the exceptionally isolated hi-hat and thinking, "You can tell this song's a hit just from the hi-hat!" The feel and vibe were so strong that it was undeniable just from that one instrument. That's what you're going for during basics.

WHAT ARE BASIC TRACKS?

Basic tracks can consist of any of the following instruments, depending on the song, artist, project, or genre of music:

- The drums by themselves
- Drums and bass
- Drums, bass, and guitar
- Drum, bass, and keyboard
- Drum, bass, guitar, and keyboard
- The entire band, regardless of how many instruments

Any of the above may be accompanied by a vocalist singing a "scratch," or guide, vocal. A scratch is a vocal that's used only as a guide so that the players know where they are in the song. It's not intended to be included in the final version, although sometimes it's so good that the singer can't beat it during overdubs.

In modern recording, sometimes the only thing that's intended to be kept for the final version when recording basics is the drums, even though other instruments are played at the same time. The theory is that if the drum track is great, everything else can be replaced as an overdub later. If that's the case, isolation of the drums becomes of paramount importance, since any leakage of other instruments such as a guitar or bass may clash with later overdubs.

That being said, most veteran producers would prefer to get a great basic recording of as many instruments as possible at the same time, since the elusive "vibe" of all the musicians playing together sometimes can't be duplicated any other way.

SETUP DAY

For a multiday session, the first day of tracking is also setup day. Usually it takes about a half day for everyone to get settled in, the engineer to get sounds, and the musicians to get their headphone mixes together.

Somewhere during the second half of the day is when the band gets to recording, even if all you really want to capture is the drums. If you're lucky, you might get a keeper take on the first day, but I find that it's usually when everyone comes in fresh the next day that the real work starts to get done. Even if you get what you think is a great take on the first day, be prepared to try it again when you're fresh on day two. You might be surprised what happens.

For a budget session in which you have only a single day to record, you want to get set up and recording as quickly as possible, certainly within the first hour after the musicians arrive. The best way to do this is to communicate to the studio all the details about the session, including how many instruments there will be, what particular mics or studio gear you'd like to use, how you'd like the outboard gear set up, whether you'll be bringing your own hard drive, what recording format should be used, and what rental gear should be expected (your engineer will usually handle this for you). If the studio is already set up before you arrive, your setup time will be cut to a minimum.

> **TIP**: *Be sure to differentiate between arrival time and downbeat time as there can be confusion between the two. If you tell everyone (especially the band members), "We're in the studio at 1pm tomorrow," at 1pm some of them will just be getting there while others will already be set up and ready to play.*

HOW LONG ARE THE SESSIONS?

In the case of a commercial studio facility, most studio time is sold on the basis of a 12-hour "lockout." This means that while you get charged for only 12 hours, no one else can use the studio for the other 12, and so all your gear and the gear in the control room can remain set up.

You can negotiate with the studio about what happens if you decide to go beyond the 12 hours. Will you be charged an hourly rate? Will you have to pay only for the assistant (the usual case)? Or will you have a 24-hour lockout, during which you can go all day and all night and not be charged extra?

The lockout mentality can play heavily on the session's consciousness. Since you're paying for a 12-hour day, it's not uncommon to want to use every minute's worth by staying in the studio long past the burnout stage. This can be counterproductive as a whole, since the burnout tends to catch up with everyone in all the successive recording days, making it harder and harder to concentrate and therefore making the useful time spent in the studio shorter and shorter.

Studio pros have found that it's best to keep your days to a reasonable eight or nine hours, pushing past that only if you're really close to something great and everyone wants to continue, or if a deadline looms. One of the producer's main jobs is to sense when the burnout point has been reached and to call an end to the session at that time.

GETTING SOUNDS

There was a time in the '70s when a few super high-budget projects would spend an entire week just trying to get the right snare drum sound. While they might've been in musical snare drum nirvana, 99.99999 percent of sessions have to move faster than that, and they should.

The more time you use before you start to record, the less time you'll spend recording, since the attention span of the players decreases proportionately to the time spent getting sounds. Although you want things to sound as good as possible, a poor-sounding track with a great vibe is a lot more usable than a well-recorded but musically stale track.

Still, dialing in sounds is a necessary evil in recording, and at least some amount of time has to be allotted for the task. A good producer knows to move on when, for example, the engineer is just trying to dial in the final five percent of the sound and it's taking too long. Similarly, he knows when to continue even when the sound really isn't working, realizing that it can easily be replaced later.

Choose the Best Instruments

Having the right equipment plays a big part in getting the best sounds, and it's the producer's role to make sure that happens. It's not uncommon for all sorts of instruments to be rented for tracking and overdubs.

For instance, one of the tricks to getting a great drum sound is to start with a great-sounding drum kit, or at least have the drummer's current kit tuned by a pro.

In major recording centers like New York, Nashville, London, and Los Angeles, companies like Drum Fetish, Drum Paradise, and Ross Garfield's Drum Doctors (see Figure 10-1) provide cartage, maintenance, tuning, and rentals for L.A.'s top session drummers as well as any band entering the studio.

Just to show that even the big-name bands with all their resources still need some help when it comes to getting drum sounds, artists like the Foo Fighters, the Red Hot Chili Peppers, Dwight Yoakam, Bruce Springsteen, and Tom Petty and the Heartbreakers (among many others) have used Drum Doctors in the studio. Similarly, bands like The Who, Yes, Bon Jovi, and Mötley Crüe and producers like the Neptunes, Don Was, Rick Rubin, and Joe Chiccarelli have used Drum Paradise on their past platinum-selling records.

Figure 10-1: Drum Doctors

Different Gear for Different Jobs

Playing a gig is distinctly different from playing on a recording session. What works on a gig won't always translate to the studio, either playing-wise or gear-wise. You choose your gear for a live gig based on its versatility, durability, and general ruggedness, but the only thing that counts in the studio is the sound.

While one size might fit all on a gig, if a player uses the same instrument for every part it will usually make for a boring recording, especially if a player is recording more than one part or playing on more than one song. The sound issue doesn't necessarily apply if you're playing on a demo (for that, the performance is what's most important), but for most other serious recording dates, gear makes a profound difference. Each player should make every effort to bring a variety of the best-sounding gear he can, because it will not only make the recording sound better, but will also make the music a lot more interesting.

While it seems like a no-brainer for most musicians to have lots of alternative sounds available, this advice especially applies to drummers. It's not uncommon for a drummer to use different kits for different songs on an album, or change the tuning or change out the snare drum according to the song. The fact that most session drummers come to a session with five or six snare drums tells you all you need to know about being prepared.

Here's the reality of today, at least with the stuff that I do. There are always budget considerations, so I generally bring six [snare drums]. I could bring 30 snares, but then the cartage bill goes up and, to be honest, you're usually way covered with the six snares because no one is ever asking, "What else you got?" past that. So I bring three different sizes of wood and three different sizes of metal drums. That's not including if I go to do an orchestral date, where I'd bring about eight different orchestral snares.

—L.A. session drummer Bernie Dresel

Well-Maintained Equipment Required

Having well-maintained gear is essential for the musician who's making a record. Everything is expected to work perfectly, with no tuning problems, no extraneous noises, and no "intermittents" (when the audio cuts in and out or crackles). Not only does everyone's gear have to work, but it also has to be in tip-top condition. The better everything works and sounds, the better the recording will sound. This is the least you should expect from each player, and it's your job to tell them this before the downbeat of day one. Of course, studio musicians and musicians who already have a fair amount of recording experience will know this already.

The drummer should, at minimum, make sure that all the drums have new drumheads, the drums are in tune, and the pedals are oiled so they don't squeak. Guitar and bass players need to make sure their instruments are properly intonated so that they play in tune anywhere on the neck, none of their cables are crackling, and their amps don't buzz or hum.

A keyboard player must know her way around each keyboard so well that she can easily get to any sound that's requested, and, as with guitar and bass players, her gear and cables must work flawlessly.

For a horn player, none of the valves or keys can stick, and no extraneous noises should come from the instrument. Like everyone else, string players should show up to a session with their best-sounding instruments for that particular application.

Is Vintage Gear Necessary?

Although not always the case, the most desirable and collectible gear does seem to have a way of sounding the best on a recording. That being said, even if the guitar player owns a '57 Les Paul or the bass player has a '62 P Bass or the drummer has a '72 Black Beauty snare or the keyboard player an original Minimoog, if it doesn't sound good or has an operating problem, you're much better off using something that's newer that works well. Just because an instrument is worth a lot of money doesn't mean that it sounds good or is going to work on a session.

That said, the fact of the matter is that a lot of the revered vintage instruments do sound great for recording, providing they're in top working order. Ever wonder why a vintage Les Paul or a Strat or a P Bass or a Marshall Plexi or a '59 Fender Bassman (see Figure 10-2) or a '60s Ludwig drum kit or a Hammond B-3 or a Mellotron (see Figure 10-3) are so coveted that they've all been reissued to sound as much like the original as possible? It's the sound, of course, and using one of these items can instantly get the sound that everyone might be looking for and therefore help the part fit better in the track.

That's why you always see or read about what seems to be some of the same gear from session to session, concert to concert, video to video, and in article to article. With some experience, players eventually learn what makes them sound their best, and certain instruments, amplifiers, effects, and accessory brands and models are just tried and true (when properly maintained, of course).

Figure 10-2: A 1959 Fender Bassman Amplifier

That's not to say that inexpensive gear isn't worth having, too. If it has a unique sound, inexpensive equipment can have a place in a session. In reality, musical gear in any price range is far better today than it's ever been. In fact, ever since about 1985 or so it's become difficult to buy a musical instrument that doesn't perform at a reasonably high level of quality. Automated manufacturing has driven down the price and raised the quality in a way we never could have imagined in the '50s, '60s, and '70s. That being said, the homogenization of manufacturing has taken the character out of much of today's low-cost instruments and make many sound pretty much the same.

One of the reasons that vintage gear has such a draw is that there's a difference from instrument to instrument because much of it was handmade and the tolerances were much broader then than they are

Figure 10-3: A Mellotron: The Sound of the Moody Blues

now. As a result, sometimes a drift in tolerance because of human error (for example, an instrument constructed on a Monday morning or on a Friday afternoon before quitting time) resulted in magic that's still difficult to duplicate. And the fact that the wood and metal are aged can't help but give an instrument a sound that's different than something new off the shelf.

Okay, so what's tried and true that usually works? Here's a quick and very incomplete list of instruments, amps, and accessories that are prized for their sound (and for their collectability the older they get). I'm not recommending that you run out and buy or rent any of these, but if you get a chance to listen to any of the instruments mentioned below for just a couple of minutes, that will give you a good reference point as to why they're so sought after.

Guitars

- Epiphone Casino (as used by John Lennon)
- Fender Stratocaster (the most widely played guitar in the world, with the models from 1957, 1963, and 1967 being the most desirable from a collector's standpoint)
- Fender Telecaster (the '52 Reissue is a good example of the best model released over the many years)
- Fender Telecaster Deluxe or Custom (with humbucking pickups)
- Gibson ES-335 (the "dot neck" versions that use simple dots for position markers are the most desirable to collectors)
- Gibson Firebird
- Gibson J-45 (also an acoustic standard)
- Gibson Les Paul Deluxe (with smaller humbuckers), used extensively by Pete Townsend during the '70s
- Gibson Les Paul Goldtop (the original Les Paul with two single-coil P-90 pickups instead of the standard humbuckers)
- Gibson Les Paul Junior (an entry-level Les Paul favored by Billy Joe Armstrong and Leslie West)
- Gibson Les Paul Standard (the most expensive vintage instrument on the market today, and some say the best guitar ever made—especially between 1957 and 1960)
- Gretsch 6120 (this hollowbody Chet Atkins–style guitar was used on a variety of huge hits, including The Who's "Won't Get Fooled Again")
- Gretsch Silver Jet
- Guild F-412 (the only acoustic built from the ground up as a 12-string)
- Martin D-28 (an acoustic standard)
- Rickenbacker 360 (the guitar responsible for the British Sound)
- Rickenbacker 360-12 (a 12-string version of the 360)
- Coral/Danelectro Electric Sitar

Guitar Amplifiers

- 1959 Fender Bassman (some think this is the best *guitar* amp ever made)
- Any blackface Fender (has a black control panel with white nomenclature, hence the name)
- Any brown-covered Fender
- Any tweed-covered Fender
- Fender Deluxe Reverb (has a different circuit design than most Fender amps that makes it sound different when overdriven)
- Hiwatt Custom 100
- Marshall 1968 Super Lead head
- Marshall JMP head with model 1960 cabinet (the sound of British hard rock)
- Marshall JTM-45 combo (the sound of Eric Clapton with the Bluesbreakers)
- Marshall Plexi (has a control panel made out of plexiglass, hence the name)
- Mesa/Boogie Mark I (as preferred by Carlos Santana)
- Roland Jazz Chorus 120
- Vox AC30 Top Boost (has extra factory-installed circuitry that gives it more overdrive than a standard AC30; the sound of Brian May of Queen)

Figure 10-4: Fender Deluxe Reverb

Figure 10-5: Danelectro Longhorn Bass

Basses

- Danelectro Longhorn (see Figure 10-5)
- Fender Jazz basses ('60s, '70s, and even '80s)
- Fender Precision basses ('60s, '70s, '80s)
- Gibson EB-2 or EB-3
- Hofner Beatle bass
- Kaye Jimmy Reed bass
- Music Man StingRay
- Rickenbacker 4001

Bass Amplifiers

Figure 10-6: Ampeg B-15A: The Studio Standard

- Acoustic 360 (the bass sound of the '70s)
- Ampeg B-15A (the standard for the studio; see Figure 10-6)
- Ampeg SVT (the standard for touring that is occasionally used in the studio; Elliot Randall played the lead on Steely Dan's famous "Reelin' In the Years" through one)

Pedals

- Boss CE-1 Chorus Ensemble
- Cry Baby Wah (Vox/Dunlop)
- DigiTech Whammy Pitch Effect
- Dynacomp (MXR/Dunlop)
- Electro-Harmonix Big Muff Pi
- Electro-Harmonix Deluxe Memory Man
- Fuzz Face
- Ibanez Tube Screamer (the older TS-808 and TS-9 are the most desirable for their sound; see Figure 10.7)
- Maestro Tube Echoplex
- Musitronics Mutron III
- MXR Phase 90
- Octavia (Tycobrahe/Roger Mayer)

- ProCo Rat
- Roland RE-101 Space Echo
- Uni-Vibe (Shin-Ei/ Univox)
- Vox V847 Wah (the original, and some say still the best)

Keyboards

- Fender Rhodes Stage 88 or Suitcase 73 electric piano
- Hammond B-3 (or A-3 or C-3, which have the same electronics in a different cabinet) with

Figure 10-7: Ibanez TS-9 Tube Screamer

a Leslie 122, 145, or 147 (which are all basically the same, except for the cabinet size or the type of connecting cable)
- Hohner D6 Clavinet
- Mellotron M400
- Minimoog
- Wurlitzer Model 120 or 200 electric piano (see Figure 10-8)
- Yamaha C7 grand piano (a studio standard)

Figure 10-8: Wurlitzer Model 200A Electric Piano

Drums

- Gretsch Round Badge kit ('50s and '60s; the logo is a round badge)
- Gretsch Stop Sign Badge kit ('70s)
- Ludwig Acrolite snare drum
- Ludwig Black Beauty snare drum ('70s)
- Ludwig Keystone Badge kit, '60s (see Figure 10-9)
- Ludwig Supraphonic 6½" snare drum
- Noble & Cooley 5½" maple snare drum

Figure 10-9: The Ludwig Keystone Logo

The broad reach of contemporary, vintage, and boutique gear appropriate to use on recording sessions runs the gamut from affordable entry-level instruments and pedals to the most expensive musical equipment on the planet. Most often, you get what you pay for, and the pricier pieces sound best.

There are exceptions though, like that time when the cheap no-name snare a drummer bought at a yard sale for 20 bucks really made a track come alive. Whatever works is always the best choice.

RECORDING THE DRUMS: THE SONG'S HEARTBEAT

If there's one instrument that producers and engineers alike seem to obsess over, it's the drum kit. And well they should, since drums are the heartbeat of virtually all modern music. Wimpy-sounding drums can make for a wimpy recording regardless of how well everything else is recorded.

The problem is that, for any number of reasons, most drummers' kits simply don't record well. Whether it's because of old beat-up heads (the worst offender), bad tuning, uneven bearing edges on the shells, or defective hardware, drums that might be adequate or even great-sounding in a live situation don't always make the cut when put under scrutiny in the recording studio.

While many producers and engineers are willing to spend whatever time it takes to make the drums sound great, most don't have the know-how or the time to improve the sound of the set before it gets under the mics. As a result, virtually all big-budget projects either rent a kit specifically for recording or hire a drum tuner, because no matter how great your signal chain is, if the drum sound in the room doesn't cut it, then there's not much the engineer can do to help (despite what the makers of outboard gear and plug-ins might tell you). But just what constitutes a great-sounding drum kit?

The Keys to a Great-Sounding Drum Kit

While the definition of *great* is different to different people on a general level, in the studio the word usually means that a kit is well tuned and free of buzzes and sympathetic vibrations. This means that when you hit the rack tom, the snare doesn't buzz and the other toms don't ring along, and when you hit the snare, the toms don't ring along. So how do you achieve this drum nirvana? It's all in the tuning and the kit maintenance.

Drum Tuning Tips

Here are a few tuning tips to tame those puppies down, courtesy of the famous Drum Doctor:

If the snares buzz when the toms are hit:

- Check that the snares are straight.
- Check to see if the snares are flat and centered on the drum.
- Loosen the bottom head.
- Retune the offending toms.

If the kick drum isn't punchy and lacks power in the context of the music:

- Try increasing and decreasing the amount of muffling in the drum, or try a different blanket or pillow.
- Change to a heavier, uncoated head like a clear Emperor or PowerStroke 3.
- Change to a thinner front head or one with a larger cutout.
- Have the edges of the drum recut to create more attack.

If one or more of the toms are difficult to tune or have an unwanted "growl,"

- Check the top heads for dents and replace as necessary.
- Make sure that the tension is even all around the top and bottom heads.
- Tighten the bottom head.
- Have the bearing edges of the drum checked and recut as required.

THE HEADPHONE MIX

The key to recording great basic tracks is to ensure the focus of the participants and comfort of the players. Although the environmental comforts are helpful, a musician will play or sing her best when she hears herself well and in the correct proportion to the other players or singers. That's why the headphone (or "cue") mix is so important.

Perhaps the greatest detriment to a session running smoothly is players being unable to hear themselves comfortably in the headphones. This is one of the reasons that veteran engineers spend so much time on, and give so much attention to, the cue mix and the phones themselves, instead of letting the assistant do it. In fact, a sure sign of a studio neophyte is when someone treats the headphones and cue mix as an afterthought, instead of spending as much time as required to make them sound great.

While it's true that a veteran studio player can shrug off a bad or distorted phone mix and still deliver a fine performance, good "cans" makes a session go faster and easier, and removes a variable that is quite possibly the biggest detriment to a session.

> **TIP**: *When players are using personal cue mix systems like Hearback or Aviom, it's best for the engineer to dial in a mix for the musicians, then explain how they can adjust it for themselves. Many musicians have a tough time getting a mix themselves that they find useful.*

Personal Headphone Mixes

Perhaps the best thing to come along in recent years has been the introduction of relatively inexpensive personal headphone systems. These systems allow the musician to control the headphone mix by supplying him with up to eight channels to control.

Each headphone mixer also contains a headphone amplifier that can (depending on the product) provide earsplitting level. Manufacturers include Furman, Oz Audio, Aviom, and Hear Technologies (see Figure 10-10). As above, it's best to provide a stereo monitor mix (what you're listening to in the control room) as well as kick, snare, vocal, and whatever other instruments are pertinent.

Figure 10-10: Hear Back Headphone System

Recording Without Headphones

Some bands new to the studio are so used to playing live on stage that they just can't get used to headphones and therefore can't perform well in the studio. Here's a way that allows them to get what they need while recording without having to wrap those tiny speakers around their heads.

- The key to not using headphones in a spread-out recording situation is to keep the amps about ten feet behind the players, and then have the players sitting or standing pretty close to the drums. Having everyone situated that close together helps them psychologically, as well as minimizes the minute acoustic delay that can occur when the players are spread out too far.
- If there are two guitar players, set them up on opposite sides of the kit. This will provide a better stereo picture for the leakage.
- At times, a floor monitor (like at a gig) will work well for scratch vocal. Sometimes if you're trying to place the singer in the same room as the band, you'll get a better performance if you use one.

Just as with the guitar and bass amps, you may need to move the floor monitor around until you find the right band balance.

- Most of the time the singer will gravitate to the spot in the room where the band's balance is best.

TO CLICK OR NOT TO CLICK

Using a click track, or recording while listening to a metronome, has become a fact of life with most recording. Not only does playing at an even tempo sound better, but it makes cut-and-paste editing between performances in a DAW possible and easy. Having a track based on a click also makes delay and reverb timing easier during mixing.

Playing to a click can present a number of problems, however, such as leakage of the click from the headphones into the mics, and exposing the fact that some people just can't play on time to save their lives. We'll cover these aspects shortly.

Making the Click Cut Through the Mix

Many times just providing a metronome in the phones isn't enough. What good is a click if you can't hear it, or worse yet, groove to it? Here are some tricks to make the click listenable but able to cut through the densest mixes, and seem like another instrument in the track too.

- **Pick the right sound**. Something that sounds more musical than an electronic click is better to groove to. Try a cowbell, a sidestick, or even a conga slap. Needless to say, when you pick a sound to replace the click, it should fit within the context of the song. Many drummers like two sounds for the click: something like a high go-go bell for the downbeat and a low go-go bell for the other beats, or vice versa.
- **Pick the right number of clicks per bar.** Some players like quarter notes, while others play better along with eighth notes. Whichever you're using, it will work better if you put more emphasis on the downbeat (beat 1) than on the other beats.
- **Make it groove.** By adding a little timed delay to the click (quarter notes, eighth notes, or triplets) you can make it swing a bit and it won't sound so stiff. This makes it easier for players that normally have trouble playing to a click. As a side benefit, this can help make any bleed that does occur less offensive, because it will sound more like a part of the song.

Preventing Click Bleed

Okay, now the click cuts through the mix, but it cuts so well that it's bleeding into the mics. You'll find this occurs mostly with drummers (who often want to hear the click at near ear-splitting levels) and string players (who play very quietly and therefore need the gain of the mics turned up). To avoid bleed, try one of the following:

- **Use a different set of headphones.** Try a pair that has a better seal. The Sony 7506 phones provide a fairly good seal, but Metrophones Studio Kans or Vic Firth S1H1s (see Figure 10-11) will all isolate a click from bleeding into nearby mics.

Figure 10-11: Vic Firth S1H1s

- **Run the click through an equalizer** and roll off the high end just enough to cut down on the bleed.

    Many times players will leave the phones loose so they can hear what's going on with the other players in the room. If they can have click in one ear (in the headphone) that's sealed closely to the head, then they get the live room sound in their free ear. One-eared phones have become almost standard for ensemble recording for horn and string sections, and are sometimes preferred by vocal groups as well (see Figure 10-12).

- **Send the click to just one player** (like the drummer or the conductor) and let him or her communicate the click to the band or orchestra.

If all else fails, try this method. It might also provide the loosest feel and best groove.

1. Put a single mic in the room.
2. Play the song three times to the click and record it on a single track only!
3. Choose the best of the three versions of the song.
4. Use this track for the drummer to play to instead of a click.

Figure 10-12: Beyer Single-Eared Headphone

Using the above method, the drummer can hear the rest of the band and play along through headphones so that there should be very little bleed. Once the drums are recorded, the session can progress as normal.

When a Click Won't Work

Let's face it, not many people like to play to a click. It's unnatural and doesn't breathe the way real players do. But in this world of drum machines, sequencers, and DAWs, most musicians have grown used to playing with some kind of metronome.

However, there are those times when a click just won't work for whatever reason. The performance suffers so much that you get something that isn't worth recording. No problem. Don't get obsessed with the click or the fact that the tempo fluctuates without it.

Many great hits have been recorded without a click and with wavering tempos ("What a Fool Believes," a Song of the Year Grammy winner for the Doobie Brothers, comes to mind). Remember, feel and vibe are what makes the track, not perfection.

LEAKAGE IS YOUR FRIEND

Acoustic spill (known as "leakage") from one instrument into another's mic is often thought of as undesirable, but it can and should be used to enhance the sound. Many production and recording novices are under the mistaken belief that during a tracking session with multiple instruments, every track recorded must contain only the instrument/source that the mic was pointed at. Since that's pretty hard to achieve, why not just use the leakage to embellish the tracks instead?

Instead of trying to eliminate leakage, great attention should be paid to the *kind of leakage* being recorded. Leakage can be used as a sort of glue between instruments in much the same way that instruments blend together in a live situation.

Keeping that in mind, when tracking with multiple instruments, try keeping the players and their gear as close to one another as possible. That will not only help the players communicate, but the leakage will contain more direct sound than room reflections, which will sound better. This might cause the overdubs to clash with the basic tracks, so it's best to have keeper tracks from all the instruments in order to get the desired effect.

THE SCRATCH VOCAL

While experienced studio players can cut a great track without a guide, or scratch vocal, almost every player would prefer to have one to play against. The guide vocal not only acts as a cue for certain sections of the song, but also adds to the groove and feel that helps a player perform at his or her best. One of the other advantages is that the lead singer can give directions and reminders to the players as the song progresses.

> *I have two separate crews that play on Carrie Underwood records, and both of them know full well what her sound is and what she likes. Once they get out to their respective positions in the studio, they'll play through the song without Carrie on the mic and get an arrangement that is fairly tight. But let me tell you something: once Carrie gets out there on that mic, everything changes. She starts singing, and the level of excitement and musicianship goes through the roof. It happens every single time. When a great singer gets on mic, it inspires everybody.*
>
> *The same thing happens with Reba. It's just that intangible thing that occurs when a truly gifted singer gets on that mic.*
> —Producer Mark Bright

There are no particular rules how to cut a scratch vocal. Some vocalists don't mind being in a vocal booth while performing a scratch vocal, but almost all vocalists want to be able to see all the players while recording a song because they dislike feeling disconnected from the rest of the band.

As a result, many singers prefer to be out in the room with the other players. The scratch track won't sound as good in that situation because of the leakage that will occur (that comes mostly from the drums), but if it helps the performance of the band and vocalist, that's what you want to do.

Many lead singers, producers, and engineers may take a scratch vocal lightly since it will be redone at a later time under better conditions, but the smart producer is always prepared just in case magic happens that can't be repeated. Treat the scratch vocal seriously, because you never know when you might capture lightning in a bottle.

DON'T FORGET TO RECORD A TUNING NOTE

It's always a good idea to include a ten-second tuning note before each song, especially if the band's sound isn't based around an instrument with a solid tuning that doesn't move, like a Hammond organ. This way, if for some reason you happened to use a tuning that was a couple of cents flat, you have the tuning note as your reference.

This seems like a small thing, but you wouldn't believe how much time it can save you down the road if a situation arises where you just can't figure out why everything sounds out of tune.

DON'T FORGET TO RECORD A COUNT-OFF

A recorded count-off is important for those times when an overdubbed pickup part is required before the song starts. Even if you're playing to a click that's being generated by the DAW itself, recording the click at least four bars ahead of the downbeat is a foolproof way to make sure that any pickup or opening part is easily executed.

If a click isn't being used, it's even more important to record the count-off. Have the drummer click two bars before the count with his drumsticks, and then count, "1, [click], 2, [click], 1, 2, 3, [silent click]." Sometimes a count with the last two beats silent is used instead like this, "1, [click], 2, [click], 1, 2, [silent click], [silent click]." This is plenty of count for the band to get the feel, and having the silent clicks on the end makes it easy to edit out later without having to worry about clipping the downbeat.

WHETHER TO USE SESSION MUSICIANS OR THE BAND

Replacing a band member with a studio musician is always one of the dicier calls that a producer has to make. There must be a strategic value involved when making this decision, because it may have long-term consequences that can ultimately sink a project unless you're extremely diplomatic about it.

If you're producing a band and someone just isn't cutting it (often the drummer during basics), you have two choices. You can either piece together an acceptable take from a number of performances (made easier today in this digital world of ours), or you can hire a ringer.

If bringing in a studio musician causes such bad blood that it will have a negative effect on the rest of the record, then it's not worth it, so using a session player is usually a last resort. It's a lot easier to hire in players for instruments that the band members don't play, like horns, strings, maybe keyboards, and percussion (but ask the drummer to do percussion first, for diplomacy's sake).

If a solo artist wants to use her backup band to record and they're not cutting it, your decision is less challenging since the artist wants the best product and the players are hired guns anyway. You probably won't get too much resistance about replacing a player in this situation.

LISTENING TO PLAYBACKS

Bringing the players into the control room to listen to a playback can be disruptive, or it can be constructive, like in the case that it's used to strategically bolster the momentum of the session. If the players listen to a playback after every take, the energy slows down as they file into the control room and then back out afterward. It usually takes a minute or two for them to get comfortable again, which can take you further away from the perfect take rather than closer.

One of the best ways to get your point across yet keep the energy high is to be selective about control room playbacks. It's sometimes best to bring the players in for a listen after a couple of takes once they've become comfortable with the sound and studio. At that point, hearing a playback can serve as a reference point for where they currently are and where they have to go.

Don't bring them back into the control room until they either have what might be a keeper take or would benefit from another listen in order to play something better. Fewer trips to the control room will help keep energy high and momentum going forward.

SESSION BREAKS

One of the best abilities a producer can develop is knowing when it's time to take a break. Sometimes a ten-minute break can pump new energy into a flagging session, so the producer always has to keep his finger on the pulse of the players to gauge their concentration.

The danger is that you'll call a break just as the players are getting in a groove and it will be difficult to get it back after the break, but usually the players will either tell you that they want to keep going, or they'll confirm that a break is needed. It's best to figure on taking some sort of a break every three hours or so, depending on how the session is progressing.

Dinner Breaks

Dinner breaks can be dangerous in that they must be handled with care so you're able to get the players back into a groove afterward. If the break is too long, it may take an equally long time for the players to get their focus back. The same applies if you allow them to leave the studio to eat somewhere else, which is why it's always better to have food brought in.

One of the biggest problems to avoid is having a large meal, since normal digestion naturally slows down a player's ability to concentrate. Keep the mealtime short, the portions small, and allow absolutely no alcohol so that everyone stays fresh and the session is kept on track.

HOW DO YOU KNOW WHEN YOU'RE FINISHED RECORDING?

Knowing when you have the keeper tracks that you need to make a great record is one of the more difficult assessments for a producer to make during basic tracking. The ultimate is a flawless performance with a great groove and lots of feel, but achieving all three attributes is elusive. Know that given enough time and enough takes, getting the perfect take is within your grasp. It's not uncommon to do dozens of takes until the perfect one occurs (Jimi Hendrix's landmark "All Along the Watchtower" was take 28).

That said, sometimes it's best to determine that although the track is not perfect, you have enough to work with. Can you cut and paste several takes together to get what you need? Should you move on to another song and return to the current song later for another try?

Once again, whoever is paying you will have dictated their needs before you begin tracking. If your job is to get a certain number of songs finished within a certain period of time, then you might have to settle on some less-than-perfect performances to meet the deadline. If your job is to get the best possible product, then you might throw the time schedule and budget out the window.

Either way, basic tracking can be over in a few hours (as in the case of recording a straight-ahead jazz project) or can continue for months or even years (like a big-budget legacy band), but it's up to the producer to make the call that the mission of capturing exactly what's needed for this phase of recording has been accomplished.

CHAPTER 11

OVERDUBS

The overdubbing stage can be something as simple as fixing or replacing some of the basic tracks (like the bass, rhythm guitar, solos, synths, or lead vocal) or as complex as adding sophisticated layering of horns and strings, multiple guitars, keyboards, and background vocals. It's also the phase of the project during which the most experimenting is done, since even the most meticulously designed parts sometimes don't work and require some alteration.

THE RECORDING PLAN

When budgets get blown out the window and the project begins to fall behind schedule, the overdubbing stage is usually responsible. If a producer is doing his job correctly, each overdub is finely crafted to complement every other musical part of the song.

This crafting takes a lot of work, since the overdub has to have the right sound and the part has to musically fit like a glove with all the others. That's why it's best to have a list of priorities that specify which overdubs are the most important and absolutely must be recorded. That way, you can make sure not to fall behind due to experimentation and extra ideas.

The overdub priority list should go song by song and might look something like the following (highest on the list being the most important):

SUNSHINE OF YOUR LIFE
Lead vocal
Lead vocal harmony (second and third B section)
Guitar solo
Keyboard, fix second verse
Keyboard line, second and third verse
Background vocals (choruses)
Background vocals (last verse)
Guitar double (chorus and bridge)

You can see just what overdubs are expected on the song and how they rank in terms of priority, with the last entry (guitar double) being the least important. Having a list like this will help you plan your overdubs and let you know just what you can eliminate if you start to get behind budget-wise or time-wise.

MAKE IT BETTER, NOT DIFFERENT

Most artists share the common trait of having a creative streak that provides them idea after idea for parts, lines, embellishments, and enhancements. The more creative the artist, the more the ideas spring forth, and that's the problem.

Sometimes an artist has so many good ideas that it takes a lot of time to try them all, and before you know it, you're behind schedule. That's bad enough, but an abundance of ideas can move a song away from its true intention, even detracting from the original inspiration.

An example would be an artist who writes a straight pop song, but then just has to hear how it sounds with a reggae feel after the pop version is complete. While the song might be great with the new style, it might not contain the essence of the artist's original inspiration. It's up to you as producer to put a hold on the experimentation and focus the energy back to where the artist shines best.

Sometimes an artist will come up with good idea after good idea for new lines and parts during overdubs, and while most of them might work, they just make the song different and not better. Again, it's up to you to focus the energy of the artist and musicians back to where it needs to be and make the decision that the original direction is the best one to follow.

Sometimes an artist's massive creativity can work in your favor, though. For example, if you're not sure about the original feel of the song, expressing that to the artist will get his creative juices flowing and before you know it, a better idea will appear. That said, usually the artist's first inspiration is the best, and it's probably the one that grabbed everyone's attention in the first place.

TIME TO EXPERIMENT

It always happens at least once in the overdub phase. A musician plays something during warm-ups or plays something by mistake during recording that lights up the whole studio and the producer says, "Can you play that again, but do something different on the end?" Or "Can you play it like that in this section instead?" The chase is then on to capture that lightning in a bottle and pour it over a part or section that was lacking before.

But things are never as simple as they seem, as the once-brilliant part is changed to fit the new section or tweaked to better serve the song. A quick pass turns into hours, and before you know it you've spent the entire day working up this single part.

That's usually the way these things go during overdubs. By the time everyone has worked out the perfect part, the player is too tired to perform it in a convincing manner.

During these times when an entirely new part is being worked out, I've found that it sometimes takes two sessions to really make things happen. The first day you take that brilliant seed of an idea and work it out so it works perfectly in the song, and the second day is when the idea flowers and you can properly execute it.

Keeping this fact in mind can save you countless extra hours at the end of a long day. Leave the idea alone and come back the next day when everyone is fresh. It'll probably be performed perfectly on the first take.

WHEN ARTISTIC BLOCK HITS

Sometimes you know the song or the part needs something, but no one can come up with a suitable idea. It's easy enough to leave it for the next day when everyone is fresh, and chances are that a new idea will indeed spring forth.

There are those few times, though, when everyone runs up against a total creative block, and that's when to call upon *Oblique Strategies* (see Figure 11-1).

First published in 1975 and now in its fifth edition, *Oblique Strategies* is a set of cards created by U2 producer Brian Eno and artist Peter Schmidt that are used by artists of all types to get beyond artistic block or to find a new direction. Each card contains a phrase or cryptic remark that can be used to break a deadlock or help resolve a dilemmatic situation.

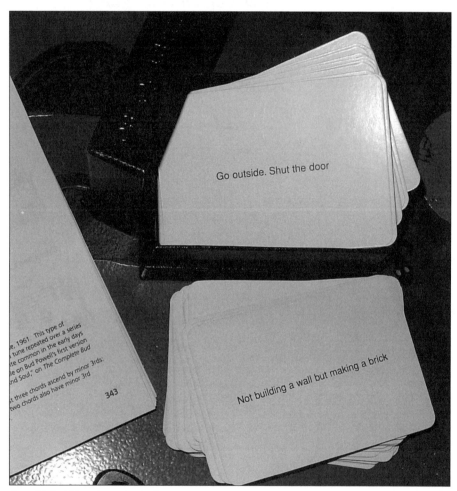

Figure 11-1: *Oblique Strategies* Cards

Here are a few examples of what a card might say:
- "State the problem in words as clearly as possible."
- "Only one element of each kind."
- "What would your closest friend do?"
- "What to increase? What to reduce?"

- "Are there sections? Consider transitions."
- "Try faking it!"
- "Honour the error as a hidden intention."

You can find out more about *Oblique Strategies* at www.rtqe.net/ObliqueStrategies. To use the strategy cards online, go to http://music.hyperreal.org/artists/brian_eno/oblique/oblique.html. There is also an *Oblique Strategies* iPhone app available.

LIMIT THE ATTENDEES

Sometimes overdubs go faster and smoother if friends of the artist or band, and their entourage are not allowed in the control room. Too many people can spook a timid performer or, worse yet, sway her into performing for the crowd instead of focusing on the job at hand. If visitors or band members must come to the studio, keep them out of the control room and have them stay in the lounge until the part is complete.

In general, it's best that any wives and husbands, girlfriends and boyfriends, friends and associates, and hangers-on and nonessential people not be allowed to come to the sessions except in extraordinary circumstances (like a playback party or delivering a forgotten instrument).

The more people directly observing the session, the more likely the gathering will become a party, and a party is not conducive to recording. There's a time and place for a group to gather, but it's not here. Unless certain people are essential to the task at hand, have them stay at home.

RECORDING IN THE CONTROL ROOM

Regardless of who's playing and what kind of instrument they're using, it's always best if you can get them to record in the control room with you. This is easy with guitar, bass, electronic keys, and even vocals, but tougher with everything else. Having the immediacy of communication, not to mention the absence of headphones, will usually get a much better performance out of the player.

Most studios are now equipped with the cables and hardware to keep an amp in another room while the musician plays in the control room. Playing in the control room is usually not an option for more than one player at a time (which probably won't happen during overdubs anyway, unless it's a horn, string, or vocal section) or with instruments that are quiet, like some percussion instruments, acoustic guitars, and strings.

Vocals in the Control Room

While it seems like recording blasphemy, many vocalists hate headphones and would much rather sing in the control room with a hand-held stage mic like a Shure SM58 (see Figure 11-2). This might not win you any high-fidelity awards for vocal sounds, but a great performance will trump audio quality any day.

Actually the sound of most stage mics, while certainly not as high-fidelity as a multi-thousand-dollar vintage Neumann, is better than you might think (as long as they're in good condition) and good enough for just about any recording purpose when routed through a high-quality microphone preamp. After all, Bono does his vocals with a 58 in the control room, and he's made plenty of hit records that way.

Figure 11-2: Shure SM58 Microphone: Popular for Live Use

OVERDUBBING TECHNIQUES

There are several commonly used overdubbing techniques that every producer should be aware of. Although the following techniques refer to vocals, they can be used for just about any instrument.

Use the Big Part of the Studio

If you're in the same studio where you tracked your basics, don't fall into the trap of keeping the exact same instrument setup in the same place in the studio as your basics (unless you're doing fixes to the basic tracks). Move the singer or instrument into the big part of the studio.

All instruments sound best when there's some space for the sound to develop. You can cut down on any unwanted reflections in the room by placing baffles around the mic, the player, or the singer.

Figure 11-3: Move to the Big Part of the Studio for Overdubs

Vocal Doubling

The technique of doubling a lead vocal has been used for as long as multitrack recorders have been around. The Beatles did it way back when they were using only 4-track magnetic tape and really didn't have a track to spare, which tells you how powerful a tool doubling can be.

Doubling a vocal (having the singer sing the exact same line or phrase twice and using both tracks in the mix) works for two reasons: it makes a vocal sound stronger, and it masks any tuning inconsistencies in the part. While the doubling technique can work for a great number of vocalists, sometimes it just doesn't sound good if both vocal tracks are replayed at the same level.

TIP: Try adding the second vocal at 6 to 10dB less than the track you deem the strongest. This will add a bit of support to an otherwise weak vocal without sounding doubled.

Vocal Stacking

An offshoot of doubling is called vocal stacking, a technique normally used on harmony background vocals. Like doubling, stacking can make a harmony vocal part sound stronger while smoothing out any tuning inconsistencies.

An example of vocal stacking would be a three-piece vocal group singing a three-part harmony section. After their first pass is complete, they double their parts, singing them exactly the same way, and then triple-track it or more, all in an effort to get a bigger, fuller sound.

One little trick that makes a stack sound bigger is to have the vocalists take a step back from the mic with every vocal pass while the engineer increases the mic gain to compensate for the drop in level that comes with the distance. The increased ambience of the room will naturally enhance the sound without artificial means.

Another trick is to have the vocalists change parts with every pass. In other words, the vocalist singing the highest part of the three-part harmony would move to the lowest, the one singing the middle part would move to the highest, and one singing the lowest part would move to the middle part.

Of course, this assumes that the vocalists are pros and capable of changing vocal parts without too much of a problem, and that their voices are capable of performing the new parts.

Instrument Doubling or Stacking

Instruments can be doubled or stacked the same way that vocals can, and while recording the exact same performance twice (doubling) can sound pretty good, you soon reach the point of diminishing returns unless you change up something to make it sound different. A different mic, mic preamp, room to record in, or distance from the mic will all help to make the sound bigger on subsequent overdubs.

For guitar, using two different guitars (a Les Paul and a Strat, for instance) and two different amplifiers (a Fender and a Marshall is the classic combination), combined with different pickup settings, will allow a multitude of guitar tracks to live together more effectively in the mix. Many times you'll find that fewer overdubs are needed if each guitar overdub has a distinctly different sound.

Vocal Comping

One of the best techniques for obtaining a great vocal is to compile a master vocal track by using bits and pieces from a number of previous passes. This is known as "comping" and has become a standard method of obtaining a great take of just about any part.

Comping is also a method preferred by a great number of vocalists, since it makes their job fairly easy. After the vocalist warms up, have her sing her part at least three times (the more the better, since you'll have more choices later), and then send her home. It's now up to you and your engineer to comp together a master track.

When we do vocal day, we're talking about upwards of 20 to 23 passes per song so it takes a long time to put a song like that together. What you get with that many passes is the perfect pass.
—Mark Bright

Tips for Comping

While you can comp a track from only two passes, the more passes the better (up to a point, that is). Using too many passes can get confusing and take too much time to sort through.

The ideal number of passes is four or five, although many producers will have the vocalist sing the song until he or she gets it almost perfect before they move on to additional passes for comping. Regardless of how many passes are made and what the quality of the performances are, if you take good notes during each pass, you'll find that your comp can be finished in no time.

Make no mistake about it, note-taking is the key to this process, and it's best done while each vocal pass is being recorded rather than during playback later. While it's possible to comp individual words or even syllables, comping by phrase is the easiest. Here's how to do it.

1. Get a copy of the lyrics. Make sure that the song is divided into clear phrases.
2. As the vocalist sings, make the appropriate following marks after every phrase:

    "↑" for sharp, "↓" for flat, "G" for good, "VG" for very good, "X" for bad, "?" for "I can't decide."

3. Create a line that's numbered "1" for "first pass" and make your marks on that line. Do the same for each pass.

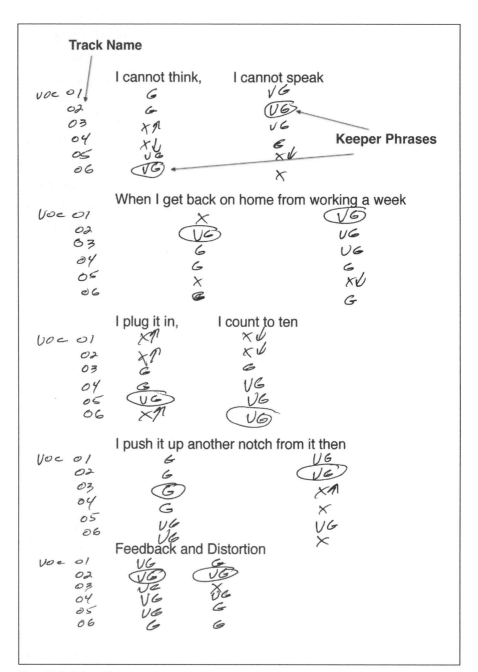

Figure 11-4: A Comp Sheet

4. After each phrase that the vocalist sings, place a mark underneath it (see Figure 11-4) to indicate your rating.

    By the end of the vocalist's last pass, you'll have a pretty good idea of which phrases are the keepers. You'll also have an idea of which phrases don't have an acceptable take, and you can ask the vocalist to just give you that line until you have what you need.

    After all the passes, see if you can piece together a vocal of all VG phrases. If a phrase with a VG mark doesn't sound as good as you originally thought, go to the G-marked vocals and see if one is acceptable. If you can't find one that works that's marked VG or G, go through the other passes to see if a ? pass works. If you still can't find an acceptable take, go through the passes again and listen to the passes that you marked with an X to see if you change your mind about one of the phrases that you considered unacceptable before.

If you still have a phrase that isn't as good as you need, either comp by word or syllable or use pitch correction to get what you need.

Comping is standard session procedure these days and is used not only on vocals but also on tracks of all sorts, so it pays to get good at it. The technique will give you great results and save you a lot of time as well.

TRACK EDITING

One of the most important parts of production in the world of DAWs is editing. Editing means creating a near-perfect track by moving the timing of a note or phrase either manually or with an app like Beat Detective, replacing a note or phrase (or even the entire track) with one from another take by using cut and paste, or using Auto-Tune, Melodyne or any of the many other pitch correction programs to correct the pitch of a note or phrase. Using these methods can make just about any track with shaky pitch almost perfect.

Timing Mistakes

That said, is perfection what you really want? It's easy to get carried away and start to edit with your eyes instead of your ears, meaning that everything gets lined up to a grid or quantized, making the track lifeless and sterile-sounding. Sometimes the unevenness of a performance is what makes it exciting, not its timing perfection. The real test of a producer is knowing when a part needs to be fixed and when to let it be, and that only comes with experience.

One method I like to use that's the best of both worlds is to only fix parts that jump out as bad timing when played in context with the other tracks. For instance, if the entrance to the song has the bass hitting before anything else, that would get fixed. Or if a guitar loses its feel for a couple bars in a verse so it becomes an obvious timing mistake, that would get fixed. Only the timing mistakes that are completely obvious get fixed.

Another method is to make sure that all of the major hits of the song (any entrances, accents, downbeats or last notes of a section) have all the instruments lined up and in time, while the other parts of the song are left as they were played. This keeps a loose feel yet still sounds tight and professional because all the major points of the song are tightened up. Of course, if anything during the song should feel out of time, that would get fixed as well as the above.

If you want everything as tight as possible, do the following:

1. Tighten up the timing of the drums either manually or, if you're using Pro Tools, with Beat Detective. This doesn't mean that the drums need to be perfectly quantized, only that they be moved enough to feel great.
2. Move the kick, snare, and bass tracks so they're beside one another on the timeline, and then solo just these tracks.
3. Listen to the entire song and move the notes or phrases of the bass as needed so it's tight with the drums.
4. Unmute the kick, snare, and bass and listen to the song with the rest of the tracks. Make sure that the timing adjustments that you just made work. If not, repeat steps 2 and 3.
5. Mute the bass and move on to another instrument that you feel has shaky timing. Solo the kick, snare, and instrument and repeat steps 3 and 4.
6. Repeat with other instruments and vocals as needed.

Vocals are frequently overlooked during editing, but they play a big part in how tight a song feels. A bad entrance (too early or too late) by a vocal can sometimes fool you into thinking that it's one of the other instruments, but by moving the vocal phrase just a little the whole passage will tighten up. Be sure to treat the vocal just like the other instruments when editing, because it's more important to the feel and timing of the song than you think.

Editing Time

The time it takes to edit a project can easily get out of hand if you're not careful. If a song is executed badly, it's possible to still make it sound great with editing, but it will ultimately take more time than it would've to just get the performance right in the first place.

That being said, it's not uncommon to spend as much time editing a project as it did both to track it and do all the overdubs! And editing doesn't come for free unless you're doing it yourself (in which case you're paying for it with your time).

DAW engineers will charge from $25 to $50 to even more, which can mount up to some significant money, even with someone who's fast. Still, editing is a necessary evil and should be budgeted for both in terms of time and money. When that shaky song comes to life with a tight groove, you'll be glad you did.

CHAPTER 12
WORKING WITH YOUR TEAM

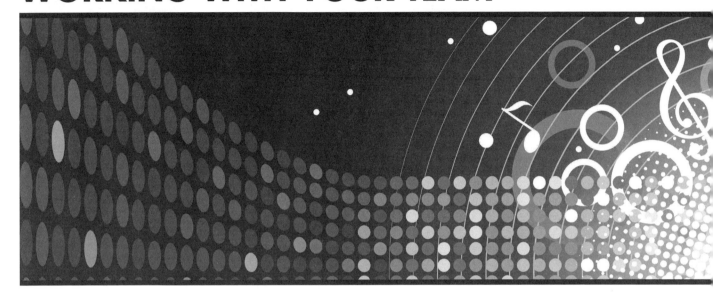

You've been hired as a producer to be the leader of the project. To do that, you've got to get the best out of your team, which includes the artist or band, any additional musicians, and your engineer. Knowing how to get them to give you their best effort in a comfortable, non-offensive way will contribute hugely toward the project becoming a success.

Making great music recordings is the result of many ingredients, but it's made up chiefly of inspiration, musicality, technology, personal interaction, and most importantly, "vibe."

The feeling that you create in the room at a session is your vibe. The more comfortable everyone is with your vibe, the better they will perform. Here's a list of things to remember that will greatly contribute to your vibe and the vibe of the session, and will show that you have a professional attitude. If you walk the walk yourself, it's easier to instill these traits on your team if they don't have them already.

BE A PROFESSIONAL

This section could just as easily be called "Be a Diplomat," "Be a Compromiser," or even "Be a Nice Guy." What it's really all about is how to interact with other people who may, or may not, want to do and play things the way you envision them.

Before we get into the issue of diplomacy, it's important that you act as professionally as possible since you're the leader and everyone takes his or her cues from you. Let's take a look at the qualities of a professional attitude.

A professional:

- **Is always on time.** Time is money, and a pro is not only on time but also usually early. If he's delayed and won't arrive at the agreed time, he calls ahead to make sure that everyone is aware of his situation, and then gives his best estimate about when he'll arrive.
- **Is always open to ideas.** Instead of arguing about the value of an idea, a pro simply says, "I haven't tried that before, but I'm really interested to hear what it sounds like!" No idea is too crazy to at least consider, because you never know when something that you initially thought was too far out will be the perfect solution to a problem or a perfect addition to a song.

I always assume that they may be going for something that maybe I'm not aware of. It's like if they'd wanted to use a Radio Shack reverb on my bass: I'd probably say, "Great, I never tried that before. Let's do it."

—Session bass player Paul Ill
(Christina Aguilera, Pink, Alicia Keys, and James Blunt)

- **Is focused only on the music.** When a pro is at a rehearsal, gig, or recording session, he's *100 percent* there in the moment and focused on getting the best results he can. He's not thinking about fighting with his girlfriend, paying the bills, or going to the party later that night. All his concentration is on the music.
- **Presents his ideas in a respectful manner.** He doesn't say, "You have to play it this way." He says, "Can you try this to see how it works?"
- **Takes responsibility for his mistakes.** A pro immediately owns up to any mistake, oversight, error, or blunder and says, "Sorry, it was my fault," and accepts the consequences.
- **Never parties on the job.** As stated previously, a pro is 100 per-

cent focused on the music at hand. While a few beers might not constitute a party, it certainly doesn't help you maintain your focus on the music if your mind isn't all there. There's plenty of time to party later, so save it until then.

- **Treats everyone with respect.** A pro treats musicians, engineers, and staff as equals and peers and would never intentionally do or say anything to disrespect any of them.

If you assume a professional attitude by following the above points, you'll find that the respect for you will grow, any interpersonal tensions will ease, and your session life will suddenly go a lot more smoothly.

THE IMPORTANCE OF DIPLOMACY

One of the greatest talents a producer needs in a team situation like a recording session is knowing how to suggest things without offending others. Artists are usually sensitive people and have "thin skins" by nature. You can be perfectly correct regarding a particular issue, yet still be completely wrong in how you present it. The object is to help get the best out of everyone, not to hurt them.

People who have a talent for choosing their words carefully can use it in a constructive manner, instead of using it to make cutting remarks that can be disrespectful and hurtful. If a player can't handle feedback and constructive criticism, the problem may well be with the one who's delivering it, not the one receiving it.

Set an example with how well you can accept the ideas from others without taking any offense, and you will likely find them accepting your ideas much more easily. Diplomacy is a discipline, and one well worth practicing.

Steps in Resolving a Conflict

Being in any relationship requires at least some compromise, and working with a group of musicians is no different from what you'd expect between family members, friends, bosses, or coworkers. There are times when you just have to bend in order to keep the peace.

While compromise is easy for some people to do, others have a personality that seldom allows it and a conflict occurs. Here are some effective steps that you can take to state your case in a way that should resolve or mediate the conflict.

1. **Cool off first.** Conflicts can't be solved when emotions are running hot. Take some time to get away from the problem for a bit and brainstorm on exactly what the conflict is, how it was caused, and most importantly, what a possible solution would be.

2. **Present accolades, support, and respect.** The first thing to do is acknowledge the person's accomplishments and talent. Something like "I want to start by saying that I think the tracks we've captured are really great, and you're playing your parts way better than I ever thought possible."

3. **Analyze why the problem occurred.** If you give a clear explanation of why you think there's a problem or why the problem or conflict has occurred, you set the initial groundwork for solving the conflict. If the other person knows exactly what your side of the story is, you might find more often than not that you're both on the same page, but on different sides of it.

4. **Take responsibility and use "I" messages.** If you are involved in a conflict that you're aware of, take responsibility and own up to it, but make sure that everything is from your point of view. For instance, it's best to say, "I think you were flat on that part," rather than "Everybody knows that you always sing that part flat," or worse, "Your singing sucks, man."

5. **Describe what "I" or "we" need so that the problem doesn't happen again.** This is the solution from your point of view. "We really need you to be here a half hour before the session so that you have time to warm up. That way we won't waste any studio time, which is costing us money."

6. **Support their success.** Tell him that you want him to win, because if he wins, so do you. "The better you sound, the better we all sound" or "Do you know how great this is going to sound once you get that part down? It's going to kill!"

GETTING THE BEST OUT OF MUSICIANS

Even if a musician is completely comfortable with his environment and headphone mix, there are additional things you can do to help him take his performance to another level. Unless they're studio pros, most musicians can be very self-conscious about what they're playing, especially after hearing a playback that uncovers some flaws they were unaware of until that moment. It's important that their confidence doesn't flag, and it's directly up to you to keep that from happening. Here are a few tricks that can help.

- **Stay positive**. Regardless of how badly things might be going, how off-key someone is singing, or how out-of-the-pocket someone is playing, never be negative in your body language or your comments. Remarks like "You suck" or "That really sounds bad" never help the situation (unless you manage to inject some humor somehow), and can even completely undermine a performance. If something isn't going as well as you think it should, give the player a reasonable chance, sit him down for a listen in the control room, and then firmly but respectfully describe why the part isn't working.

- **Explain what's wrong**. Players hate it when they're told, "Do it again" without being given any explanation as to why you think what they just played wasn't good enough. If the take wasn't a keeper for some reason, explain what was wrong in a kind and gentle way. Statements like "I think you have a better one in you," or "I've heard you play it with more excitement before" might work if you can't put your finger on the problem. Players appreciate it if you can be specific when critiquing their performance so they can concentrate on that part the next time they play it through. "You're falling behind the beat every time we come out of the chorus," is an example of a specific statement. If the player continues to get it wrong, make sure you play back the part for him so he can hear it clearly and understand what you're going for.

- **Keep the studio talkback mic on**. Communication is one of the most important yet often overlooked parts of a successful session. Players hate it when they're speaking to you from the studio and either you're unaware that they're trying to get your attention, or you simply can't hear them. Make sure that the engineer puts up a dedicated talkback mic in the studio and that it's turned on immediately after every take. It's important that you don't miss a single word.

- **Keep the control room talkback mic on**. Players also hate it when there are long periods of silence from the control room after a take. They might see a conversation going on, but if they can't hear it, they can get insecure and feel isolated. You may be having a conversation about what kind of take-out food to order, but as far as the player can tell, you're talking about how bad his performance was and how you'd like to replace him. Get rid of the insecurity by latching the control room talkback so he can hear you all the time between takes. Once again, communication is the key to a successful session.

- **If a player asks to play a part again, let him.** You may think that the player just nailed the ultimate take, but if he feels he can play it better, he usually can. Players inherently know when they've messed something up, were late on a chord, misfingered or ghosted a note, or slowed down during a roll. Maybe you didn't hear it, but the player knew it. Let him go again. Thanks to digital recording, this is a much easier decision to make nowadays than it was back in the analog tape days. Back then, you might only have space on tape for a single take, and you could lose a take that was great if the next take didn't work. That kind of pressure on the producer has now been lifted, thanks to your favorite DAW.

GETTING THE BEST OUT OF SINGERS

One of the hardest things about making a record is trying to record a vocalist who is uncomfortable. Even a seasoned pro sometimes can't do her best unless the conditions are just right. Consider some of these suggestions before and during a vocal session.

- Make sure the lighting is correct. Most vocalists prefer the lights lower in the studio and the control room when they are singing.
- A touch of reverb or delay in the headphones can help the singer's comfort level with the headphone mix, since it makes the vocal sound more like the finished product.
- If you need to have the vocalist sing harder, louder, or more aggressively, turn down the vocal track in the phones or turn the backing tracks up slightly.
- If you need to have the vocalist sing softer or more intimately, turn his or her track up in the phones or turn down the backing tracks.
- Keep talking with the artist between takes. Leave the talkback on if possible. Long periods of silence from the control room can be a mood killer.
- Try lowering the lights in the control room so the vocalist can't see you. Some people think that you're in there judging them, when you might be talking about something completely different.

- If the take wasn't good for whatever reason, explain what was wrong in a kind and gentle way. Something like "That was really good, but I think you can do it even better. The pitch was a little sharp." This advice goes for just about any overdub, since players generally like to know what was wrong with a take rather than receiving a "Do it again" blanket statement.
- Keep smiling.

The Three Ps: Pitch, Pocket, and Passion

When it comes to vocals in the studio, engineer/producer Ed Seay's "Three Ps" are what a producer lives by. You've got to have all three to have a dynamite vocal. And while pitch and pocket problems can be fixed by studio trickery, if you don't have passion, you don't have a vocal. Let's take a look inside the three Ps.

Pitch

Staying on pitch means singing in tune, and not just with some of the notes—with every single note! They're all equally important. Singing in tune requires real concentration and awareness. If you know your singer has a constant pitch problem and tends to sing either sharp or flat, there are some really simple things to try that might help.

Singing sharp is usually caused by the power of your voice blanking out any background pitch reference. You're singing too hard to hear yourself! The fix is easy. Just turn up the lead vocal in the headphones a little.

Singing a touch flat is easily fixed by asking the singer either to lift his eyebrows or to smile. Smiling is not only recommended, it's required—and that's because it provides proper relaxation of the facial, cranial, and neck muscles (this is where it helps to have a good sense of humor).

Correct head position and correct position of the abdomen are needed to have enough air to stay on pitch. Learning correct positioning is the best reason for any singer to consult a vocal coach for at least a few lessons.

The more relaxed a singer is, the easier it is to hit the higher notes in her range. Yawning is a recommended warm-up exercise because it promotes relaxation.

Pitch also means following the melody reliably. There's a trend these days to scat-sing around a melody, and while that might be desirable in some genres, it doesn't work in any genre if it's done all the time. Scatting might show off a singer's technique and ability, but a song has a melody for a reason. That's what draws the listener in, that's what they can sing to themselves, and that's usually what they want to hear.

THE SINGER MUST HEAR HERSELF

In order to stay in tune, a singer must hear herself. How much she can hear herself will determine if she can stay on pitch.

As I stated previously, some vocalists sing sharp when they sing too hard. They push themselves over the top of the correct pitch when they can't hear themselves in the headphones. The solution is to have either more vocal or less of everything else in the phones, but be aware that pitch and timing problems can also occur if you hear too much of yourself in the mix.

If your vocalist is singing flat, give him a little less of himself or more of everyone else in the mix, since it's not unusual for pitch to change with intensity. Less vocal in the headphones makes you want to sing harder (and possibly raise your pitch slightly) and vice versa.

Sometimes the mix can be too dense with instruments, and thinning it out a little can help correct pitch problems. First, add more bass (the root of all chords) and kick (the root of all rhythm) to help with pitch and pocket. Next, turn down anything that is heavily chorused and turn up anything that has a more "centered" tonal frequency (like a piano).

Sometimes listening to only the rhythm guitar instead of multiple guitar parts (if there is more than one guitar part) can be helpful, since some vocalists can hear their own pitch better when singing with a simple tonally centered instrument than when singing with screaming guitars or airy synth patches.

Pocket

Being "in the pocket" means singing in time and in the groove, or rhythm, of the song. You can be on pitch, but if you're wavering ahead or behind the beat, it won't *feel* right.

All of the things advocated throughout this book that help instrumentalists apply to vocalists as well. Concentrate on the downbeat (beat 1) to get your entrances. Concentrate on the snare drum (beats 2 and 4) to stay in the pocket.

Quincy [producer Quincy Jones] *used to say that some singers have a pocket in their voice. Supposedly Michael Jackson had such an amazing pocket that he could sing a line and you could build a groove around it.*

—Producer Frank Fitzpatrick
(Jill Scott, Dave Hollister, *High School Musical*)

Passion

Passion is not necessarily something that can be taught. To some degree, you either have it or you don't. What is passion? It's the ability to sell the lyrical content of the song through performance. It's the ability to make the listener believe in what you're singing and feel that you're talking directly to them and not anyone else.

Passion can sometimes trump pitch and pocket. A mediocre singer who can convey his emotion through his voice is way more interesting to listen to than a polished singer who hits every note perfectly but with little emotion. In fact, just about any vocalist you'd consider a star has passion, and that's why he or she is a star.

On stage, passion can sometimes take a backseat to stamina, since you have to save yourself for a whole show and you can't blow it all out in one song. That's why many singers have only one or two big "production numbers," when they totally whip it out. In the studio, however, there's never any cruising. You've got to give all the passion you can give to every song.

A few paragraphs ago I said that you either have passion or you don't, but sometimes a singer has it but doesn't know it, and it's the job of the producer to pull passion out of her.

That could mean getting the singer angry to stir some emotion, building her up by telling her how good she is, or making her laugh to loosen her up. Anything to sell the song! Once she knows how to summon it up from inside herself, she can do it again and again.

BACKGROUND VOCALS NEED ATTENTION TOO

It's too easy to take background vocals lightly and say "Just throw a background part on this" or "Hey, can you sing a little background here?" That can be a trap though, as background vocal parts are so important that they can make the difference between a record sounding polished or sounding as though it just came out of the garage.

Background vocals are integral parts of the song that require the same amount of attention as the drum, bass, guitar, keys, and lead vocals get. In fact, a bad background vocal part can easily sink a recording that otherwise sounds great.

You can't have someone sing background just because they're used to doing it live. If it's a part worth doing, then it's a part that must stand on its own. It either sounds great or you can't let it get by.

Harmony Vocals Take More Time

Unless you're hiring in a vocal group whose members sing with each other all the time, or the lead singer is doing them all herself, it usually takes more time to get a blend on harmony vocals than you might think, especially if the group is composed of singers who haven't sung together before. Regardless of the amount of time they've spent together, here are some tricks to make those harmony vocals sound as tight as possible.

Phrasing Is Everything

Singing together means that you really have to sing together—exactly. Each vocalist has to sing exactly the same way as the other singers, complete with the same inflections, slurs, attacks (starts), and releases (stops). Usually this means that one vocal part will be the reference part, and all others will follow.

The way that I've seen great background singers work is for one to say, "Sing it to me. Show me what you're doing," and then the others would try to match that exactly. It works for them and it will work for you, too.

Attacks and, Especially, Releases

Whether you're playing it or singing it, attacks and releases are the secret to tight music. While it's usually easy to get the attack part (where everyone starts at exactly the same time), the release part (everyone ending at the same time) is often overlooked.

The releases are just as important as the attacks, and polishing up this one area will make a vocal group sound so tight you won't believe it. So remember, everyone starts and stops at the same time.

A great example of background vocal with a tight release is the end of the theme song for the television show *American Dad*. Listen to how tight "Good Morning USA" is, especially the end of the phrase. That's what you're going for.

Gang Vocals

Gang vocals are background vocals in which the vocalists sing the same thing that the lead singer sings, and in unison. This usually happens in the chorus.

An example can be heard in Kiss' classic hit "Rock and Roll All Night," or a number of hip-hop songs like Jay-Z's "99 Problems." It's not uncommon for a band to get some of its members who don't usually sing to sing for a gang vocal.

You might think that singing a gang vocal would be easy because you don't have to worry about a harmony, but that can be a big mistake, because you still have to be concerned about pitch and phrasing, just like with harmony vocals. Don't make this mistake.

When working on vocals, place the same importance on all parts. Every single part needs the same attention as the lead vocal. Remember, if it doesn't sound great, work on it until it does, try something else, or eliminate it!

WORKING WITH THE ENGINEER

Most often, engineers are congenial professionals who manage to combine artistry and technicality at the same time. It's important to have a meeting with the engineer prior to the first session to discuss the parameters of the project so you each know what to expect from one another.

It's best to let the engineer do the job he's hired to do, but don't be afraid to tell him what you need. Don't be afraid to ask any technical questions, or even to ask for production opinions. You hired him for his expertise, so take advantage of it.

Remember to be specific about what you need, and you and your engineer should easily make a great team. You're both aiming for the same outcome, and rarely should there be any dissonance between the both of you if you've hired an experienced pro.

These are the things to look for in an engineer:

* **Credits and experience.** Credits don't always tell you what you want to know, but it's a start. An engineer can have a major credit on his resume even though he assisted on an editing session when the artist wasn't there, so take those credits with a grain of salt unless you see the CD cover yourself. That said, experience in terms of time on the job is a pretty good indicator about the competence

and attitude of an engineer. Most engineers don't stay around too long if they're difficult to get along with or are short on talent.

- **Experience in the type of music you're about to produce.** Sometimes this matters a lot and sometimes it doesn't. If you're able to hire an engineer who has a lot of experience with the music you're working on, then that's the guy to get, all things being equal. If you're not able to hire an expert in your genre, an engineer with a lot of experience and credits who doesn't do much of the type of music you're doing is usually a better choice than a newbie who has a little experience with your music style.

- **Technical expertise.** Most engineers have a fair amount of technical expertise; it comes with the job. Where an engineer's level of technical knowledge would be especially pivotal in your hiring decision might be if you were planning on recording at 192 kHz or using magnetic tape or anything else that was out of the norm. Someone with that kind of specific experience will save you both time and money.

There are some major engineers I know who have big-time hits under their belts that frequently work with a client only once. Their personalities are abrasive enough that they get passed over for the "next record," since their clients are generally unhappy with the experience. Save yourself that kind of grief. Talk to other engineers and artists prior to hiring anyone.

WORKING WITH THE ARTIST

It's best to show a quiet, friendly respect to the artist at all times. While recording, you're a valued asset to their creative and business process, and are usually considered at least a peer and at most a parental figure or teacher. During the time you're involved in the sphere of activity with the project, you inhabit the artist's musical, professional, and social universe as a cross between an honored guest and a partner in their musical enterprise.

Once an artist begins to trust you on a musical level, that trust may carry over to a personal level, as well. It's easy to become a confidant as the intimate bond between you and the artist grows, but there may be danger in getting too close. It's easy for personal issues to get in the way of the music, and while the producer has to deal with them, it's easy for the focus to drift away from the music if the producer becomes too personally involved. Many producers are careful to set boundaries that allow them to stay focused on the job at hand, and become engaged in the artist's private matters only if those things are having a negative impact on the music.

With respect to all the tangential interactions that may occur on a session, consider anyone associated with the artist (like a spouse, family member, boyfriend or girlfriend, guest, driver, personal assistant, or staffer) an "artist," too. Treating them improperly can bring the scorn of the artist upon you!

There are many other music-production gigs where the person who is considered the "artist" is a slightly different entity. If it's a jingle date, for instance, view the client or anyone from the ad agency in the same light as you view an artist-musician. If it's a film or a TV date, the director, producer(s), music supervisor(s), studio execs, and any of their representatives can be considered akin to an artist.

CHAPTER 13
SELF-PRODUCTION

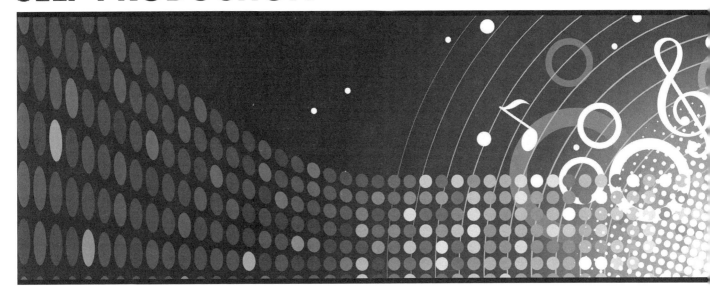

Self-production is simultaneously one of the most difficult things to do in music and at the same time perhaps one of the easiest. Every artist hears what their music should sound like in their head (that's the easy part), but it's sometimes difficult to get it to actually sound that way when it comes to real-life recording.

For many singer-songwriters, that can lead the artist to overwork a song until it's limp like a dishrag, or overproduce it until it has so many layers that it sounds like there's a 30-piece band backing them up. Indeed, it's difficult to get it to sound somewhere in between, where a project is both exciting and vital, and still meets the artist's vision.

Working in a vacuum can sometimes lead to new discoveries, since you're not beholden to any previously learned "rules," or it can lead to frustration from not being able to get the sound that you want and not having anyone to turn to for help. Let's look at some ways to stay out of the self-production rut.

OVERCOMING THE SELF-PRODUCTION BLUES

One of the biggest problems for an artist is creating in circles. This means that the artist has so many good ideas that the production is never finished. As soon as a version is complete, the artist thinks, "Maybe the middle eight should have a ska feel." Then after that's recorded, he thinks, "Maybe the entire song should have a ska feel." Before you know it there are versions in 6/8, speed metal, and reggae (and maybe more), with each one sounding different, but not necessarily better. If this is what's happening to you, there are two words to keep in mind to help you out of your rut.

Instinct. Usually, the very first inspiration is the right one, especially if you've gone through more than a couple of different versions. You've got to repress the urge to keep changing things and learn to follow your initial instinct. That doesn't mean you shouldn't tweak or perfect what you're doing; it means that you shouldn't make a completely opposite turn in a direction that goes against your initial inspiration.

The exception to this is if you think it might be cool to have multiple different versions of the song available so you can give the alternate versions to your core fans as an exclusive gift, use them as a promotional vehicle, or because it's been specifically requested by a music supervisor for a television show or movie. In any of those cases, a wholesale change in direction can actually be particularly useful and even profitable.

Deadline. One of the biggest problems with producing yourself is the fact that your project is usually open-ended, time-wise. As a result, you end up with the "project that wouldn't end" that keeps going for years (no exaggeration here).

The surest way to keep that from happening and to actually accomplish something is to set a deadline for the project's completion. Many people do their best work on deadlines because they don't have a chance to second guess themselves.

The final product may not be 100 percent of what you want, but remember that it seldom ever is, even with all the time in the world available to finish the project. Save yourself some heartache and impose a deadline on yourself so you can finish that project and get it out the door where it can do you some good.

Two Key Production Concepts

There are many great artists, bands, musicians, engineers, and producers, and much written about how they work that's pretty accessible to anyone who wants to find it. The problem is that after reading some of these articles, it's easy to get the impression that recording great music is an easy process, and that can make producing yourself much more difficult than it already is.

There are certainly times when the planets align and you can catch lightning in a bottle, but just like anything else done well, producing a project usually takes a lot of work. Whether you're recording yourself or your band with your own gear or using a commercial studio, the goal is the same—to make the songs and the recordings sound as big, as polished, and as accessible to your audience (however large or small) as you can. With that being said, here are some things to be aware of that can help the self-production process go a little faster:

1. **You Hardly Ever Sound Great the First Time**

    Contrary to what you might have heard about hit records done on the first take, most recordings of any type require more work than that to be any good. It takes time to get both the right sounds and performances, and unfortunately, these things usually can't be rushed.

    Perhaps the most difficult thing to learn when recording is not to expect gold-record-quality playing right off the bat. One of the worst ideas that you can get is that you have to be perfect every time you play. It just doesn't happen that way, so don't let imperfection discourage you.

    Even the best studio players make some flubs or have slightly erratic time when they're playing. They just go back and fix the problems afterwards, and you can too. Yes, it does happen occasionally that someone gets extremely lucky and plays something terrific on the first take, but it's a rare exception even for studio-savvy and expert musicians.

    Recording is hard work. It's not uncommon for people to slave over a part for days or even weeks until it feels right in the track. If pros won't settle for something that's not the best it can be, why should you?

The Hits of the Past

I know you're probably thinking about all those hit records in the '50s that were done in just a few takes, how the first Beatles album was done in one twelve-hour session, and how in the glory days of Motown in Detroit they used to crank out three #1 hits in three hours. All true, but don't forget that all those famous '50s artists honed their act by playing months and years on the road. The Beatles played six sets a night for a year in Hamburg before they hit the studio, and the Motown studio musicians were the best of the best jazz musicians in Detroit with some hall-of-fame song-writers and arrangers.

That being said, the bar is set much higher for recording these days. Sad but true: many of those incredible tracks just wouldn't make it through the recording process if they were done today because of defects in the playing and recording.

The fact of the matter is that recording today on any level is a demanding process, so don't fool yourself into expecting great results too soon. Just like a band learning a new song together, everything takes some time before it actually gels, so be prepared to work until you get it.

As stated previously in the this book, I really believe that a typical overdub takes at least two days to record. The first day you work out the part until it's a perfect fit for the song. The second day you actually perform it well, since now you know how to play it and can just concentrate on performance. The whole trick is to follow your gut. If you think deep down inside that you can do it better, then you probably can.

2. It's a Lot of Work

In the majority of cases, making a record is hard work. It takes more time than most people think to work out parts, make them sound great, and play and/or sing them well. Sure there's been a handful of records that have been done on the first take or in a couple of hours (mostly in the 50's and early 60's), but that's a rare occurrence that involves as much luck as winning the lottery.

During the recording of one of my early bands' demo tapes, we became increasingly frustrated because it seemed to take forever (a whole four hours!) to record six songs from our set. Now these were songs that we'd been playing at gigs every weekend for about a year so we knew them backwards and forwards. Or so we thought!

"We must really suck," is what we told ourselves from that point until the band broke up. Only later, when I began to regularly work in studios, did I learn the real truth. Recording is hard work and takes a lot of time to make something that will sound good.

First of all, you never really know exactly what you're playing and exactly what you sound like until you record yourself. Almost always you'll find that something that you thought was gangbusters live is in fact just a buster. You might be playing a line differently from the other guitar player, or maybe your rhythm pattern is different from what the drummer is playing. Maybe you just can't hit that high note in the chorus like you thought you could.

The secret here is to be brutally honest with yourself about your playing and singing, just like in the previous chapters. If it doesn't sound great, either rehearse it until it does or don't play it at all!

SMALL STUDIO PRODUCTION

If you're producing yourself, chances are that you're doing it in either your own studio or a friend's. The chances are also good that the studio is small and not the equal of a commercial studio of any size.

If that's the case, there are probably a number of problems that you'll be facing (some without you even being aware of) that could potentially hinder the quality of your production. Not to worry, this section will take a look at some of those problems and provide some possible solutions, so your production can end up sounding as close to the commercial studio sound as possible.

> **PROBLEM**: Poor acoustics or none at all.
> Most small- or home-studio owners usually think about gear first and give no thought to the acoustics of the recording and listening spaces.
> **SOLUTION**: Sometimes you can get lucky and come up with a great sounding space with little thought, but that's not usually the case, so here are a few quick and easy suggestions that won't cost of ton of money.

1. **For recording, stay in the middle of the room.** Stay away from the walls, where you can get unwanted reflections or low frequency build-up.
2. **Keep the monitor speakers away from the walls.** It's best to place them equidistant between side walls, with the rear of the speakers at least six inches away from the front wall for the smoothest response with least amount of unwanted reflections (see Figure 13-1).
3. **Add some acoustic treatment.** For as little as $100 or so you can make your own acoustic panels or buy them from a number of

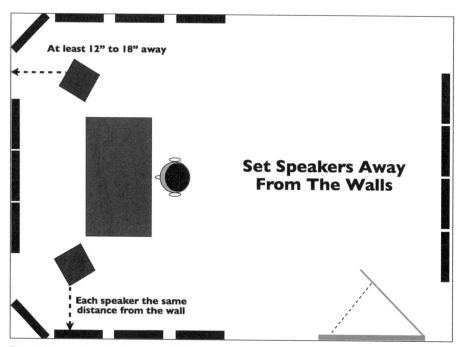

Figure 13-1: Keep Speakers Away from Walls

suppliers (see my *Studio Builder's Handbook* for more info). You'd be surprised how much better a little acoustic treatment can make almost any room sound (see Figure 13-2).

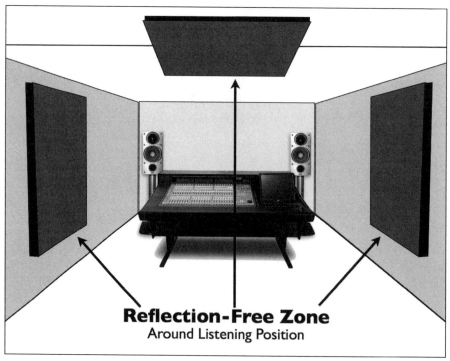

Figure 13-2: Acoustic Treatment Around the Listening Area

PROBLEM: Low ceilings (see Figure 13-3).
The majority of small and home studios have ceilings between 8 and 12 feet high. Most commercial rooms have ceilings that are far higher than that, and that's one of the reasons they sound better. The ceiling height adds volume and dimension to the room and helps to keep down the nasty reflections.
SOLUTION: You can't raise the ceiling, but you can stay away from a low ceiling's unwanted effects. This usually comes in just one situation—overhead mics on drums (although recording strings could be another). Instead of using one of the many overhead techniques that require the mics to be placed above the drummer's head, mic the cymbals fairly closely instead, just two to three feet above the bell of the cymbals. This will keep all those bad-sounding reflections off the ceiling to a minimum.

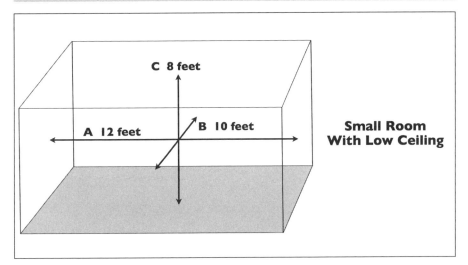

Figure 13-3: A Small Room with Low Ceilings

PROBLEM: Not enough recording space.
SOLUTION: Once again, you can't change the physical space, but you can use it to your advantage. Instead of trying to record multiple instruments at a time (like a rhythm section), just go for one. An example would be to record the drums, and use a guitar and/or bass guide track going direct through amp simulators.

Another example would be to have the rhythm section play the track live a few times, pick the best take, and have the drummer overdub to the prerecorded instruments for totally clean drum tracks.

PROBLEM: No recording space or iso room.
SOLUTION: Lots of records have been done in that type of environment. In fact, most overdubs are routinely done in the control room even in a big studio these days. A good example would be Bono, who records his vocals on most U2 records that way. Just turn the output level of the monitors down and listen on headphones along with the player, or turn the monitors to just the level where the player can hear it without causing any mic leakage. (Hint: experiment with turning the mic to find the point of most rejection.)

PROBLEM: Inexpensive gear.
SOLUTION: You'd be surprised how many great records have been recorded on less than the best gear. It's all in the technique, or to put it another way, "it's not the hammer, it's how you swing it." That said, here are a couple of tips to get the most out of inexpensive gear.

1. **Watch your levels.** A major problem with running digital gear (or analog for that matter) too hot is that you run out of headroom quickly and compromise the sound. In these days of 24-bit audio resolution, there's little advantage to recording above -10 dB.

2. **Give the mic some space.** Not everything needs to be, nor should it be, close-miked. You'd be surprised how much more natural an instrument or vocal can sound with a foot or two of space between the mic and the source.

3. **Don't use the same mic on everything.** Every microphone has peaks and valleys in its frequency response and those frequency peaks are emphasized as you use the mic on more and more tracks, regardless of how good it is. Try instead to match the mic to the instrument. For instance, an instrument with a dull sound would get a bright-sounding mic, and a bright sound would get a mic that had the opposite sound.

PROS AND CONS OF MIXING ON HEADPHONES

Many producers using home or small studios are forced to use headphones late at night so they don't disturb the family or the neighbors. Believe it or not, it's possible to get great mixes out of virtually any set of speakers in just about any room, and that includes headphones. The trick is that you have to have enough listening time using the headphones so you can get a reference point as to what sounds good or bad when you play your mix back elsewhere.

That's why mixers began to take their own speakers wherever they went (or asked for something like Yamaha NS-10s) in the first place. It was a reference point that they were familiar with, and since the speakers were nearfields, the room didn't come too much into play during the mix so they could be surer of the result.

Mixing on headphones does have four significant downsides, though:

1. You can't wear them for as long as you need to (which is somewhere between 8 and 12 hours) before your head and ears get tired from the extra weight.
2. You have a tendency to turn them up, which can lead to some quick ear fatigue, again limiting your ability to mix for long periods.
3. Although most of the more expensive professional headphones really sound great, you can get a false sense of what the mix is like (especially on the low end), and it causes you not to work as hard getting the frequency balance in that part of the mix right.
4. Much of the audience won't listen on phones after the mix is completed. Since a mixer is always aiming for a mix that sounds great on any speaker that the material is later played on, you want to stay in that realm if possible, and even listen on some crappy speakers if possible as a check. Headphones just sound too good for that.

That said, headphones do have their place. They're great for editing in that you can hear clicks, pops, and inconsistencies that you may otherwise miss while listening on speakers, and they're a great check for panning and checking reverb tails when mixing, but it's best not to use them for an entire mix of possible.

But if you're mixing in your bedroom and don't want to wake the kids, significant other, or the neighbors, then by all means, go for it. Just make sure that you listen to some other material that also sounds great on your speakers first so you have a reference point of what sounds good and what doesn't.

CHAPTER 14
MIXING: WHERE IT'S MAKE IT OR BREAK IT

An ever-important aspect of production is mixing, which can make or break a song. A brilliant mix can put an otherwise average production over the top, while a mediocre mix can bring down a brilliant production (although sometimes the song is so brilliant that nothing can detract from it).

If you're not an engineer (or don't have a lot of mixing experience), the more you know about the process of mixing and how the mixing engineer thinks will definitely help you during the process. Even if you're already an engineer and an experienced mixer, here are a few concepts that may help you visualize the final product a bit better.

THE MECHANICS OF MIXING

Although most engineers ultimately rely on their intuition when doing a mix, there are certain mixing procedures that they all consciously or unconsciously follow.

Hearing the Final Product

Most mixers and many producers can hear some version of the final product in their head before they even begin to mix. If an engineer is mixing a project that he's tracked, sometimes this is a result of countless rough mixes during the course of a project that gradually become polished. Even if an engineer is brought in specifically to mix, many won't begin until they have an idea of where they're going.

Engineers who can hear the finished product before they start normally begin a mix the same way. They become familiar with the song by either listening to a previous rough mix or putting up all the faders on the DAW or console and listening for a few passes.

Sometimes that is harder than it seems, though. In the case of a complex mix with 50 or more tracks, the mix engineer may have to spend some time muting the tracks that aren't desired in certain sections before the song begins to pare down and make sense.

For better or worse, the engineer's vision will end up changing, thanks to input from the producer and the artist. Although today it's common for a major mixer to complete a mix unattended by the producer or the artist, most mixers prefer to have the input. However, a vast majority prefer to start the mix by themselves and have the producer and the artist come by to offer suggestions five or six hours later, after the mix begins to take shape.

Tall, Deep, and Wide

Most great mixers think in three dimensions. They think "tall, deep, and wide," which means they make sure that all the frequencies from low to high are represented (tall), the mix has depth (deep), and it has stereo dimension as instruments are panned within the sound field (wide).

The tall dimension (the frequency range of the mix) is the result of knowing what sounds correct timbre-wise as a result of having a reference point. This knowledge, or reference point, can come from being an assistant engineer and listening to what other first engineers do, or it can come from comparing your mix to CDs, records, and files you're familiar with and consider to be of high fidelity.

Essentially, you're trying to make sure that all the frequencies are represented in the correct proportions. Usually that means that all of the sparkly, tinkly highs and fat, powerful lows are there. Sometimes some mids need to be cut, but whichever frequencies are adjusted, clarity is what you aim for. Again, having experience with instrumental and vocal elements that sound good really allows you to establish your own a reference point.

The deep, or effects, dimension is achieved by introducing new ambience elements into the mix. This is done with reverb and delay (and offshoots like flanging and chorusing), but room mics, overheads, and even leakage play an equally big part.

The wide, or panning, dimension is placing sound elements in the stereo sound field in such a way as to make a more interesting soundscape, and, to a lesser degree, so that each element is heard more clearly. That brings us to the nitty-gritty of mixing, which requires more detail about all the elements of a great mix.

Before we can talk about the elements that make a great mix, it's good to be aware of the signs of a mix that's not up to that standard. Does your mix have any of these characteristics?

SEVEN CHARACTERISTICS OF AN AMATEUR MIX

1. **NO CONTRAST.** This problem is a result of the same musical textures being used throughout the entire song. This is generally an arrangement issue, which the mixer can affect somewhat since mixing is so much more than balancing. It's influencing the arrangement by what you mute, emphasize, or lower in the mix.

2. **A FREQUENT LACK OF A FOCAL POINT.** Sometimes during a song, there are holes between lyrical phrases in which nothing is brought forward in the mix to hold the listener's attention. Granted, this is an arrangement issue, too, but it's the job of a mixer to find some point of interest and emphasize it. Of course, the producer should catch this problem way before the project gets to the mixing stage.

3. **MIXES THAT ARE NOISY.** Clicks, hums, extraneous noises, song count-offs, and sometimes lip smacks and breaths are all things that the listener will find distracting. It may be a pain to eliminate these distractions, but you've got to do it to take the mix to where it has to be. It will save you time and money if this is accomplished by editing them out before the mixing stage.

4. **MIXES THAT LACK CLARITY AND PUNCH.** With this problem, instruments aren't distinct, and low-end frequencies are either too weak or too big. This is really the number one indication of an amateur mix, especially in the low end: it's either way too heavy or way too light. The way around this is to listen to other records that

you think sound great and try to emulate the sound. Sure, it takes time, but doing so will get you in the ballpark.

5. MIXES THAT SOUND DISTANT AND ARE DEVOID OF ANY FEELING OF INTIMACY. Sometimes a mix sounds distant because it has too much reverb or other effects have been overused. This is another common trait of an amateur mix, since a newbie mixer thinks the plug-in effects are so cool (because they are!) that they should be used on everything all the way through the song. You'd be surprised just how many effects are used in a great mix sometimes, but the use is so subtle that you can't tell they're there unless you have the original unaffected mix to compare it with. In an amateur mix, you hear all the effects screaming at you all the time. If you can make the mix first sound great without effects, you'll automatically moderate their use.

6. INCONSISTENT LEVELS. This involves instrument levels that vary from being balanced to being too soft or too loud, or lyrics that can't be distinguished. Once again, a newbie mixer often sets the faders and forgets them, but mixing can be just as dynamic as the music. Every note of every solo and every word of the vocal must be heard, and this may require riding the faders. Even with parameter automation as sophisticated as it is these days, it still takes some time and a critical ear to be sure that everything is heard.

7. DULL AND UNINTERESTING SOUNDS. This problem happens when generic, dated, or overused sounds are used. There's a difference between using something because it's hip and new and using it because everyone else is using it. One example is the Auto-Tune keying trick initially used by Cher, and then copied by NSYNC, T-Pain, Kanye West, and others. They've already used it, so give it a rest. It doesn't mean you're cool if you use it, just a copycat. The same goes for using generic synth patches from whatever the latest hardware or software synthesizer is. We've heard all those sounds a thousand times already. Time for something new. Most great artists and producers strive for something that no one has ever heard before.

Although some artists, producers, and mixers get lucky by flying through a mix, making and mixing records usually takes a lot of time and attention. We'd all like it to go faster, but there are some things that you just can't let get by. Eliminate the seven characteristics of an amateur mix, and you'll be surprised just how good your song can sound.

THE KEYS TO A GREAT MIX

Although it's always easier to do with great tracks, solid arrangements, and spectacular playing, a great mix can take okay tracks and transform them into a hit so compelling that people can't get enough of it. It's been done on some of your all-time favorite songs. So how can you get a mix to that point?

More than being just technically correct, a mix must be as interesting as a good movie. It must build to a climax while having points of tension and release that keep the listener subconsciously involved. Just as a film looks bigger than life, a great mix must sound bigger than life. The passion and the emotion must be on a level that sucks in the listeners and forces them to focus on the sound.

Most great mixers, whether they know it or not (and many mixers aren't conscious of how they do it), have a method in the way they approach a mix. Although the method can vary a little depending on the song, the artist, the genre, or even whether the mixer tracked the song from scratch or is just coming in for the mix, the technique remains constant.

> **Figure out the direction of the song.**
> **Develop the groove and build it like a house.**
> **Find the most important element and emphasize it.**

The last point may be the most important in creating an outstanding mix. As famed Latin music mixer and 18-time Grammy winner Benny Faccone so succinctly states:

"It's almost like a musician who picks up a guitar and tries to play. He may have the chart in front of him, but soon he has to go beyond the notes in order to get creative. Same thing with mixing. It's not just a thing of setting levels any more, but more about trying to get the energy of the song across. Anybody can make the bass or the drums even out."

Find the Direction of the Song

The first thing that the mixer must do before delving headfirst into the mix is to find the direction of the song, and that's determined by both the artist and the performances. For instance, if the song is folksy in nature, then it probably won't need big, bombastic drums and long reverbs and delays, but if the artist is a loud arena rock band, then you probably won't want a close, intimate sound.

Although it's absolutely possible to change the direction of a song and have a hit, a song usually works best with one artist only one way. A good example of this is Marvin Gaye's "I Heard It Through the Grapevine," a hit covered over a hundred times by everyone from the Kaiser Chiefs to Tina Turner to Amy Winehouse. If we consider only two of these covers, the direction of Creedence Clearwater is very different from the direction taken by Gladys Knight and the Pips, yet the song works equally well for both groups. Another example is Green Day's version of Bob Dylan's "Like a Rolling Stone." Its direction is a function of the artist and the performance.

Develop the Groove and Build It Like a House

We talked about the groove of a song in Chapter 6, and while the producer has to make sure that a song has a strong groove to begin with, the mixer has to identify the main instrument or instruments associated with the groove and make them stand out in the mix so the pulse of the song is strong.

As stated in Chapter 6, sometimes it isn't the bass and drums that are the main instruments holding down the groove. It could be a percussion instrument like a shaker, a rhythm guitar part, or an arpeggiated synthesizer line. Regardless of what's supplying the groove, the trick for the mixer is to find the instrument that defines the groove, and then build the rest of the mix around it.

Find the Most Important Element and Emphasize It

Equally as meaningful, and in some cases even more important than finding the instrument responsible for the groove, is finding whatever element is the most important to the song. In some cases (like dance and hip-hop), the most important element is the groove. Yet in other genres (like country and pop), it's the vocal.

Even though the most important element in a song is often the lead vocal, it doesn't necessarily have to be. It could be a riff as in, say, The Rolling Stones' "Satisfaction" or "Start Me Up," or the synth line of Maroon 5's "Moves Like Jagger," or the intro to Coldplay's "Clocks." It's always a part so compelling that it forces you to listen to the song.

Whatever part is most important, the mixer must identify it and emphasize it in the mix in order for the mix to be elevated to beyond the ordinary. Like most other creative work that requires some divine inspiration for success, you can't underestimate the importance of talent and experience.

THE MASTER MIX

Gone are the days of manual mixing, when the hands of not only the engineer but also the producer and all of the band members manned a fader or a mute button or a pan control in order to get the perfect mix. Gone are the days of massive amounts of takes of your mix in order to get your "keeper." Thanks to the digital workstation, the mix is (or should be) perfect before it gets committed to hard disk, analog tape, solid-state memory, or any other format yet to be devised. Regardless of the format used to deliver the music to the record label, the mastering facility, and, ultimately, the public, the mixing engineer must make several decisions right before and right after achieving a mix that lights up the speakers.

Competitive Level

Since as far back as the '50s, mixers have strived to make their mixes hotter than those of their competitors. That's because if two songs are played back to back, the louder one is sometimes perceived as sounding "better." But the limitation on how loud a mix could be was determined by the type of medium delivered to the consumer.

In the days of vinyl records, if a mix was too loud, the stylus would vibrate so much that the record would skip. When mixing too hot to analog tape, the sound would begin to softly distort and the high frequencies would disappear (although many engineers and artists actually liked this effect). When digital audio and CDs came along, any attempt to mix beyond 0 dBFS would distort terribly as a result of digital "overs." (Nobody likes this effect.)

But over the years mixes have become hotter and hotter in perceived level, mostly because of new digital technology that has resulted in better and better limiters. Today's digital "look ahead" limiters make it easy to set a maximum level for the mix (usually at -.1 dBFS) and never worry about digital overs or distortion again.

Raising the competitive level (the mix level that's as loud as your competitor's mix) used to be left to the mastering engineer. The mix engineer would hand off a mix that was acceptable and the level would get raised from there, regardless of whether the ultimate delivery medium to the consumer was a record, a cassette, a CD, or a DVD. Part of the voodoo of the mastering engineer was his ability to make your mix louder than the mixer was able to.

That process doesn't cut it these days. Artists and A&R people want the mix to not only immediately sound "like a record," but also to be as loud as anything commercially released, from the first rough mix onward. This is one of the reasons that the famous mix bus compressor built into every analog SSL console became so popular. It was built like a typical mastering compressor to give your mix that "radio sound" as soon as you inserted it into the signal path.

Today, with many powerful plug-in compressor/limiters available, it's all too easy to raise the level of your mix as loud as it will go, but just because you can do it doesn't mean you should. Raising the level too much results in a condition called "hypercompression" (see Chapter 15 for an in-depth explanation), which can rob the song of any life, cause listener fatigue, and not give the mastering engineer much to work with. It's still best to leave any major mix compression and level boosting to the mastering engineer.

MIXING WITH MASTERING IN MIND

Whether you master your final mixes yourself or take them to a mastering engineer, things will go a lot faster if you prepare for mastering ahead of time. Nothing is so exasperating to all involved as not knowing which mix is the correct one or forgetting the file name, which preparation will help you avoid. Here are some tips to get you mastering-ready.

THINGS TO REMEMBER BEFORE MASTERING

- **DON'T OVER-EQ WHEN MIXING.** Better to be a bit dull and let your mastering engineer brighten things up. In general, mastering engineers can do a better job for you if your mix is on the dull side rather than too bright or too big.
- **DON'T OVERCOMPRESS WHEN MIXING.** You might as well not even master if you've squashed it too much already. If your mix is hypercompressed, that will deprive the mastering engineer of one of his or her major abilities to help your project. Squash it for your friends. Squash it for your clients. But leave some dynamics for your mastering engineer. In general, it's best to compress and control levels on track by track basis and not on the stereo bus.

- **GETTING THE LEVELS OF DIFFERENT SONGS TO MATCH IS NOT IMPORTANT.** Just make your mixes sound great. Matching levels between songs is one of the reasons you master your mixes.
- **HAVING HOT LEVELS IS NOT IMPORTANT.** You still have plenty of headroom even if you print your mix peaks at -10 dB or so. Leave it to the mastering engineer to get you the hot levels. That's another reason you go there.
- **WATCH YOUR FADES.** If you trim the heads and tails of your track too tightly, you might discover that you've trimmed a reverb trail or an essential attack or breath. Leave a little room and let the mastering engineer perfect it.
- **DOCUMENT EVERYTHING.** You'll make it easier on yourself and your mastering person if everything is well documented, and you'll save yourself some money, too. The documentation should include any flaws, digital errors, distortion, bad edits, fades, shipping instructions, and record company identification numbers. Finally, make sure that each file is properly identified for easy recognition (especially if you won't be at the mastering session).
- **ESPECIALLY DON'T BE AFRAID TO MAKE A NOTE OF ANY GLITCHES, CHANNEL IMBALANCES, OR DISTORTION.** The mastering engineer won't think less of you if something got away from you (that happens to everybody at one time or another), and it's a whole lot easier than wasting a billable hour trying to track down an equipment problem when the problem is actually on the mix master itself.
- **ALTERNATE MIXES CAN BE YOUR FRIENDS.** A vocal up, a vocal down, or an instrument-only mix can be a lifesaver when mastering. Things that aren't apparent while mixing sometimes jump right out under the microscope of mastering, and having an alternative mix around can sometimes provide a quick fix and keep you from having to re-export the mix. Make sure you document any alternative mixes properly, though.
- **CHECK YOUR PHASE WHEN MIXING.** It can be a real shock if you get to the mastering studio and the engineer begins to check for mono compatibility, and then the lead singer or guitar disappears because something in the track is out of phase. Even though this was more of a problem in the days of vinyl and AM radio, it's still an important point to make now since many so-called stereo sources (such as television) are either pseudo-stereo or are stereo only some of the time. Check it and fix it before you get there.

MIXING IN THE BOX

Where once upon a time it was assumed that any mix was centered around a mixing console, that's no longer true, as most mixes are primarily done using a DAW. It's now so much cheaper and faster to mix "in the box" (ITB) that even engineers that have a console available for mixing will do most of the processing and automation in the DAW.

Many old-school mixers who grew up using consoles initially disliked mixing in the box because either they found it hard to mix with a mouse or they didn't like the sound. While it's true that the early workstations (or rather their A/D/A converters) didn't sound very good, that's no longer the case. Indeed, even the least expensive converters have come a long way, so that's not the issue it once was.

Another objection has been that the sound of the internal mix bus of a DAW degrades the signal, and once again that isn't quite the case. It's true that each DAW application uses a different algorithm for summing, which makes the sound of a particular software application vary from the next a little to a lot, but a bigger issue is the same one that mixers in the analog world have faced almost from the beginning: it's how you drive it that counts!

Suffice it to say that whether mixing in the box or with a traditional console, the principles are the same. Although you or your engineer may have a preference for one or the other, you can expect to get a similar quality from either mixing method.

THE MIXING ENGINEER'S STYLE

Most mixing engineers excel at working on a certain type of music. Some work better in R&B, some are great at rock, while still others shine at acoustic music. While music is music to some degree, and most mixers can manage to achieve a reasonable mix in a genre they're not used to, it's important to match the correct mixer with the type of music you're doing.

For instance, an engineer who is used to doing acoustic jazz may not be able to get the punch required for a rock record or the low end needed for an R&B track. Conversely, someone who mixes primarily hip-hop may be lost when confronted with an orchestral track. That being said, some of the finer mixers just have that special touch that lifts a track up beyond what you thought it could be, and that's why they get paid the big bucks to mix.

HOW MUCH SHOULD MIXING COST?

Mixing engineers are all over the board price-wise, especially in the current depressed music market. At one time there was a mixer (who shall remain nameless) who was charging as much as $10,000 per mix, plus a percentage of the sales, to mix just one song. Even more outrageous was the fact that he'd do as many as three mixes a day, since his setting for each instrument never changed because it was his "sound." Very few budgets can support that kind of excess anymore, and virtually all mixers' prices, although still at a premium, have come down in recent years.

While some mixers charge by the song, others charge a daily rate, and so the price can escalate quickly if there are fixes or the mix goes longer than expected. The rates might be as low as $250 a day, and can run up to $2,500 or more (although most rates are somewhere in the middle these days). These rates may not include the studio costs if a mix using a studio console is desired, which are separate from the mixer's rate. That means that mixing could theoretically cost as much as $5,000 a day with the mixer included, although this is a rate that only a very few A-list projects can support.

Because budgets are so small these days compared to what they once were, mixing specialists have been caught in a dilemma—the client (you, the producer) can afford only the studio or the mixer, but not both.

As a result, many mixers have resorted to creating their own mixing environment and giving an all-in price that makes the process much more affordable for the producer. This is one of the advantages of the digital age and DAWs: it was impossible to build and equip a suitable mixing room for less than a half-million dollars back in the analog days.

Since the music business is weak at the moment and budgets are way down, present an offer to your mixer. If you're willing to wait for when the mixer can fit you in during his or her down time, or if you agree to let him mix alone without you or the artist attending, you might be surprised at the rate you can get. Even if the price you offer is below his rate, chances are you can work something out that will get you a great mix for a price you can afford.

HOW LONG SHOULD MIXING TAKE?

As stated in Chapter 3, it used to be standard to figure that a mix would take anywhere from a day to a day and a half per song, especially if you used an A-list mixing engineer. The first day was to get the mix about 95 percent of the way finished, and the second half day was to try to get those last 5 percent with a fresh set of ears.

Of course, the time it takes to mix something depends on the song, the type of material, the way it was recorded, and the style of the mixer. If, for instance, the recording were a live concert given by a three-piece band and a vocalist, with all the songs sounding pretty much the same, an entire album might take only a day to mix if there are no fixes or complications. An R&B song with 100 tracks, however, could take a few days just to get a handle on. A song that has poorly recorded tracks and needs a lot of editing and fixing to bring it up to snuff might take even longer than that.

On the other hand, producer/engineer Kevin Shirley has been known to mix entire albums in a single day, such as the best-selling Journey records he worked on in the '80s. Of course, he was mixing each song as he went along during the project, instead of doing rough mixes. The final mix amounted to making only minor tweaks.

Regardless of how long the initial mix took in the analog days, tweaks or changes after the fact were once dreaded by all involved because resetting the console and all the outboard gear (see Figure 14-1) usually resulted in a mix that sounded slightly different (not to mention how long it took to set up the equipment). As a result, producers and mixers did everything they could to avoid any redos, which mostly consisted of spending extra time on the mix to be sure it sounded right, making multiple versions of the mix (more on this in a bit), and doing just about anything to assure that the finished version was in their hands when they walked out of the studio door.

Now that people can mix "in-the-box" in a DAW, it's easy to bring a mix back from exactly where you left it—days, weeks, months, or even years before—thus making fixes fast and easy. As a result, this has taken some of the pressure out of the mixing process, unless you're still mixing in the analog world with a console and outboard gear. In that case, it hasn't really changed much at all.

In the end, it's best to figure at least a day per song regardless of whether you're mixing in the box or on an analog console. Consider yourself lucky if it goes any faster.

Figure 14-1: Reconnecting the Patch Bay: One of the Reasons That Remixing Is Unpopular

ALTERNATIVE MIXES

It's now standard operating procedure to do multiple mixes in the hopes of avoiding having to redo the mix later because an element was mixed too loudly or softly.

Even with today's ease of calling up a digital project in a DAW, a producer does not want to revisit a completed project if at all possible. This means any element that might be questioned later (such as lead vocal, a solo instrument, background vocals, or any other major part) is mixed with that track recorded slightly louder and again slightly softer. These mixes are referred to as the *up mix* and the *down mix*. Usually these increments are very small—.5 dB to 1 dB—but usually not much more.

With multiple mixes it's also possible to correct an otherwise perfect mix later by editing in a masked word or a chorus with louder background vocals. Many times an instrumental mix is used to splice out objectionable language (see Chapter 13).

Although many record companies may ask for more or different versions, here's a typical version list of a rock artist's mix. Other types of music will have a similar version list that's appropriate for the genre.

1. Album version
2. Album version with vocals up

3. Contemporary-hits radio mix—softer guitars
4. Album-oriented radio mix—more guitars and more drums
5. Adult contemporary mix—minimum guitars, maximum keyboards, and orchestration
6. TV mix (the mix minus the lead vocal but with background vocals)
7. Instrumental mix (no vocals at all)

You or the artist or A&R person may also want additional versions, such as a pass without delays on the vocals in the chorus, a pass with more guitars in the vamp, or a version with the bass guitar up. If you're working with a hit artist, there's also a good chance that any singles will also need a shortened radio edit. Thanks to the virtues of the digital audio workstation and modern console automation, many mix engineers leave the up and down mixes to their assistants, since most of the hard work is already complete.

CHAPTER 15

MASTERING:
THE FINISHING TOUCH

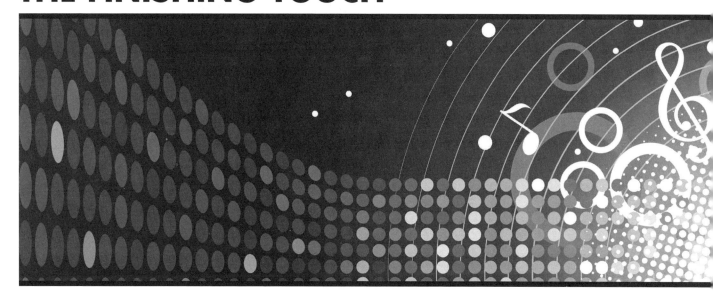

astering is one of the most misunderstood operations in production, but also one of the most important. While it might be tempting to consider not mastering a project, a good mastering job can make even a great production sound even better. Let's take a look at what mastering is and what a producer has to know about it.

WHAT IS MASTERING?

Technically speaking, mastering is the step between taking the audio fresh from mixing and preparing it to be replicated or distributed. But it is really much more than that.

> **Mastering is the process of turning a collection of songs into a record, making them sound like they belong together by unifying their tone, volume, and timing (spacing between songs).**

Mastering isn't a set of tools or a device that music runs through and automatically comes out mastered (despite what the adverts for mastering plug-ins and devices say). It's an art form that, when done well, relies on an engineer's skill, experience with various genres of music, and good taste.

WHY IS MASTERING SO IMPORTANT?

Mastering should be considered the final step in the creative process because it's your last chance to polish and tweak your project—at least, that's the case in the United States. In Europe, mastering is viewed as the first stage of the manufacturing process, and that's because it's the stage where the digital bits get transferred to either a mechanical medium (such as vinyl) or another electronic medium better suited for mass production (like CDs).

Both of these views are accurate, but it's a shame to overlook the creative aspect involved in mastering. The issue has become a moot point anyway, with many music releases now completely bypassing CDs and other legacy mediums.

A project that has been mastered, especially at a top-flight mastering house, simply sounds better. It sounds complete, polished, and finished. The project that might have sounded like a demo before now sounds like a "record."

This is because the mastering engineer has added judicious amounts of EQ and compression to make the project bigger, fatter, richer, and louder. He or she has matched the levels of each song so they all have the same apparent level. He's fixed the fades so that they're smooth.

He's edited out bad parts so skillfully that you don't even notice them. He's made all the songs blend together into a cohesive unit. In the case of mastering for CD, he's inserted the spreads (the time between each song) so the songs flow seamlessly together. He's sequenced the songs so that they fall in the correct order.

He's proofed your master before it's sent to the replicator to make sure it's free of any glitches or noise. He's also made and stored a backup clone in case anything should happen to your cherished master, and he's taken care of all the shipping to the desired duplication facility, if you're using one. And all of this happens so quickly and smoothly that you hardly know it is happening.

The Reason Why a Pro Makes It Sound So Good

There are many reasons why a commercial mastering facility usually produces a product that's better than one mastered at home. First of all, the mastering house is better equipped. It has things available that you probably won't find in a simple home- or small-studio DAW room, such as high-end A/D and D/A converters, ultra-smooth outboard compressors and equalizers, and an exceptional listening environment and monitoring system.

The monitoring system of these facilities sometimes costs far more than many entire high-end home studios. Cost here isn't the point but quality is, since you can rarely hear what you need to hear on the commonly used near-field monitors in most home and small recording studios. The vast majority of monitors, and the rooms they are in, just aren't precise enough.

Figure 15-1: A Professional Mastering Studio

Experience Is the Key

It helps to have great equipment, but the mastering engineer is the real key to the process. Mastering is all he or she does, day in and day out. He has "big ears" because he masters for at least eight hours every day and knows his monitors the way you know your favorite pair of sneakers. His reference point for what constitutes a good-sounding mix is finely honed thanks to working hours and hours on the best- and worst-sounding mixes of each genre of music.

Finally, if mastering were easy, wouldn't you think that all the big-time engineers and producers (and record companies, for that matter) would do it themselves? They don't, and mastering houses are busier than ever, which tells you something.

While all of the above may seem as though I'm trying to discourage you from doing your own mastering or from finding a place that's inexpensive, that's really not the case. In fact, I'm trying provide a reference point that shows how the pros operate and why they're so successful. From there you can determine whether you're better served by doing it yourself or using a pro.

The Mastering Engineer's Sound

All mastering engineers have their own style and their own sound. Some specialize at R&B, some excel at dance music, some are known for their low end, and some are known because they can cut songs louder than anyone else. Most have experience in all types of music and can do a good job regardless of the genre.

It's not uncommon for a producer with a track record and a top-flight artist to ask for a "shoot-out" between mastering engineers to see which one can do the best job on a particular project. That means the producer will ship the same mix to different mastering engineers, who then master the song (usually for free). The winner gets the mastering job for the album.

Mastering engineers intensely dislike this practice and will do it very reluctantly (since they only get paid if they win the shoot-out) and only for high-end clients. Even if you have such a project, you'll have a much happier engineer if you don't ask him to prove himself. You'll also get a better job if you develop a relationship with your engineer.

Treat your mastering engineer well today, because he could be saving your next project tomorrow.

The Mastering Engineer as a Security Blanket

Sometimes a mixer will send a rough mix to a mastering engineer for an opinion on how it sounds. Many times that simple procedure can save a lot of time and money, since the mastering engineer can tell the mixer where things might be off in the mix.

Sometimes the mastering engineer might say something like, "The midrange is a dB or two hot, but otherwise it's okay" or "You're plus 12 at 60 Hz! You've really got to check the level of your subwoofer." Either way, it's great to have a working relationship with a mastering engineer so you can work with him in this way.

HOW LONG SHOULD MASTERING TAKE?

Mastering done by a pro usually moves at a rate of two or three songs per hour, although it can take longer if you have a song that requires a lot of fixes or edits or you have trouble finding or choosing a mix. Most mastering jobs are finished within five hours, and few rarely go beyond a full day (although a hit artist might have a song mastered several times in the event of fixes or a picky producer or A&R person).

Sometimes a mastering engineer will reject a mix, saying that it's so far off that it's better to remix. This ultimately saves money, since it's easier than asking the mastering engineer to try to resurrect a bad mix that will end up being an inferior product anyway.

When booking mastering time, be sure to tell the studio manager about any deadlines you might have and the type of masters needed (for example, a 48 kHz/24-bit AIFF file for video, a vinyl master, etc.). The more information the studio has beforehand, the less time the project will take, which means the less money you'll spend.

HOW MUCH SHOULD MASTERING COST?

Mastering prices at pro facilities vary wildly but are, for the most part, broken down into three areas: EQ time, production time, and the cost of the master.

EQ time is the creative time spent by the mastering engineer to EQ and compress your tracks. The price in a major facility can run from about $250 to $750 per hour (see why it's so important to come prepared?). The price in a small indie mastering facility might only be $50 per hour (or per song), but you get what you pay for, since you're paying for the mastering engineer's ears and experience.

Production time is the time that the mastering engineer or assistant spends doing the actual sequencing for vinyl or CD, making the master for the CD replicator, vinyl duplicator, and online distributor, and making any reference files or CDs for the producer and the artist. The price for production time is usually about half the cost of the EQ time.

The master, or the final product that gets sent off to a replicator to make CDs or the vinyl duplicator, costs between $250 and $1,000. These days, the master is a file that contains the audio, the spread information (the timing between the songs), and the IRSC codes (which identify one song from another), and it's delivered to the replicator by FTP, CD, or even Exabyte tape. You can also request a CD-R of the master, but don't make the mistake of playing it; even the slightest smudge on the disc can cause a problem during replication. Some facilities offer a package that includes the CD master, an online master, and reference copies—all at one price.

All told, a full mastering job at a top-notch facility for a ten-song record can cost as little as $1,500 and as much as $5,000 or more.

PREPARATION FOR MASTERING

The mastering process will go a lot faster and smoother if you prepare for it ahead of time. Nothing is so exasperating for all involved as not being able to identify the correct mix file or forgetting the file name. Here are some tips to get you mastering-ready.

THINGS TO REMEMBER BEFORE MASTERING

• **MAKE SURE TO BRING MIXES WITH THE HIGHEST RESOLUTION POSSIBLE.** Lossy formats like MP3s and AAC won't cut it, and will give you an inferior product in the end. Bring the highest-resolution WAV or AIFF mixes you can, and make the other formats for online distribution later from the mastered project. If you DAW session is at 96k/24 bit, that's the master file resolution you should use. If it was set at 44.1/24, that's what you should use.

• **GO TO THE SESSION IF AT ALL POSSIBLE.** Most producers and engineers will go to the first few sessions with a new mastering engineer to see if he has the same musical and technical sensibilities. After that, a bond of trust develops, and they will simply send the master mixes, along with any instructions as to their preferences, to the mastering engineer. That being said, you should go to all of the mastering sessions if possible, because things will always sound a bit different (and probably better) than the way they sounded during mixing. Attending the session also allows you to make some final creative decisions that only you could add ("The kick is a little loud; see if you can deemphasize it a bit," or "Let's squash the whole mix a little more to make this tune punchier").

• **COME PREPARED.** Make sure that all documentation, shipping instructions, and sequencing is complete before you get to the session. Sequencing (the order that the tunes appear on the CD or vinyl record) is especially important, and checking that the order is correct beforehand will save you some money in mastering time.

Many producers have the mistaken impression that once the final mix is finished, it's off to the mastering studio. It's best if there's one additional session known as the sequencing session, in which you take a day and do any editing that is required (cheaper to do it here than during mastering) and listen to the various song order possibilities. This is really important if you will be releasing in multiple formats such as vinyl and CD or in different countries or territories (since they will probably require a different song order due to having two sides on the record).

• **HAVE YOUR SONGS TIMED OUT.** This step is important because you want to make sure that your project can easily fit on a CD or vinyl record, if that's your release format. Most CDs have a total time of just less than 80 minutes (78:33, to be exact), although it is possible to get an extended-time CD (but be careful—you might have replication problems). As discussed previously, just because you have all that time available doesn't mean that you need to fill it.

Vinyl records may be around for a while (but in limited quantities), so the following will apply if you intend to cut vinyl. Cumulative time is important because, due to the physical limitations of the disc, the mastering engineer must know the total time per side before he starts cutting. You are limited to a maximum of about 25 minutes per side if you want the record to be nice and loud. Since you can have only 25 minutes or less on a side, it's important to know the sequence before you get to the mastering session. Cutting vinyl is a one-shot deal, with none of the undo functions that a workstation has. It'll cost you money every time you change your mind.

COMPETITIVE LEVEL, TAKE TWO

As stated in Chapter 14, the volume/level wars began way back in the vinyl era of the '50s, when it was discovered that if a record played louder than the others on the radio, the listeners would perceive it to be "better" sounding and might make it a hit as a result. Since then it has been the charge of the mastering engineer to make any song intended for radio as loud as possible in any way they can.

That also applies to situations other than the radio. Take, for instance, the Spotify playlist, the CD changer, and, in the very old days, the record jukebox. Most artists, producers, and labels certainly don't want one of their releases to play softer than their competitors', and that's because of the perception (and not necessarily the truth) that it won't sound as good if it isn't as loud.

But as said in Chapter 14, the limitation of how loud a song can sound is determined by the delivery medium to the consumer. If the mix on a vinyl record is too loud, the stylus can vibrate so much that it will lift out of the grooves and the record will skip. With digital audio and CDs, any attempt to mix beyond 0 dBFS results in distortion (although many artists, producers, engineers, and labels no longer seem to mind). Trying to squeeze every ounce of level out of the track is a lot harder than it seems, and that's where the art of mastering comes in.

HYPERCOMPRESSION: DON'T GO THERE!

Over the years it's become easier to make a record that's hotter in perceived level than in the past, mostly because of new digital technology that has resulted in better compressors and limiters. Today's digital "lookahead" limiters make it easy to set a maximum level (usually at -.05 or -.1 dBFS) and never worry about digital overs and distortion again, but this usually comes at a cost in audio quality.

Too much bus compression or over-limiting when either mixing or mastering results in what's become known as "hypercompression." Hypercompression should be avoided at all costs because of the following:

- It can suck the life out of a song, making it weaker-sounding instead of punchier.
- Lossy codecs like MP3 have a hard time encoding hypercompressed material, inserting unwanted side effects as a result.

- It's known to cause listener fatigue, so the consumer won't listen to your record as long or as many times.
- A hypercompressed track can sound even worse over the radio because of the behavior of broadcast processors at the station.
- A hypercompressed track has no dynamics, leaving it loud but lifeless and unexciting. On a DAW, it's seen as a constant waveform that fills up the DAW region.

Here's how the levels of a typical 1985 rock song have changed on recordings over the years as it has made its way to hypercompression on its subsequent rereleases.

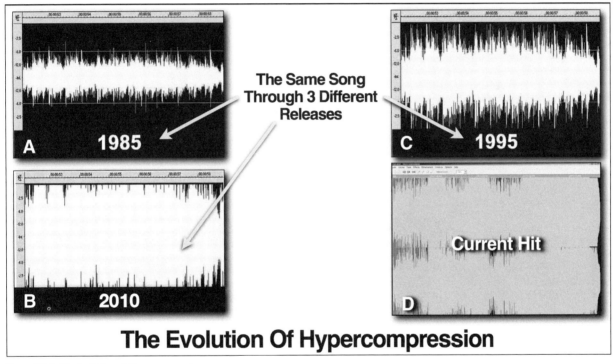

Figure 15-2: The Evolution of Hypercompression

This practice has come under constant fire for the last decade or so, since we've just about hit the loudness limit thanks to the digital environment where audio now dwells. Still, both mixing and mastering engineers try to cram more and more level onto the disc, only to find that they end up with either a distorted or over-compressed product (go back and listen to Metallica's 2008 CD release of *Death Magnetic* for a most egregious example).

While this might be the sound that the producer and artist were looking for, it does violate the mastering engineer's unwritten code of keeping things as natural sounding and unaltered as possible while performing his level magic.

That said, getting the most level onto the disc or file is not the only level adjustment that the mastering engineer must practice. Just as important is the fact that every song on the disc must be perceived to be just as loud as the next. "Perceived" is the key word, since this is something that can't be directly measured and must be done by ear.

SHOULD YOU USE A PRO OR MASTER AT HOME?

The temptation may be great to do your own mastering instead of using a pro, especially when money is tight. If an online release is all that's in the artist's game plan, there may be even more pressure to save the money.

While it's very possible to master the project yourself (meaning that either you or your engineer do it), that increases the chances for the project to come out a lot worse instead of better. Today's mastering tools (like iZotope's Ozone, for instance) are extremely powerful, and could even cause a lot of harm to your project in the wrong hands.

If you do decide to master yourself, here are a few tips to keep you out of trouble:

SELF-MASTERING TIPS

• **LISTEN TO OTHER SONGS THAT YOU LIKE BEFORE YOU EVEN TOUCH AN EQ PARAMETER.** The more songs you listen to, the better. You need a reference point to compare your work with, and listening to other songs will prevent you from over-EQing. EQing is usually the stage when engineers who are mastering their own mixes get in trouble. There's a tendency to overcompensate with the EQ, adding huge amounts (usually of bottom end) that wreck the frequency balance of the song completely.

• **A LITTLE GOES A LONG WAY.** If you feel that you need to add more than 2 or 3 dB, you're better off remixing! That's what the pros do. It's not uncommon at all for a pro mastering engineer to call up a mixer, tell him where he's off, and ask him to do it again.

• **BE CAREFUL NOT TO OVER-COMPRESS OR OVER-LIMIT YOUR SONG.** This can lead to hypercompression. Instead of making a song louder, hypercompression sucks all the dynamics out of it, making it lifeless and fatiguing to listen to.

- **CONSTANTLY COMPARE YOUR MASTERING JOB TO OTHER SONGS THAT YOU LIKE THE SOUND OF.** Doing this is one of the best ways to help you hear whether and how you're getting off track.
- **CONCENTRATE ON MAKING ALL THE SONGS SOUND THE SAME IN RELATIVE LEVEL AND TONE.** This is one of the key operations in mastering a collection of songs like an album. The idea is to get them to all sound as though they're at the same volume. It's pretty common for mixes to sound different from song to song, even if they're done by the same engineer with the same gear. It's your job to make the listener think that the songs were all done on the same day in the same way. They've got to sound as close to each other in volume as you can get them, or at least close enough so none stand out.
- **FINISH THE SONGS.** Edit out count-offs and glitches, fix fades, and create spreads for CDs and vinyl records.

MASTERING FOR DIFFERENT DELIVERY FORMATS

Different formats require slightly different mastering techniques. What works for a CD most times won't work for vinyl (it will probably be too loud and the stylus will jump out of the grooves), and may not work well for MP3s, either.

Encoding an MP3 of your mix is easier than it's ever been as encoders have gotten better and higher available bandwidth has made the need for small files a lot less stringent.

That said, here are some tips to get you started in the right direction so that you won't have to try every possible parameter combination. Remember, though, the settings that might work on one particular song or type of music might not work on another.

The Source File

Using lossy coding such as MP3 (which actually throws away some of the digital data to make the file smaller) makes the quality of the master mix *even more* of an issue because high-quality audio will be damaged much less by this type of encoding than low-quality audio will.

Therefore, it's vital that you start with the best audio quality (the highest sampling rate and most bits) possible. That means it's better to start with the 24-bit mix master or to make the MP3 while you're exporting your mix than to use something like a 16-bit CD master as the source for your MP3 encodes.

It's also important to listen to your encode and perhaps even try a number of different parameter settings before settling on the final product. Listen to the encode, do an A/B comparison with the original, and make any additional changes you feel necessary.

Sometimes a big, thick wall of sound encodes terribly and you need to ease back on the compression and limiting of the source-track master. Other times, heavy compression can make it through the encoder better than with a mix with more dynamics. There are a few predictions one can make after doing it for a while, but you can never be certain, so listening and adjusting is the only sure way.

Here are some things to consider if your mix is intended for MP3 encoding:

MP3 ENCODING TIPS

- Start with the highest-quality audio file possible.
- Filter out the top end at whatever frequency works best (judge by ear). The MP3 format has the most difficulty with high frequencies, and cutting them out liberates a lot of processing for encoding the lower and middle frequencies. You trade some top end for better quality in the rest of the spectrum.
- A busy mix can lose punch after encoding. Sparse mixes, like acoustic jazz trios, seem to retain more of their original audio punch.
- Don't totally squash your mix with a compressor/limiter. Leave some dynamic range so that the encoding algorithm has something to look at.
- Use multiband compression or other dynamic spectral effects very sparingly. They tend to confuse the encoding algorithm.
- Set your encoder for maximum quality, which will allow it to process for best results. The encoding time is negligible anyway.
- Remember, MP3 encoding almost always makes the resulting material slightly hotter than the original material. Limit the output of the material intended for MP3 to -1.1 dB, instead of the commonly used -.1 or -.2 dB, so you don't get digital overs.

CREATING FILES FOR STREAMING SERVICES

Submitting song files to the various streaming services is usually done either through an aggregator like Tunecore or CD Baby, or direct from a record label. Regardless of who submits the files, the requirements are the same in most cases—44.1 kHz/16 bit audio, the same as CD. In some cases a high quality MP3 at 320 kbps is also acceptable for submission, but obviously this doesn't represent the best that the music can sound.

After the file is submitted, the streaming service then encodes it to their specifications, which vary considerably. It's good to know how the music will be encoded in order to provide the best-sounding source file, so here's a chart with the current streaming specs of the most popular services.

Submitting to Online Stores and Services

If you want to distribute your work via online stores, you might want to consider one of the many distribution services. While you may be able to submit your songs to some online stores, others (like iTunes) require a large record label account, meaning that you need a digital distributor in order to get your songs placed in the store. Plus, each online store has different file format requirements, which can cause you to spend a lot of time with file preparation, when submission is just a single click away with CD Baby, Tunecore, Distrokid, or ReverbNation (among others).

	CD Baby	Tunecore	Distrokid	ReverbNation
Single Fee	$12.95	$9.99	$19.99 for unlimited songs	$34.95 annual fee
Album Fee	$49	$29.99 first year $49.99 each year thereafter	$19.99 for unlimited albums	$34.95 annual fee
Sales Commission	9%	0%	0%	0%
Number of Digital Partners (iTunes, Amazon, etc)	95	74	4 (Amazon, iTunes, Spotify, and GooglePlay)	40

	CD Baby	Tunecore	Distrokid	ReverbNation
CD Sales	Yes	No	No	Yes
Commission on Physical Sales	$4	n/a	n/a	$5.49
CD and Vinyl Distribution	Yes	No	n/a	No

In a nutshell: Tunecore, Distrokid, and Reverbnation charge annual fees but don't take a percentage of your sales. CD Baby takes a 9 percent cut but doesn't charge an annual fee. And if you want physical distribution, only CD Baby and Reverbnation offer that service.

EXPORTING FOR ITUNES

iTunes uses the AAC (Advanced Audio Coding) format for its store and streams. Contrary to popular belief, AAC isn't a proprietary format owned by Apple. In fact, it's part of the MP4 specification and generally delivers excellent-quality files that are about 30 percent smaller than a standard MP3 of the same data rate. iTunes does all the encoding, and music destined for the iTunes Store must be at least CD quality, with a 44.1 kHz sampling rate at 16 bits.

Submitting to the iTunes Store

It's not possible to submit directly to the iTunes store if you're an indie artist, band, producer, or even a small label. Apple reserves that feature for larger labels with large catalogs that release titles on a regular basis. You can easily get your music on the iTunes store by using a digital distributor like Tunecore, CD Baby, Distrokid, ReverbNation, Nimbit, or others.

In order to submit directly to the iTunes store, labels must pass the requirements for submission, and then use a program known as iTunes Producer to submit individual songs and albums. This free program not only allows uploading product to the store and iTunes Radio, but allows the label to set the price and input all the metadata associated with the project.

This is one of the reasons why mastering engineers can't directly submit songs to iTunes on behalf of their clients. The use of the program is exclusive to the label for their product only, and any payments from sales will only return to the bank account associated with that particular iTunes Producer account.

The "Mastered for iTunes" Format

"Mastered for iTunes" (MFIT) is an alternative to the standard iTunes quality, where the iTunes store accepts high-resolution master files, and provides higher quality AAC encodes as a result. Music files that are supplied at 96 kHz/24 bit will have a "Mastered for iTunes" icon placed beside them to identify them as such, although any sample rate that's a 24 bit file is also considered high-resolution (see Figure 15-3).

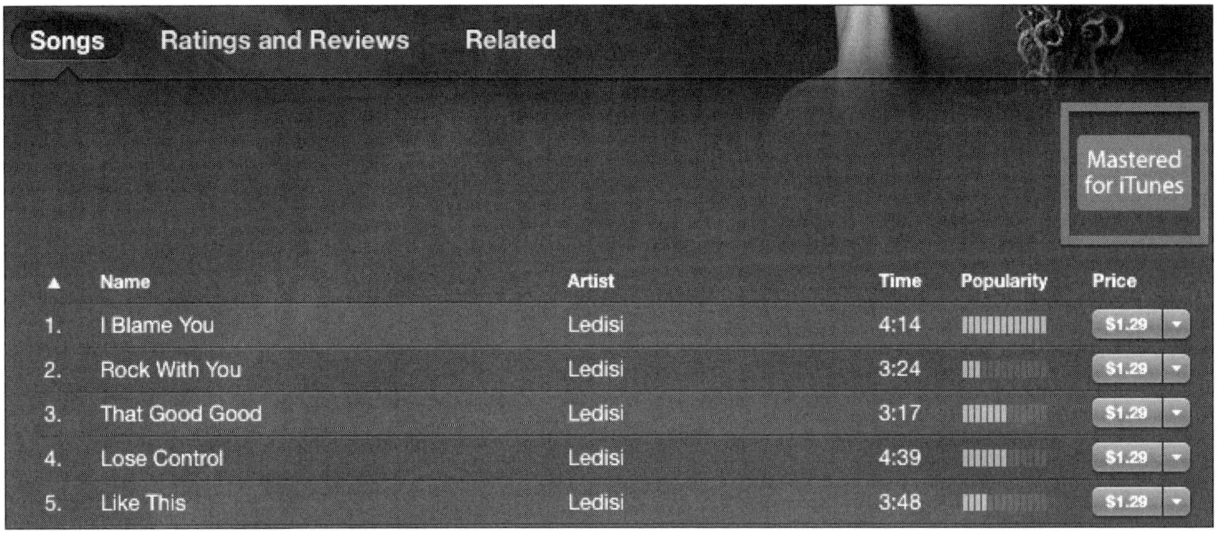

	Name	Artist	Time	Popularity	Price
1.	I Blame You	Ledisi	4:14	‖‖‖‖‖‖‖‖‖‖‖	$1.29
2.	Rock With You	Ledisi	3:24	‖‖	$1.29
3.	That Good Good	Ledisi	3:17	‖‖‖‖‖	$1.29
4.	Lose Control	Ledisi	4:39	‖‖‖‖‖	$1.29
5.	Like This	Ledisi	3:48	‖‖	$1.29

Figure 15-3: Songs Indicated as Mastered for iTunes

"Mastered for iTunes" (or MFIT for short) doesn't mean that the mixer, producer, or mastering facility does anything special to the master except to check what it will sound like before it's submitted to iTunes, and perhaps check it later again before it's posted in the iTunes store. All encoding for iTunes is still done by Apple, not by the mastering engineer, record labels, or artists (see Figure 15-4). According to Apple, the reason for this is to keep the encodes consistent and to prevent anyone from gaming the system by hacking the encoder, but also to avoid any potential legal problems that might occur when a mixer, producer, or mastering house sends the files directly to iTunes without the label's permission, or uses different submission specs.

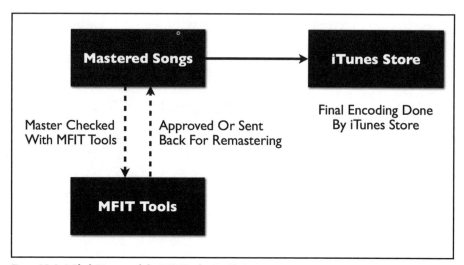

Figure 15-4: A Block Diagram of the MFIT Production Chain

"Mastered for iTunes" is only an indication that a hi-res master was supplied; it's not a separate product. There will always be only one version of the song on iTunes and it will be available at the same price regardless of if it's "Mastered for iTunes" or not. "Mastered for iTunes" doesn't mean you get to charge more, or that iTunes charges you more. Everything is like it was before, you just supply a hi-res master so it sounds better.

CHAPTER 16
EDM, POP, AND HIP-HOP PRODUCTION

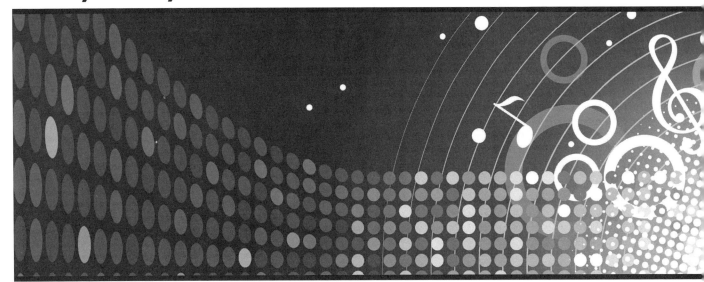

lectronic dance music (although many practitioners hate the term), pop, and hip-hop production have a lot in common in that they've moved the emphasis away from the artist and placed it squarely on the producer. In these beat-driven genres, the producer is the primary songwriter, and many times will only plug a singer into the track at the end of the process, or have the singer collaborate after most of the basic track has been created. This, of course, is totally opposite to the way production has worked in most of the rest of this book.

HOW EDM IS CHANGING MUSIC

Both mixing engineers and mastering engineers are tied at the hip, though many don't realize it. Yes, it's true that many mastering engineers are dependent upon a mixer's business to keep the doors open, but that's been changing, since many times there's a shoot-out between mastering engineers to see who gets the gig. Usually, the one who can provide the loudest master wins (there's that loudness war again).

But that's not the real issue, nor is it where mixing and mastering engineers are mostly tied together. In fact, the concept of a separate specialized mixing engineer and a creative mastering engineer both began at nearly the same time during the late '70s, and has continued to grow in prominence from that point until today. Before then, engineers were somewhat interchangeable and came with the studio that you rented. Usually the same engineer that recorded the project would mix it, since the projects were generally short (a few weeks long) to begin with.

As for mastering engineers, they were just part of the process of transferring the audio signal from tape to vinyl disc (and later CD). It wasn't until legends like Bernie Grundman, Doug Sax, and Bob Ludwig began to make mixes sound better and louder than the mixer could, that the mastering engineer came to be what he is today—the last part of the creative process.

EDM is changing all of that, though. Today there's less perceived need or pressure to hire an outsider to mix an EDM track. The writer/programmer gets the sound he wants right from the start of the track, and since the kick and bass are already out in front and have a lot of impact, most feel that there's no reason to hire a specialized mixer for that particular bag of tricks.

The same goes for mastering engineers. Thanks to some great tools from a variety of plug-in companies like Waves, Slate Digital, Universal Audio, and iZotope, to name a few—the same tools that many mastering engineers use—EDM mixers can pretty much make their mixes as loud as needed, so it's not surprising when they ask, "Why do I even need to use a mastering engineer?" (See Figure 16-1.)

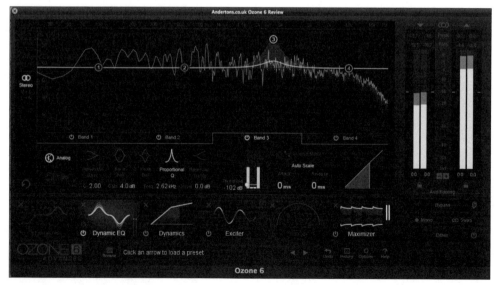

Figure 16-1: iZotope Ozone Mastering Software

Coming from a Different Place

The kind of finesse involved in the creation of EDM is different from what a great many industry veteran producers are used to. In this genre, manipulation of sound is encouraged and celebrated, and distortion is viewed as simply a byproduct of that manipulation. That's the antithesis of most mix and mastering engineers that don't deal in EDM, where in their world, distortion is something to be avoided. In fact, getting impact from the rhythm section without it is almost revered.

As mixing legend Dave Pensado recently expressed, "We've (mixers) been too concerned with sonic quality, and it's hurt mixers when it comes to EDM as a result." It should be noted that Dave is one of the few mixers who mixes a fair amount of EDM, so he can speak with some authority on the subject.

Is this trend going to kill the market for mix and mastering engineers? Probably not. When it comes to music made by recording live instruments and players instead of using prerecorded samples and loops, it takes a great deal of expertise that only comes from experience with that type of recording. Throughout the genre you'll find producer/engineers who create fantastic electronic music, but are hopeless when it comes to either recording or mixing real instruments (especially the drums).

In many ways, though, it's apples and oranges. EDM is an ever-growing musical genre that now dominates the music business. As Aaron Ray (a principal in the management company the Collective) recently revealed, "EDM has decimated rock. It's now an entirely different business."

Not only have recording, mixing, and mastering changed, but basic songwriting as well. Let's look at the creation of a typical dance-oriented pop song to get the idea.

A Look at the New Song Structure

If you look at classic pop or rock songs from a decade ago or more, most relied on only one or two hooks. Usually that consisted of an intro hook that might be repeated in subsequent interludes, choruses, and bridges; and a vocal hook that was part of the melody or lyric that usually came in the chorus. As a matter of fact, back in the Tin Pan Alley and Motown days, the theory was that all you needed was a single killer hook to make a song a hit.

Today it's felt that a new hook or at least a new song peak must happen every seven seconds, which is the average length of time a listener will give a radio station before changing the channel. It's not enough to have a single or even two hooks anymore—you've got to have some sort of a hook in just about every section to keep the attention of today's listeners.

The Modern Pop Formula

The absolute master of the modern pop formula is Max Martin, followed by his protégés Stargate, Dr. Luke, and Ester Dean. The formula was primarily developed by Martin's mentor Denniz PoP in Stockholm during the early '90s, according to author John Seabrook, in his book *The Song Machine*.

According to Seabrook, the formula consists of "ABBA's pop chords and textures, Denniz PoP's song structure and dynamics, '80s arena rock's big choruses, and early '90s American R&B grooves." The sound is intentionally mechanical and automated and virtually free of real musicians, while the songs are frequently written by committee, with the idea that anything less than a hit is discarded.

Many of the current crop of top 40 hits are intentionally very similar just up to the point of plagiarism, with the successful beats frequently used for different songs. The reason? Today's listening audience embraces familiar sounds.

This violates the adage of "art is something that you do for yourself; a craft is something you do for everyone else," since the focus is always on creating a hit instead of just good expressive music. Most songwriters follow their hearts and souls when writing, but not here. It's cold and calculated with an aim of success or nothing.

The Formula to the Extreme

Korean pop, or "K-pop," takes the pop formula to a new extreme, where a step-by-step manual created by former pop star Soo-Man Lee guides composers, producers, and choreographers on everything from what chord progressions and what eye shadow to use, to even what hand gestures work in a particular country.

What's more, most K-pop performers attend a "pop academy" for as long as seven years before debuting as either an artist or part of a group. Getting into the academy doesn't assure success, however, as only about one in ten actually "graduate."

While many might look at the above and think that music has become too manufactured, it should be noted that Motown once had a similar academy back in the '60s for all of its artists, and much of its music ran through a musical director that also employed a formula. We saw something similar on the music side in the '80s and '90s with Stock, Aitken, and Waterman in the U.K. It turns out that what's old is new again, only in a different language.

FIFTEEN TIPS FOR DEVELOPING YOUR OWN SOUND

While the previous sections seems completely contrary to what the traditional songwriter, artist, and producer try to create, it's a by-product of not only the times that we live in, but also the tastes in music as well as the technology. Many successful pop/EDM/hip-hop producers got their start as DJs, and because there's no need to play an instrument particularly well, learn music, or even know how to record with some of the latest tools, they can still create killer tracks that the world loves.

That doesn't mean it's easy, by any means, just that there's a new road into the production world that many are taking. While making beats and the intricacies of producing electronic beat-based music can take up an entire book by itself, here are a few more or less universal tips that can apply to all facets of this type of music.

1. **Analyze the groove and programming of your favorite tracks.** Before you can be unique, it's best to learn what works either on hits or songs you like first. You can change the rules after you've made the tried and true work for you.

2. **Set the perfect tempo.** Be sure to select the right tempo for the style of music that you're creating, since many electronic music genres have specific tempo ranges. For instance, house is between 125 and 128 bpm, dubstep around 140 bpm, and drum & bass at 170 or 180 bpm. Also, consider slight tempo variations around these ranges, as sometimes just a bpm slower or faster can make a huge difference in the feel.

3. **Consider using syncopation.** Having some of the rhythm elements or the bass play on the unaccented parts of the rhythm can be very powerful and can change the song's feel considerably.

4. **Utilize dynamics.** All music works best around tension and

release, meaning loud against soft, complex against simple, fast against slow, or any other set of contrasting qualities.

5. **Get great sounds come first.** No matter how sick your beat is, if your sounds aren't there, the song's not going to get the reaction you want. Get the sounds to work well together before you mix, because you most likely won't be able to fix it there as much as you think.

6. **Focus on the kick.** In these genres of music, if the kick isn't working, then neither will the song. Don't be afraid to mix different sounds to get the sound you want. A typical Skrillex trick is to use a short clicky-sounding kick for the transient attack, one centered around 200 Hz for the body, and another for the release of the sound.

7. **Limit the number of sounds.** Infinite variation is nice, but if you want to develop a signature sound, it helps if at least some of the elements that you use are limited to only three or four sounds. This can be the kick drum, the bass, or a particular effect, but it goes a long way to putting your personal stamp on the sound.

8. **Use velocity and modulation during programming.** Slight variations in velocity and sometimes modulation can change a flat feel into something exciting.

9. **Don't forget about instrumental loops.** All of your loops don't have to be based around just drums and percussion. Many hip-hop producers like Dr. Dre and Timbaland use both synth and ethnic loops as a big part of their sound.

10. **Make loop variations.** A loop is a lot more interesting if it's not the same over and over throughout the song. Make a variation or two that's slightly different to keep the interest high.

11. **A live player can add interest.** If you want to add a touch of realism, just add a single live player to the track. It's surprising how much better a track can feel as a result.

12. **Repeat the hook on a different instrument.** Sometimes just by changing the instrument or sound, the same hook can sound completely different.

13. **Don't be afraid to clear out the mix.** Sometimes just the drums and a lead synth can sound bigger and louder than having dozens of other tracks playing at the same time along with them.

14. **Pay attention to lead sounds.** Most lead sounds use either a saw or square wave as the basic sound, since these tend to cut through

in a mix. Use the other flavors of oscillators to add color to the sound to make it unique.

15. **Everything doesn't have to be exactly on the beat.** Considering pulling back snare, clap, hat or bass tracks a few ticks to change the feel. Many times, this makes the track sound larger as well.

Following these tips will take you a long way to developing your own sound.

CHAPTER 17
PRODUCTION CHECKLISTS

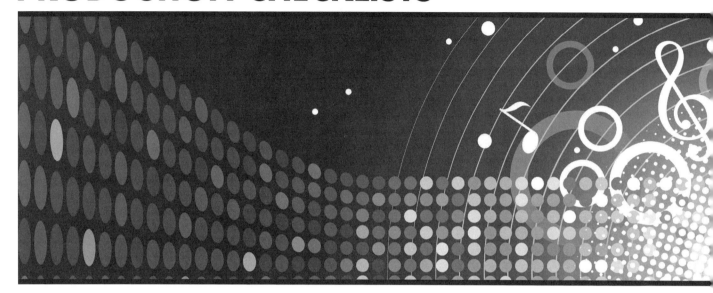

Here are a number of checklists that cover most situations you will encounter during the production process. Remember that each project is different and that the outcome ultimately depends on the players, the instruments, the recording environment, the songs, the arrangements, and the budget. Of course, sometimes things are just out of your control. Also, these are not hard and fast rules, just a starting place. If you try something that's different from what you read below and it works, then it's good thing! Remember—take risks, experiment, take notes on what works for you and what doesn't, be creative, and most of all, have fun!

PRODUCER CHECKLIST
Getting Paid

Before any serious work on the project can begin, there are a series of important questions that the client must answer about your compensation.

1. **Who's paying?** Is it a record label, the artist or band, or an investor?
2. **How are you getting paid?** Will you be paid per song, on spec, by the hour, or with a flat fee for the project?

3. **What's your compensation?** Do you get some money up front (an advance)? Do you get a percentage of sales? Do you get a combination? If so, how many points?

4. **Do you get paid from the sale of the first unit onward?** Or will you be paid after the advance is recouped?

5. **Will you get an advance?** How much is it? Does it come out of the recording budget? Can you get at least half up front?

6. **Will you be paid on something other than music sales?** Since sales are pretty low these days, can you get a piece of merchandise or publishing?

Assembling the Budget

Assembling the budget is a major part of the producer's job, but before that can be determined, the producer must know some information about the project that will determine what it will ultimately cost.

1. **How many songs will be recorded?** The more songs that are recorded, the higher the budget required.

2. **What kind of sound are you looking for?** This will determine the studio, the engineer, the players, and the rentals—all of which will impact the budget.

3. **What kind of studio is the artist comfortable in?** Some artists prefer new, high-tech studios, while others like something old and funky, and others prefer their own production environment. No matter which way, the decision impacts your budget.

4. **Does the budget include my fee?** A budget could shrink noticeably if your fee is included.

5. **Are the manufacturing costs included in the budget?** A budget could shrink noticeably if CD or vinyl manufacturing costs are included.

6. **Are the mastering costs included in the budget?** Once again, a budget could shrink noticeably if the mastering costs are not accounted for in the budget.

7. **On what format** (streaming, CD, vinyl, etc.) **will the final product be released?** The choice may impact your mastering costs.

8. **On what format will you be recording?** This choice will determine if you require any additional rental gear or hired-in expertise.

9. **Are you sure you don't have a budget in mind?** A band, artist,

or investor will usually know what they want to spend, but may be afraid to say it.

PREPRODUCTION
Questions for the Artist or Band

The more you know about what influences an artist or band, the easier it is to help shape the sound that he's trying to achieve.

1. **What are some of your favorite records?** Why?
2. **What are your biggest influences?** Why?
3. **What recordings do you like the sound of?**
4. **What kind of sound are you looking for?**
5. **What is it that you like about the projects I've done?**

Song Analysis

When a song doesn't seem to be working, it's usually because of one or more of these common problems.

1. **Are the sections too long?** Sections of a song that are too long cause the listener to rapidly lose interest unless there's something in the arrangement that tweaks the ear.
2. **Is there a clear distinction between sections?** For instance, can you tell the difference between the verse and the chorus? Once again, listener interest wanes if a song goes too long without something new happening.
3. **Does the song have a bridge?** A bridge adds tension and release, keeping the interest high and enabling the song to build to a peak.
4. **Does the song have a hook or an identifiable riff?** A strong hook or riff develops listener interest.
5. **Does the song have dynamics?** Dynamics (places in the song that are more and less intense and/or loud and soft) develops listener interest.
6. **Does the song have a tight arrangement?** See the Song Arrangements checklist.

Song Arrangements

Just like with the songs themselves, the song's arrangements also tend to have common problem elements.

1. **Have you limited the number of simultaneous elements to a maximum of four?** More than four musical elements happening at the same time causes the listener to become confused and fatigued because they don't know what to focus on.
2. **Does each instrument have its own sonic space?** Instruments that play in the same frequency or register will either bury one another or clash for attention.
3. **Do the guitars sound different?** In order for each guitar to stand out and make the recording sound bigger, they need to be in different registers, use different rhythms, play different lines, or have different sounds.

Rehearsal Guide

Here are a number of tips to help rehearsals be more productive and efficient.

1. Practice in the round.
2. It's the little things that count. (This includes dynamics, turnarounds, builds, and attacks and releases).
3. Stop when there's a train wreck.
4. Work on the most difficult part first.
5. Start with the out chorus.

Preparing for the Session

Save yourself some time and some possible hassle by knowing the answer to the following questions before the downbeat of the first session.

1. Who's the engineer?
2. Is any rental gear required?
3. What's the best time of day to record?
4. Are there any additional musicians required?
5. On which format and at which sampling rate will the project be recorded?
6. What's the song recording order?
7. What studio or studios will you be using?

Selecting a Studio

Ask yourself these questions before selecting a studio for the project.

1. **Does the location work for the artist?** Is it too far or too close for the artist? Is it in an area where the artist will feel safe?
2. **Does the studio have the right vibe?** Does it have a kitchen? Does it have a comfortable lounge? Is it clean? The longer you stay, the more important the vibe will be.
3. **Is the studio staff competent, helpful, and professional?**
4. **Will the deal for the studio fit within my budget?** Is there a way to book the studio during off-times when it's not as busy?
5. **Is the studio size right for the project?** Do you need a larger control room? Do you need iso booths?
6. **Are the acoustics right for the project?** Is the studio too live? (You can often dampen it down.) Is it too dead?
7. **Does the available recording gear meet the needs of the project?** Does the console have enough inputs? Is there enough outboard gear? Are there enough mics? Can you get the sound you need? Are personal monitor mixes available for each player?

PRODUCTION
Basic Tracks

Before the basic tracks even begin, ask yourself the following questions to make sure your players will be happy and the sounds will be great.

1. **Do the drums sound great acoustically in the room?** If they don't, change the heads, rent a new kit, or hire a drum tuner.
2. **Are the drums tuned properly?** Before recording begins, the drums should have new heads put on and have all buzzes and sympathetic vibrations removed.
3. **Do you have a variety of instruments available?** The greater variety of instruments you have, the better the arrangement elements will fit together and the more interesting the recording will sound.
4. **Are all the instruments in tip-top condition?** Is the intonation set correctly? Is the instrument clean of any buzzes, hums, and intermittents?
5. **Are all of the players happy with their headphone mixes?** Can you give each musician his or her own mix? Is a personal headphone mixer available for each player?
6. **Does the click have the right sound?** Does it cut through the mix? Is it musical enough that the drummer can play along? Is it so "musical" that the drummer can't groove to it?

7. **Does the click groove?** Does it work better as quarter notes or as eighth notes? Is there a different sound for the downbeat?
8. **Is the click bleeding into the microphones?** Can the drummer use isolating headphones? Can you roll the high end off so that it doesn't leak as much?
9. **Do you have the studio talkback mic on?** Can you hear the musicians in the studio at all times between takes?
10. **Is the control room talkback mic always on?** Can the musicians hear you at all times in between takes?

Music Troubleshooting

Here are a number of questions to ask if the song just doesn't sound as good as you think it can.

1. **Do all the players in the band know their parts inside out?** Is there a part that someone is unsure of?
2. **Are all the players performing their parts the same way every time?** (This assumes that you aren't recording some form of jazz or blues in which you want a different performance for each take.) Any variation can lead to a section not gelling or not being tight.
3. **Is the band playing dynamically?** Does the music breathe volume-wise? Does the verse have less intensity than the chorus or the bridge?
4. **Does the band lose its drive when playing with less intensity?** Do the band members forget about attacks and releases when they play more quietly?
5. **Is everyone playing the song and section starts and stops the same way?** If not, ask every player, "How are you playing it?"
6. **Does the band sound tight?** Are the attacks and releases of phrases being played the same way by everyone? Are the builds, turnarounds, and accents being played the same way by everyone? If not, ask every player, "How are you playing it?"
7. **Is the band in tune?** If not, make sure that everyone uses the same tuner and tunes the same way.
8. **Does the song have a groove?** Is the rhythm section playing in the pocket? Is the drummer or the bass player wavering slightly in tempo?

9. **Is the tempo right for the song?** Try playing the song a beat per minute or two faster or slower and see if that feels better.

10. **Are all vocals in the best range for the singers?** Does the vocalist have trouble hitting all the notes? Does he or she sound comfortable singing, and is the sound right for the song?

Overdubs

It's easy to spend too much time and money recording overdubs, and these questions will not only prevent that from happening, but help make sure you get the best sounds as well.

1. **Do you have a list of overdub priorities?** Do you know which overdubs absolutely must get done and which ones are less important? A list will keep you on track budget-wise and time-wise.

2. **Can you record in the control room?** Most players prefer to record in the control room because they like to hear what you're hearing and they like the immediacy of the communication.

3. **Are there too many people in the control room or studio?** The fewer the people, the fewer the distractions. It's best to keep all friends, associates, and hangers-on out of the studio when you're working to keep the distractions to a minimum.

4. **Did you move the vocal or the instrument into the big part of the studio?** All instruments sound best when there's space for the sound to develop, so move the vocal or the instrument into the big part of the studio for overdubs (after you've done any basic track fixes). You can cut down on any unwanted reflections from the room by placing baffles around the mic and player.

5. **When doubling, are you trying to do something a little different on each track?** Using a different mic, mic preamp, room, singer, or distance from the mic will all help to make the sound get bigger.

6. **When doubling or adding more guitars, do you have a variety of instruments and amplifiers available?** Two guitars (a Les Paul and a Strat, for instance) and two amplifiers (a Fender and a Marshall is the classic combination) combined with different pickup choices will allow a multitude of guitar tracks to live in the mix together more effectively.

7. **Are you making it sound better, not just different?** Changes aren't always for the better. Is there a big difference between what

you just recorded and the original part? Does the new part make everyone in the studio go crazy in a good way?

8. **Would it be better to try recording the part tomorrow?** You'd be surprised how much more you can accomplish when you're fresh.

9. **Do you have the studio talkback mic on?** Can you hear the musicians in the studio at all times between takes? If they're talking to you but you can't hear them, they'll feel isolated.

10. **Do you always have the control room talkback mic on?** Can the musicians hear you at all times in between takes? Periods of silence can be a mood-killer.

11. **Does a musician want to play his or her part again?** If a player feels strongly about playing it over, he probably can do it better. Be sure to keep the last recorded part before recording again.

Vocal Recordings

Getting a great vocal take comes from having a comfortable vocalist. Here are a number of things to check to ensure a great performance.

1. **Would a handheld mic work better?** Some singers aren't comfortable unless they feel as though they're on stage. Give him or her an SM58 and don't worry about the sound. A great performance beats a great sound any day.

2. **Is the headphone mix at the correct level?** If the track is too loud, the vocalist may sing sharp or too hard. If the track is too soft, the singer may not sing aggressively enough.

3. **Is the room ambience conducive to evoking a good vocal?** Are the lights too bright? Does the singer feel claustrophobic?

4. **Is the sound of the headphones conducive to producing a good vocal?** A touch of reverb or delay in the headphones can help the singer feel more comfortable with the headphone mix.

5. **Did you explain to the vocalist exactly what you need or where he or she was wrong?** If the take wasn't good for whatever reason, explain what was wrong in a kind and gentle way. Something like "That was really good, but I think you can do it even better. The pitch was a little sharp."

6. **Does the singer have the three Ps: pitch, pocket, and passion?** A great vocal needs all three.

7. **Do you have the studio talkback mic on?** Can you hear the musicians in the studio at all times between takes?

8. **Do you have the control room talkback mic always on?** Can the musicians hear you at all times in between takes? Periods of silence can be a mood killer.

Mixing

If you're not sure if your mix is finished, ask yourself the following questions. You must have a positive answer for each one.

1. **Does your mix have contrast?** Does it build as the song goes along? Are different instruments, sounds, or lines added in different sections?
2. **Does your mix have a focal point?** Is the mix built around the instrument or vocal that's the most important?
3. **Does your mix sound noisy?** Have you gotten rid of any count-offs, guitar-amp noises, bad edits, and breaths that stand out?
4. **Does your mix lack clarity or punch?** Can you distinguish every instrument? Does the rhythm section sound great by itself?
5. **Does your mix sound distant?** Try using less reverb and fewer effects.
6. **Can you hear every lyric?** Every word must be heard.
7. **Can you hear every note being played?** Automate to hear every note.
8. **Are the sounds dull or uninteresting?** Are you using generic synth patches or predictable guitar or keyboard sounds?
9. **Does the song groove?** Does it feel as good as your favorite song? Is the instrument that supplies the groove loud enough?
10. **What's the direction of the song?** Should it be close and intimate, or big and loud?
11. **Are you compressing too much?** Does the mix feel squashed? Is it fatiguing to listen to? Is all the life gone?
12. **Are you EQing too much?** Is the mix too bright or too big?
13. **Are your fades too tight?** Do the beginnings or endings of the songs sound clipped?
14. **Did you do alternate mixes?** Did you do at least an instrumental-only mix (TV mix)?
15. **Did you document the keeper mixes?** Are all files properly named? Are you sure which file is the master?

Mastering

Whether you're mastering the mix yourself or using a professional, these five points will ensure not only a better master, but a faster and more efficient mastering session.

1. **Are you using the highest-resolution mix?** The higher the resolution, the better the final product will sound.
2. **Did you bring all the documentation, sequencing, and shipping instructions?**
3. **If mastering the mix yourself, are you comparing your mastering to other mixes that you like?** Keep referring back to CDs that you like to make sure you're not drifting away instead of getting closer.
4. **If mastering the mix yourself, do all the songs have the same relative level?** Drop into each of them in your DAW for a couple of seconds to make sure they're all equally as loud.
5. **If mastering the mix yourself, did you fix any fades and edit out all count-offs?** If a fade sounds unnatural, make it sound smooth. If a fade sounds chopped, make it sound smooth.

PART 2

INTERVIEWS

MARK BRIGHT

Enjoying a hit record with his very first production of Blackhawk in 1994, Mark Bright has gone on to become one of the architects of the modern contemporary country sound. With production credits on hugely successful albums by superstar acts Rascal Flatts, Carrie Underwood, and Reba McEntire, Mark continues to blend cutting-edge production techniques with traditional country values and his love of a great song into a sound loved by all music fans.

Did you become a producer as a result of writing songs?
I've always written songs, but as I was songwriting I learned how to become a recording engineer in Texas. I moved here (Nashville) in 1981 with engineering skills, where I got work at House of David (a historic studio on Nashville's Music Row) as an assistant while attending classes at Belmont College (now Belmont University). I spent three years at Belmont while I honed my engineering skills and continued to write songs.

Right next door to where I was working was a publishing company called Screen Gems/Colgems Music, where I eventually got a job in the tape room. I was really interested in working there because it put me closer to great songwriters and I felt that if I ever was going to be a great producer, I had to get close to great songs.

Was being a producer your aspiration from the beginning?

Yeah, from the very beginning. When my sister brought home Beatles records I was completely smitten, and when I started seeing George Martin's name on them I thought, "Wow, I want to be George Martin someday." So from that point on I watched for other producers' names on records, like Phil Ramone, David Foster, and Mutt Lange, and I just dreamed of being that guy every night.

Do you start making a name for yourself as an engineer or jump right into production?

The deal I got from Screen Gems (which was later bought by EMI) was that they'd give me the use of the studio if I engineered and produced their publishing demos. Every day I continued to work with songwriters, hone my skills, and develop a sound.

In the early '90s I was introduced to Henry Paul, who was the former lead singer of the Outlaws. Henry had come to town to make a record with (producer/industry executive) Tim DuBois, who had just opened Arista Records Nashville. Tim didn't necessarily see Henry as a solo country artist and set him up with a couple of songwriters named Dave Robbins and Vance Stevenson (who eventually became the group Blackhawk) and gave them a development deal. They recorded some songs with another producer that weren't very good, so I asked them if I could work with them on my own time in the EMI publishing studio. After several months, we figured out an incredible vocal sound for Henry and recorded five songs, three of them not even published by EMI at that point.

When Tim heard the songs, he loved them and called me in to see him. He said, "Mister, I don't know what you did, but this stuff sounds like a hit so I'm going to give you a shot. Whatever you do, don't screw this up!" [Laughs.] He put his name on the record as a producer to give me some credibility and was available when needed, but he gave me all the points and the whole deal. So it was Tim Du-Bois that gave me that first shot when nobody else in town would. And that's the critical thing—there always has to be someone who's willing to give you the shot, and Tim did. And our first single ("Goodbye Says It All") was a hit.

Do you consider him your mentor?
Absolutely, I consider Tim to be the biggest catalyst and mentor in my career.

Have you continued to engineer since then?
No, but I certainly can. I have a Pro Tools rig and a few pieces of outboard gear at home, but that's mostly for my own demos while I'm writing. I have an engineer that I've had a long-term relationship with named Derek Bason, and we work together on everything.

What are the budgets like that you're working with these days as compared to five years ago?
Honestly, with the big stars, budgets are not something that we worry about. Yes, there is a budget, but it's more important that we make a great record. I do occasionally work with a new artist that I really believe in, and in those cases the budget does very much come into play.

When that happens, I don't even bill for most of what I do. I don't take an advance but get more points on the back end instead. I've worked on a bluegrass record with a five-thousand dollar budget at the same time I was working on a Carrie Underwood record. It doesn't matter to me because it's about the music.

For me it's never been about money, ever. It's always been about passion for music. That's always been the thing that's driven me. I never thought I'd make a nickel in this business, so if you go in with that point of view, any money that comes is just icing on the cake.

The budgets are smaller in general and so are royalty streams because sales are way down. How does that affect how you look at a project, taking into account what you just said? I mean, at some point you've got to think, "I'm working really hard here for what amounts to be a lot less money."

That's an interesting conversation that I have with some of my other producer friends who live and die by how much they make because they're used to making a whole lot of money and their lifestyle reflects that. Yes, I have a nice lifestyle too, but I'm also involved in many other aspects of the music industry.

For most of my adult life, I've had a very successful publishing company joint venture, so I've always stayed close to the music. That's very important—to stay close to the music and the songwriter. It's a primal need for me to have access to the hit song. Honestly, that's always brought in money, so I've never had to worry about the royalty stream from the records I've produced.

One artist might sell a few million and another might not sell anything, but it all seems to even out for me. I'm involved in so many different areas that if one part isn't making money then hopefully another somewhere is. In the end, I'm just working on stuff that I love and as long as I'm honest about that with myself, it all seems to work out. I have been truly blessed to make a living in a business that I love.

Publishing is still the one facet of the music business that's doing well.

Publishing has always been a blue-chip business. It's not sexy but it's always been strong.

What's your preproduction like?

It's very artist- and budget-dependent. For instance, if I'm working with someone like the Isaacs, who are a southern gospel group, we go into a rehearsal room and we'll rehearse the music over and over and over again. Since there's very little money to work with, it becomes very important to know what you're going to do once you get on the clock.

With an artist like Carrie Underwood, preproduction becomes very song-dependent. If we're tracking with a live band, we don't do any preproduction. We get the band together and they've never heard the song before. While most of the band is listening to it in the control room, I take Carrie and the piano player into the keyboard booth and spend anywhere from 20 to 45 minutes finding the correct key for her. After that, I'll just spit out a bunch of ideas to the band as they're listening, since I've listened to the song many times and have ideas in my head that I have worked out in my home studio.

I have two separate crews that play on Carrie Underwood records and both of them know full well what her sound is and what she likes. Let me emphasize, we're not making my records—we're making Carrie records. Once they get out to their respective positions in the studio, they'll play through the song without Carrie on the mic and get an arrangement that is fairly tight. But let me tell you something—once Carrie gets out there on that mic, everything changes. She starts singing and the level of excitement and musicianship goes through the roof. It happens every single time. When a great singer gets on mic, it inspires everybody.

The same thing happens with Reba. It's just that intangible thing that occurs when a truly gifted singer gets on that mic.

Do you ever keep the tracking vocals?

Yes. I'm not at liberty to say which tracks we've kept, but for both Reba and Carrie we've kept both portions of the tracking vocal and in Carrie's case, even all of the tracking vocal. But that's not what the story is about. The story is about how great that artist is overall. Both of them exhibit the kind of behavior where they sound like a record when they're singing their tracking vocal. It's really frightening how great that is. You feel like you should be paying someone money to be sitting in there listening to them.

The sessions must go quickly then.

No, that's not true at all. I think with both of them, because they can do what they can do, you want to get it to where you're doing very little to no tuning of the vocal at all. In order to accomplish that, you sometimes need many, many passes.

When we do vocal day, we're talking about upwards of 20 to 23 passes per song, so it takes a long time to put a song like that together. What you get with that many passes is the perfect pass.

Twenty-three passes? That makes for a long comping date then.

Yes it is, but that's why these records are expensive. That being said, we're spending our money on actual recording instead frivolous things like eating and traveling.

How long does it take to comp a vocal then?

It takes us anywhere between 8 and 12 hours.

What's your process? Is it something like mixing where you let the engineer start it and you come in towards the end and tweak it?

Yes. We've developed a system that's finely tuned after this many years. When we're tracking vocals, I mark my favorite pass or parts of passes or lines on my numbered comp sheet and Derek marks his and we compare them. The ones that we agree on are obviously the ones that we comp out first. Then we go to the ones that I like, but if they don't work then we do the B option. I don't have to sit in there the whole time because Derek knows what I'm looking for during that process, and because of that, there may even be a C option that he'll find and drop in for me to listen to. Sometimes I'll go, "Wow, that's incredible. I don't even want to hear what the other options are," and sometimes they don't work.

The other thing with a lot of great singers is that I let them know when the last pass is coming, and I'll ask them to do whatever they want on it. Whatever comes into their mind and out of their mouth, just do it. A lot of time, assuming that the vocalist is not too tired, you'll get some incredible stuff out of that pass.

Do you have any particular techniques of getting a great performance from a vocalist?

That's the whole thing for me, I don't want to work with singers that are marginal. I come from the David Foster school in that I want to work with really excellent singers and all I want to do is coax the best performance that I can out of the them without telling him or her how to sing the song. That would include making sure that the singer is comfortable with the headphone mix, that they're comfortable in the room, and that they feel secure and happy. Just put them in the best environment you can put them in and let them go. If they're swallowing a word, I might say, "At line 25 you're swallowing that word a little bit, but you're sounding great!", and just be honest about it.

But telling them to "sing this line this way because it's my way," I don't believe in because it's their record.

How long does it take you to track a record?

Generally in Nashville it works a little differently than it does in New York or Los Angeles. We're a union shop here in Nashville so we work in three-hour sessions that start at 10 a.m., 2 p.m., or 6 p.m.. Typically we'll do one song per three-hour session, but that's just the basic track. Over the course of the next four to five months we'll be adding other instruments and the vocals to it.

How large is the band that you use for tracking?

Depends on the artist. Sometimes it's a very stripped-down band that's only drums, bass, electric guitar, and piano. Sometimes it's drums, bass, acoustic guitar, two electric guitars, steel guitar, and violin. Basically what I'm doing is casting it not only per artist but per song.

How long do your overdub sessions last then, excluding vocals? Is it in the same three-hour increments?

No, you can book a special where it's only an hour and a half, or it could be a lot longer. Like in the case of "Jesus, Take the Wheel"

(Carrie's first single, which was a 14-week #1 record), we had a string player come in and play all the orchestral parts from first violin to second violin all the way down to double bass and it took about nine and a half hours.

An hour and a half is pretty fast by L.A. standards.
Yeah, but we're more structured. We have templates already set up here. If we're going to record Jonathan's violin, we don't have to rent any gear. I work in one studio only (Starstruck) and I have the overdub room booked 24 hours a day. When you're staying in that one room, you know how every nook and cranny works and you know just how it sounds, and we have templates set up for every player and every instrument. If it's this fiddle player, then it's this particular signal path. If it's someone else, then we're going to use this other signal path. Maybe we'll use a plug-in to make it sound different, but we're not starting from scratch with these guys every time, so it's much more efficient.

Whenever I record in L.A., it's à la carte and I have to rent everything I want to use because they're not going to have the compressor or preamp or mic that I want.

I like the mindset of Nashville where you're not afraid to track with eight or nine players. That's pretty taboo here (L.A.).
It's unheard of, but I will say this—we're not afraid to do track builds, particularly with Carrie Underwood. We might start with programming and stay in the virtual world for several weeks, and once I get comfortable with where the track is virtually, I'll bring in a drummer to play on top of it. When I get comfortable with that I'll bring in a guitar player, just like you'd do it out there.

What are you looking for in a song?
It's the perfect marriage of the perfect melody married to a great lyric. Number one, it's got to be suitable for the artist. It's got to have a story for the artist to tell or an emotion that the particular artist can actually convey.

How much time do you spend looking for songs?
Just hours and hours. I have my own A&R person, Kirsten Wines, and all she does is spend her days looking for songs. I also have songwriters who are my go-to people that will call me up whenever they've got

a hot song. I'm always going to stop what I'm doing for some of those big-hitter songwriters.

How long do your mixes generally take?
Generally two days minimum up to five days max. The first one is usually harder than the rest because that's setting up the whole template for the sonic character of the album. In country, you have a single sonic imprint for the whole album.

We don't try to make one song sound too different from the next song because culturally that's not how it works here. We're going to go for a texture that runs through the whole album. Maybe in the next album it'll be texturally way different than the album before, but we won't alter that texture drastically within an album.

So once you set up your sounds, you're keeping it that way for each song then?
Yeah, you'll change reverb decay rates and stuff like that, but you won't all of a sudden go from one sonic palette to another from song to song. There are some artists that do that, but not so much with the bigger artists. Our fans want to hear consistency and they want to hear "great."

It's really crazy. What's considered cliché in country is considered ridiculously cliché in pop, and what is considered cliché in pop is considered ridiculously cliché in country. I have plenty of country records that cross over into the Hot 100, but the cultural subtleties are incredibly subtle and they're not so subtle at the same time.

That being said, Carrie does not like remixes for different formats. Reba doesn't mind, and most of the artists I've worked with over the years don't mind. Carrie does not do different mixes because artistically that's just not where she's at, so if it's going to cross, it's going to cross on its own merit. We don't do a Hot AC mix, we don't do an Urban mix, and we don't do a pop mix. We don't do any of that kind of thing.

How many alternative mixes do you do?
We do different versions for mastering, but not for public consumption. We do TV mixes and all the same versions that everyone else does, but that's not for the public to hear.

Do you have a particular mastering engineer that you go to, or doesn't it matter to you?

It does matter to me but it depends on the sound we're going for. Country mastering guys make it sound a certain way because country radio programmers set their broadcast compressors a certain way, which is different from what Hot AC guys do and what pop guys do.

You have to take that into consideration because you wouldn't want to get a mastering guy who does primarily Hot AC if that's not where you're going to be played. I'd say a go-to guy for me is Hank Williams (at MasterMix) here in town. If we have a lot of contemporary stuff, I like Gateway, and we use those guys quite a bit.

Do you attend the mastering session?
It depends. Gateway, definitely not (it's located in Portland, Maine), but we send WAV files back and forth and we tweak things that way. It works just as well and in fact, I prefer hearing the songs on my own speakers because I know them like the back of my hand.

What's the best piece of advice you've ever received?
A long time ago someone told me to thrive on rejection, and I've always taken that to heart. I think it's particularly relevant now. If someone tells you "no," you figure out another way to get it done.

JOE CHICCARELLI

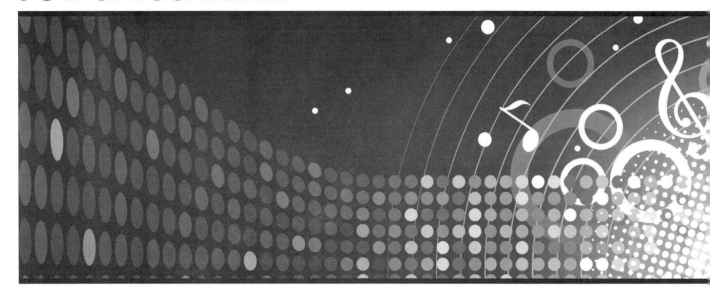

Joe Chiccarelli is a ten-time Grammy winner who's known not only for his production prowess, but his engineering and mixing skills as well. Joe has a ton of great credits including Spoon, My Morning Jacket, Morrissey, the White Stripes (he won a Grammy with them for *Icky Thump*), the Killers, the Shins, the Strokes, and many more.

It seems like you're pretty prolific by the looks of your credit list.
It's probably three albums production-wise and a couple of mixes per year, which is pretty typical. Part of it is that projects roll over from year to year. It seems like every album takes longer to do now and takes longer to be released, so something that you do in 2013 won't show up until 2015.

How hands-on are you when you're producing in terms of working with the band?
To me, engineering is one-tenth of the total picture. It doesn't mean that much because anyone can make a record now since the bar of quality has been lowered so much, so to me the engineering is the lowest part of the art form.

The most important thing is getting in there working with the band on songs, arrangements, concept, lyrics—all that stuff. It's months of work before I ever get in the studio. It means at least two weeks of eight-hour rehearsal days for preproduction working on song arrangements, rhythm section arrangements—all of it.

We all geek out and have our favorite pieces of gear, but that's so insignificant to getting the musical part of it right and getting the artist to stand out from the pack of other artists. There's so much music out there but so much of it isn't ready to be seen on a global scale. Getting people to weed through it and find stuff is very difficult, so we have to come up with a song, a character, a sound, or a melody that really vibrates with people, and that's hard.

I'm involved with every note of a project, even when I collaborate as well. For instance, on a project I'm collaborating on now, I'll work with the band in the morning, then they send me rough mixes at night and I'll make comments on them. I spent about a week by myself working on the arrangements, then about a week on the tracking, then I handed the overdubs off to my coproducer. I'm still involved with every note of it, I'm just not physically in the room for two or three weeks of the record. Even when I'm sharing the duty I'm still very active.

Do you engineer the tracking yourself or get another engineer for that?
It depends on what's best for the album. Usually I'm doing it myself, but that's pretty much dictated by budget. The budgets are cut to about a quarter to a tenth of what they once were, so it demands that I assume two roles.

There are times when I'll feel that I'm not the best engineer or mixer for the project, so then I'll bring in someone else. If I do three projects a year, I find that on one of those there's someone sharing some of the duties with me.

I always found that it was difficult to be the tracking engineer and the producer at the same time.
Yeah, it's definitely hard and that's why I insist on the preproduction before going into the studio. If I can sort of sign off on all the arrangements, then I can concentrate more on getting sounds and getting performances, as opposed to worrying about the bass line in the chorus. We'll have worked that out in preproduction.

Is there a mentor that you feel you got a lot of your chops from?
There were a lot of people over the years for a lot of things. I started at Cherokee studios when I was 20 years old and the Robb brothers [the owners of Cherokee] were very good to me. David Anderle [former A&R exec at A&M Records] was the first one that ever gave me a production project, and that was Oingo Boingo. I learned a lot from David, especially how to deal with artists. I worked with Jimmy Iovine for long time and I learned a lot from him.

I was pretty much a pop/rock kind of kid when I started, but I worked with Roy Thomas Baker on a number of albums and he taught me how to push the limits. Up to that point, I had learned that there was only one way to make records and it was a somewhat conservative approach. I learned from Roy that records could be a lot more dynamic and cinematic and abstract. He really opened up my eyes. He understood how things had to be bigger than life. They had to jump through the speakers and the performances had to rip your heart out. I don't think I've looked at making records the same way since my time with Roy.

There are a zillion ways to make a record, but it's even more important these days to do something impressive and unusual, yet keep in mind the specific vision of the artist. That, to me, is the first goal and first part of the job—to help them achieve that while along the way hiding their weaknesses and enhancing their strengths. The more I bond with an artist and understand and agree with what they're trying to achieve, the better the results are.

I always come at an album with a very specific vision in mind. I even can hear the finished product in my head before I start it. I hope that my picture is in sync with the artist's picture, and the more that it is, the better the record turns out. Hopefully it's commercially successful, or at least artistically successful, but I want the artist to walk away saying, "This is the album that I had in my head that I was trying get out and Joe really helped me achieve that."

You mentioned about how you're trying to find something that stands out in a production. Do you have a process to do that?
I think it's something you hear in a song or the lyrics or their voice or approach. For instance, I'm attracted to artists that push boundaries or blur genres and combine different styles of music, so that might be something about an artist that I might really enhance.

If the artist had a love for classical music, for instance, I might ask them to write a classical-oriented piece in the middle of a song. I like albums that take a left turn or surprise you or catch you off guard. Albums take you on journeys and bands take you on journeys. If you think you have them figured out, you find out you don't when they suddenly incorporate something that you didn't hear on the first three songs of the album.

As a result, I always try to push artists to take some chances. I think it's important that they grow. As a music fan, I always hate it when an artist does the same thing over and over again. Even if they fail, it opens up doors creatively.

I agree with you, but isn't that at odds with record label thinking?
I don't know, maybe not so much with label thinking, but more at odds with the way the marketplace is right now. Everything sounds the same with the same pop formula, and that's kind of a sad thing.

Producing means managing the record company desires and management expectations along with the band's specific ones. Sometimes you're stuck in the middle, but sometimes everyone's on the same page.

There are still some A&R guys out there that encourage artists to take chances, believe it or not. Just as you watch the artist's back, a great A&R guy can watch the back of the producer as well and see the flaw in the song that you totally miss. Unfortunately everyone has a boss that they have to answer to and the major labels have to have hits.

At indie labels it's a different situation. The good thing about an indie is that they want to make sure that they have their core audience covered and branch out from there, so in that way they're looking out for the artist's best interest. They want them to reach their people and get them psyched first, then broaden the base.

What I've noticed is that most people running indie labels are fans themselves, almost like it used to be way back in the early days of the record business. They signed artists they loved and it made a difference.
Yep, but back then those execs were able to give an artist two or three albums to grow and try different things to help develop a career. There's not a lot of artist development these days, even at the indie-label level. You get your $25,000 to make a record and that's it. They kind of hope that you'll build a fan base from that.

Is that the typical budget that you find these days?
That's typical with most indies. There's a next level up with indies that
are associated with major labels and those budgets are two or three
times that. The budget for a baby artist on a major label is not much
beyond that.

*How do you reconcile a small budget like that? It has to impinge
upon how much time you're able to spend on the project and also
on how much money you can make.*
Yes, on all fronts. I find that I have to spend more time on the preproduction part of it, and usually that means working in the band's basement or rehearsal room because it's inexpensive. I make sure that the
band is really ready to record and that all the song arrangements are in
good shape so the tracking process becomes simpler and cheaper.

When it comes to overdubs, they just take what they take. Typically it's three or four weeks of a record, although sometimes it might go
to two months, while mixing takes ten days to two weeks,. Everyone's
got home studios or access to friends' studios these days, so you're not
using major studios all the time. I'm fortunate in that I'm camped out
at Sunset Sound and can use it for tracking or mixing, but I'm always
moving to a smaller room for overdubs because the smaller budgets
can't handle the cost of a big room.

If I know that the artist needs some extra time to experiment,
then I have to budget for that and maybe go to an even smaller studio
where we can spend a couple of extra weeks working.

Do you have a secret for keeping everyone happy in the studio?
It varies with every project. One of the fun things about being a
producer is that every artist is different and has different needs, so it's
more a matter of scoping out the artist and finding out what the artist
requires. For some you have to be their cheerleader, others you have
to sit them down and tell them the truth about stuff, and others are in
between. It changes from project to project.

I always spend some time with the artist before going to the studio.
It might mean a few dinners together, or hanging out listening to music, and then a couple weeks of preproduction, so by the time you get
into the deep end of the pool you kind of see what they're all about.
They become your family for months, and then you might not see
them for years afterwards until you make another album with them.

With the My Morning Jacket guys, we just had the best time together in New York and Nashville, and then I didn't bump into them until a couple of years later on the road.

Do you have any techniques for getting the best performance out of musicians or vocalists?
I try to stay on the positive side of things, always encouraging them and putting them in a safe environment where they can try things and go beyond what they're used to. It's important to really give people the freedom to experiment if that's what they need to do. Even if you only use a tenth of it, they'll feel really great about the record.

What's the thing you find the toughest to do?
Sometimes the lead vocal is tough. You put it all together and think, "We got it," and then you sit back and listen to it and go, "Hmmm. Is it really right for the song?" Maybe it's not big enough or too big, or not emotional enough, or not connecting.

It's tough to go back to someone and say, "I know that you worked your ass off getting this vocal, and I was really excited about it then, but I'm not sure it's there yet. You have to try it one more time." It takes a lot of energy for a singer to get up, especially if they're personal songs that may have a lot of pain in them, and it's hard to put yourself back in that moment sometimes.

What do you do with a player that loves his performance, but you don't feel the same way about it?
It's hard to go back to somebody who loves their performance and tell them that it's really not working. Usually if you've developed some level of trust, at the very least you can ask, "Give it one more shot." I've found that maybe they might not do the whole thing better, but maybe they'll improve a few parts of the song, and that's enough so it improves the whole picture. That seems to work really well.

How much do you do in the box these days?
A lot, even mixing in the box sometimes. I'm not a fan of it and I don't feel that I make the best-sounding records that way, though. I still love the big analog studios. I find that the process and the end result are a lot more satisfying and I don't get that from an in-the-box mix. That analog magic just isn't there.

When you mix in the box, where are you doing it?
Sometimes at Sunset, sometimes with other engineers. Sometimes I'll use a hybrid system of some in the box and some analog summing. Sometimes I'll do it all in the box and take it back through an analog chain to get the tone I feel I'm missing. I find that I can never get the low end and the size and the warmth that I want from being just in the box.

Even when I mix on an analog console like at Sunset, it still becomes somewhat of a summing box, meaning that I may have a hundred tracks of music, but it's broken out to 24 or 32 faders.

I remember running into you a lot in various studios in the past and you always had an RTA (real time analyzer) hanging across the mix buss. Do you still use it?
Oh yeah, all the time, just to get my low end right. Things like sibilant S's show up on it, and I kind of know where that fine line of what I can get away with and what I can't. When there's a lot of electronic tracks in a mix with a lot of subsonic information, it helps to know what's messy and over the top, so I found that to be a really helpful tool for mixing.

Are you mostly looking at the low end?
Yeah, mostly between 50 and 100 Hz. I know the curves of records that I like the sound of, so there's a certain curve that I aim for. What's interesting is that curve has changed over the years. Pop records are brighter and more aggressive now. What I prefer as an overall tone might tend to be a little dark for a lot of pop records.

I like to push the bottom as much as I can. I think that you can never have enough low end on a record. I've never heard of anyone complaining about a record that has too much bottom end. *[Laughs.]*

Are you trying to make a really loud record or does it matter to you?
I could care less. To me it's what's right for the song. Sometimes a loud mix is important for a song, like a heavy band with loud guitars where the midrange has to be nasty and in your face.

I'm not competing with anything though, especially now that everything gets so processed after the fact, because it only hurts you to be the loudest mix in the game. All that processing stuff is going to knock your mix down and make it sound smaller, just like what happens on the radio. I don't see loudness being the big thing that it was a few years ago.

When I deliver a mix, of course I give everyone a bumped up version because they're listening on their laptops and everything else, so it has to be loud, but I leave the rest of the battle up to the mastering engineer, the artist, and the record label.

What's the best business advice you ever received or learned?
Number one, you have to be doing this because you love it and you want to be in it for a long time.

Also, being honest with people goes a long way. Managers and A&R people keep coming back because they trust that you'll tell them the truth as you see it. I'd rather people know where I'm at instead of tap dancing around and being dishonest about something. Building relationships is about the best thing you can do.

I find my career has gone through five-year cycles. You have some hits and then you work nonstop for five years, and then you don't have a hit for a year and you're back to the basement trying to get gigs. You have another hit and it builds back up again. Maybe the style of music changes and the music that you like to make no longer commands the biggest bucks, but you have to weather that. Times change and there are cycles of music, so you have to learn to ride those waves.

RICHARD FELDMAN

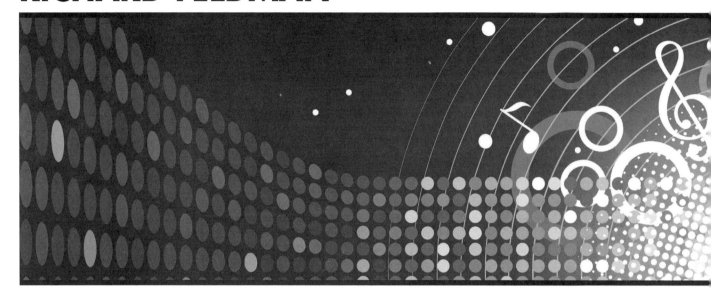

Although featured in my *Music 4.0* book for his chops as a music publisher with his Artist First Music, as well as being the former president of the American Independent Music Publishers association, Richard Feldman has an equally rich history in reggae music production. With credits of amazing reggae music stars like Andrew Tosh, Joe Higgs, Junior Reid, the Congos, I Threes, and the Wailing Souls, he also won a Grammy award for his 2005 production of the legendary Toots and the Maytals' *True Love*. While his non-Jamaican credits are formidable, producing artists like Keith Richards, Ben Harper, Willie Nelson, No Doubt, Eric Clapton, Bonnie Raitt, and many more, it's the reggae connection that truly makes Richard unique.

How did a kid from Oklahoma like you get into Jamaican music?
In 1970 I went to Jamaica on vacation and fell in love with reggae music because there's some essence of Jamaican music that captures the nitty and gritty of all kinds of soul music, which I was already into. My interest was probably ahead of a lot of people, because reggae really wasn't that popular at the time. There were a few Jamaican singles out at that time like "My Boy Lollipop" (a 1962 pop hit by Millie

Small) and "The Israelites" (a 1968 hit by Desmond Decker), which I didn't even know were Jamaican. It was the rhythm and heavy bottom end that I heard in the clubs and at outdoor sound systems that really knocked me out.

I came back to Tulsa with a lot of records, and in 1973 started a band called "Guava." The band included some members of Eric Clapton's band at the time (when they weren't on the road) and we actually started playing our hybrid version of reggae music in Tulsa, so I slowly learned how to play it. In fact, Family Man (Bob Marley's bass player) stayed at my house when they came through Tulsa, and he and I recorded two records on my little four-track recorder. Working with a guy like that who really knows it taught me a lot, because I was learning from a master.

Then in 1978 I went down to Jamaica to play on Inner Circle's record as a guitar player and I actually got fired. They really wanted a rock player but I naively thought that they were hiring me because I could do all the picking guitar stuff that they did. In hindsight, I was pretty stupid because there were hundreds of guys in Jamaica that could do that, so why did they need me to play it?

I remember as I was overdubbing on their new album, they kept asking me to "model it," and I just couldn't make out exactly what they meant. When the session was over I asked them, "What were you trying to tell me?" and they said "model it" meant to swagger like a model down a runway, or blast your licks out. It turned out to be a good experience and a good education, and I made some connections, but it really wasn't until the '80s that I did production.

How did that happen?

Lee Jaffee, who I had met in Tulsa with Bob Marley and who had brought me to Jamaica to record with Inner Circle, hooked me up with the Wailing Souls. I did an album with them which won a Grammy nomination and led to more work. He also referred me to a record label that wanted to do a potpourri of reggae artists. I produced a wide variety of artists for them, and some things like volumes one and two of reggae versions of Grateful Dead songs.

In the spirit of Bob Marley, reggae had open arms to everyone who loved it, although that began to change when dancehall (a more sparse and hardcore genre of reggae) came around. There's a tradition of producers that weren't Jamaican that goes all the way back to Chris

Blackwell (who released many of the early reggae hits on his Island Records label). In fact, some of the famous early Jamaican producers like Leslie Kong were Asian, so you don't have be of that race to produce that music.

There weren't that many people around that were doing it at the time, so I became sort of a go-to guy for labels that wanted to release reggae music. I began to know the studios and how to work down in Kingston, which is such an amazing place to record. If you need a percussion player, you can sort of yell out the window and there'll be a line of guys ready to do it, and they'll all be great and affordable. [Laughs.]

Jamaican studios have a reputation of putting out these great-sounding records with the most marginal equipment. Have any idea about that?
They pushed their gear as hard as they could and got every ounce of sound that they could get out of it. I did a live session at Tuff Gong where I wanted to use a real Hammond organ to get a "bubble" (style of playing) going and along with the organ comes a guy who was their Hammond organ guy. That was his only job—to keep that Hammond working, so there's a reverence for some of that equipment that you don't even get here sometimes.

Some of the studios are better than you think though. Tuff Gong studio has an amazing-sounding room with an SSL console. Studio One and Federal are both pretty good. There are lots of them. I've heard that there were more studios per square mile than anywhere in the world for a while and they all had their own flavor. Now it's just like here, where everyone has a studio in their house with Pro Tools, but there are still a lot of commercial studios in Jamaica.

How much have you recorded in Jamaica?
Probably around 20 times, but I've never totaled it up. I'd do parts of records here, but to get the real flavor, I'd have to go back down there. For example, I did a record with Willie Nelson where Willie doing his country stuff but with a Jamaican flavor. Another producer started it, but it never sounded right. I think one reason was that no one took it down to Jamaica. The album had been cut up here with Jamaicans that I knew, and they're really good players, but it just didn't have the full flavor that it needed and you could only get it down there.

Believe me, taking multitrack tapes down to Jamaica and back is not an easy job! *[Laughs.]* Their tape machines run at different speeds down there because the power is different, so you have to jump through hoops just to get things in tune. Then there's the ever present brown-out or black-out, where you're finally getting something going and everything in the room goes dark.

Are you tracking the entire band?

Yes, except in the case where I was using a drum machine. I'd get Sly (producer Sly Dunbar, half of the famous Sly and Robbie rhythm section) to come over and he'd just sit there with the original Linn drum machine and pound out a beat. It would be a single two-bar phrase that he'd slowly add to.

There'd be about 15 guys in a control room that's meant to hold 6, just listening to him making this beat with everyone stoned out of their box. That's definitely a different kind of vibe than you see up here.

Would you rather track the entire band or just go for a good drum track and replace everything later?

I guess the key word is "depends." Toots' band is rock-steady. Their tempo does not budge! Why wouldn't you want to cut with that band? They're just incredible. I know that Sly and Robbie have the same thing going.

What's your preproduction like?

Non-existent. With Toots, we'd get to the studio, then there'd be the ritual hour and a half with his "chalice" (pipe), and then you're on. You just better have your shit together, improvise, and go quick after that.

It's mostly your preparation then.

Yeah, I would do my homework and come up with some grooves and different things in my head, but I would always defer to the masters in the room that not only had the musical knowledge, but also the musical history knowledge that was way beyond mine. I'd always trust them, but I'd have a few other ways ready to go if needed.

Do you have any secrets to keeping everybody happy?

That's a very subtle thing. I'm certainly not the best at it or I'd be more famous as a producer. In the larger scheme of things, the tricks that you'd employ with Jamaicans are no different than what you'd employ with anyone else.

One of the tricks I like is to record a bunch of tracks, get the artist out of the way, and put it together after the fact. You don't want to burn out an artist and some of the first takes will be the best anyway. I've had complete disasters with Jamaicans trying to work a way I thought was best where it just didn't work at all, but you could really say the same thing about any kind of music. You really can't predict how an artist is going to relate to an idea.

The only thing that you could probably do in Jamaica was make the excuse that you didn't understand what they were saying (which is the case a lot of the time), so you have an excuse in your back pocket because there is a language difference.

How long do the sessions there normally last?

You don't see the normal amount of tracking and retracking that you see in pop stuff. These guys know when they've got it, so there's a lot less second-guessing. When I was working with Ben Harper for the *True Love* record, we had players from Ben's band and the rhythm section from Toots' band. After a take, Ben's guys wanted to go into the control room and judge it, but Toots' guys just said, "That track done, mon. It finish!" and they were right.

That makes your job a lot easier.

Yeah, it does. It's a real pleasure working with those guys, but let's face it, they're playing straight-ahead grooves with little variation. But what a groove!!

Generally it's a day of tracking and then another day of overdubs and stuff, so in that way it's pretty much like any kind of session. That being said, Jamaicans have a love of recording and they don't mind doing a lot of takes if necessary. and with many Jamaican I've worked with it's always a different take.

Do you have any techniques for getting best performance out of singers?

Number one, before you ever say anything to a singer or touch that talkback button, really think about what you're going to say so it isn't taken the wrong way. I say that from experience, and I still screw up.

You've got to really get in their head to feel what they're doing, what they're trying to go for, and what they're dealing with.

Sometimes you really have to be aware of what they're listening to in the phones, because if there's something that's competing with them in the track or throwing them off time-wise or pitch-wise, you have to get rid of it. They won't think of it because they're trying to connect with their part, so it's up to you.

A lot of things that I've done in the past producing non-Jamaicans wouldn't apply to Jamaicans, like giving sort of acting tips to help a singer get into the mood of the song. Something like, "Pretend you just saw your boyfriend with someone else and really sing to him," to get them into the emotion. That technique wouldn't work with Jamaicans. They'd take it as being disrespectful.

What do you look for in an engineer?
In Jamaica, you don't get a choice, since you get whoever's with the studio. You just have to hope that they don't screw up. I've had some real disasters. In the early days of Pro Tools, I've gone home with a hard drive with nothing on it because the engineer saved it to the wrong drive. Pro Tools and Jamaicans didn't mix for while. *[Laughs.]*

Generally, it's the serendipity of working with a true recording master. When you work with an engineer that really understands what he's doing, it makes recording such a pleasure. It's pretty cool when you work with a guy who says, "Wait a minute. I've got just the mic for this," or "Wait a minute. Let's compress it after the input," or some other suggestion that just works perfectly for the situation. I'm an old dog so I've seen it all, but I'd still never trust myself to put it all together, which is why people hire engineers who know this stuff.

Would you mix down there or come back here?
I've done both. It kind of depends on the project. Even though there are now lots of Jamaican mixers who live in the States, it still comes down to a flavor that is unique to Jamaica. Don't forget, Jamaicans invented dub and are the true originals at dropping out sections of a song, so if you want to get something like that right, that's where you have to go.

Another area Jamaicans are masters are delays and delayed feedback. They have a style and it's part of their language as to opposed to here, where it isn't, so if you had a record that needed that flavor, you'd better mix down there.

It's funny because low end is such a critical thing in music and just turning up the bass is not how to do it, obviously. Trying to get a guy over here that understands the Jamaican thing, I'd say forget it. You'd have to go down there for that, but most of my records didn't need that pure dub sound.

Would the mixes go faster?

Sometimes, but usually it's the same tedious process as everywhere. In the early '90s, studio time was scarce and guys would work around the clock, so there were places where you could not leave the mix up overnight like they do here.

How about mastering?

I never did master down there. Most of the stuff I've done is hybrid, which is why I've always said, "If you want a 100 percent Jamaican sound then you don't need me," so my stuff was always mastered for U.S. and European audiences.

One of my philosophies in producing any kind of music, either to my credit or discredit, is that I always want to do something a little different. So with Jamaican music, I tried to combine it with something else.

For example, we put the Wailing Souls on a house track. It wound up getting a great deal with Sony and a Grammy nomination, but it wasn't pure reggae. For those early Wailing Soul mixes, we sent all the dub stuff down there to mix, and for mastering as well.

What's the best piece of advice you've ever been given?

Most advice that applies to music is mostly universal. I still think the best one I've heard is something that I think (legendary country producer) Billy Sherrill said and that's, "The most important word in music is the word 'next.'" Meaning, you've got know when to move on. Don't spend two years mixing a song, or if you're overdubbing and not getting the part, maybe there's not an overdub needed, or you have the wrong guy overdubbing it.

I know that Denny Cordell went through 18 bass players trying to play the part on (Procol Harem's) "A Whiter Shade of Pale," which he produced. His point was that you know in the first two minutes whether the guy was going to get it, so you might as well move on and get a new guy right away if you think he won't work out. That's a nice piece of advice I've always tried to keep in my head. Thanks, Denny!

GARETH JONES

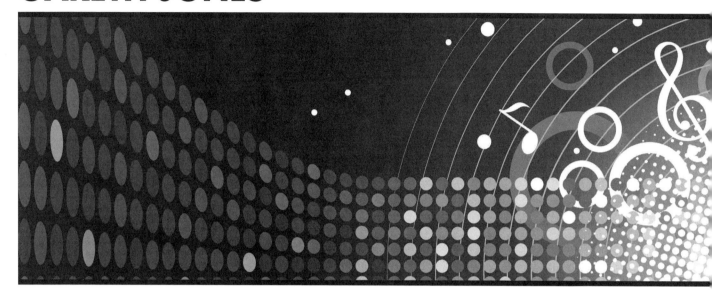

Beginning his career as an engineer and mixer, Gareth Jones soon made the transition up the ladder as a coproducer with superstar band Depeche Mode. While producing such eclectic acts as Erasure, Can, Madness, Devo, Tackhead, and Nick Cave and the Bad Seeds, among many others, Gareth's high-tech, no-nonsense production approach has won him acclaim and admiration from all corners of the industry.

How did you become a producer?
I had a hit with Depeche Mode as an engineer, so I negotiated a coproduction with them. I didn't know very much about production at that stage as I was very junior, but they were gracious enough to include me in the production team, so that was my first toe in the water. I was not responsible for the whole production in the way that I am today, but it gave me an opportunity to develop my production skills later as the lone producer with other bands because I'd been a coproducer on some famous records.

When I look back on my starting out in the production world, I was a glorified engineer who the artist respected enough to invite me to be a producer. It was a very long but ongoing learning curve for me because I had to learn to take care of the schedule with the artist, work with the artist in preproduction, keep them in a very emotionally creative space, and attempt to get records finished on time and on budget. I realized that there was a lot more to the producing job than being taken seriously by the artist and making good recordings.

Is there a technique that you have to do that?
I think so. It's not rocket science but what I try to do now is to work as fast as possible. If I'm lucky enough to be working with a full team of an engineer and an assistant, I make sure that everyone is working fast because over the years I've developed a lower and lower boredom threshold. [*Laughs.*] I want to keep recording and doing new stuff and I feel that most of the artists I work with really appreciate that, so I don't take any time to technically fiddle when the artist is around. I try to keep the whole process as transparent as possible, so they can set up and get working quickly.

The other thing is that with younger artists, I try to schedule things so the sessions are not open ended and everyone knows that we start at 12 o'clock and work until 8 or 9, and in that time we're working and creating. That means that we don't waste time in the studio, which I think the artists enjoy.

When I started my career, I know that a great deal of time was wasted in the studio because we were all learning and less experienced. Now when I'm in the studio, I just want to get music done as fast as possible and keep a flow going. In that way, I think it's a good space for the artist and me to try out new ideas so it doesn't take too long. If I suggest that the artist try an idea, they know that we're only going to spend 10 or 15 minutes on it and we'll know by then if it's working or not, as opposed to trying an idea for 5 hours, so I like to work as fast as I can.

What does that mean in terms of the amount of time you spend on a project?
It's so budget-driven that it makes them all different. Right now I'm working on a project that we're probably going to spend a month on because they came to me with recordings that they made at home. We're going through the demos and keeping the good bits and replacing the rest.

If I work with an artist where there's a higher budget, we might spend a really long time. I did a project recently where I sort of did "additional production," where I produced the vocals and mixed it and that was an extended process. We took blocks of time over 18 months to get it right because we were inventing a sound with the artist, so time scales are really variable in my world, which I really pride myself on, actually.

I enjoy the luxury of going into great detail and spending a long time on the project, but I also enjoy getting in the studio and going really fast. The record I'm making at the moment is very instinctive because we really don't have the time to deliberate too much. We're just going for it, and that's very creative sometimes because there's not too much thinking going on. It's very exciting because it shuts off all the monkey chatter *[laughs]* and you just react to the moment.

What attracts you to an artist?

Their energy, their songs, their personality in a meeting. I've been lucky in that after 30 years I've got a discography that makes a certain kind of artist gravitate towards me and that kind of fits with my sensibilities.

Before we really commit to work together, it's really important to get to know people a bit and that's a crucial time, I feel. If a band has a recording budget, they're out there meeting a bunch of producers, so the first meeting with me will be one of a number of meetings that they'll be doing. If we like each other, every subsequent meeting we'll chat in more detail and make some notes and listen to some things and get some ideas where we want to go with everything. After that we'll have sort of a personal relationship moving already, so we'll go into a rehearsal room.

It's great to be able to see a band live even before we go into rehearsals, but that's not always possible. It gives me a better picture of what they're trying to do.

What are the budgets that you're working with like these days?

Budgets have shrunk massively in the last 20 years. Budgets of the projects that I'm working on range from 25,000 pounds (about $41,000 USD) to 100,000 pounds (about $165,000 USD). It's very different depending upon if they're an established band or a total newcomer that I'm keen to work with, so I work across a big range of budgets.

I just want to make it clear that I'm not a hitmaker. I've been lucky to work with some great artists and had the privilege of making some great records with them, but I'm not a producer with a designed sound where people come to me to give them a hit. That impacts the budgets I see.

The sheer power of the technology has enabled a lot of us to do projects that we ordinarily couldn't do because now we don't have to do them in expensive facilities. Actually, the studios are really suffering because they're the next down the food chain. I'm not booking studios like I used to. I may only book a studio to track drums for a few days, then after that I'll work in a little production room somewhere.

Has your deal significantly changed with the budgets?

For me, it means that I'm making less money because the royalty stream is not as rich. I'm not in a position where I can say, "The royalties are not going to be as much, so I need a bigger advance," so that's something that has had an effect.

I've been looking at different types of deals with my management that involve publishing because, in fairness, it seems almost the only way to make some projects work. I can see that being a fair argument because it's the only part of the revenue stream that's still available, so some artists will have to share out. Traditionally, a portion of the publishing was dedicated to arrangement and obviously part of my job is helping the artist arrange their tunes both musically and sonically, so sharing fits in that sense. Of course some artists will say no to that. Negotiating deals is all about a power hierarchy in that if you're in a powerful position you can get a better deal. If I'm approached by an artist that's already had some measure of success, they're less likely to want to give me a piece of their publishing stream than if I'm working with a new artist that hasn't broken through yet.

How long do you like to have for preproduction?

I've really come to value preproduction and I like to spend a couple of weeks in the rehearsal room with the band before we go into the recording studio. I think that pays great rewards. One of the main reasons why it's so productive is because we all get to know each other in a relatively low-stress environment, so when we get into the recording studio, we all know where are strengths and weaknesses lie and there's already a level of trust that's been developed with the band. In the studio, that band is more willing to take what I'm saying seriously if we've done a lot of preproduction because they've worked out that some of my ideas are worthwhile, and that's really important.

What I like to do during preproduction is to make a very small multitrack recording on my laptop to help work on arrangements and sounds. We make sure that everyone listens to everything and we hone arrangements before we get in the studio. That's a big timesaver, but I feel it's the psychological foundation that's so important. It means that we can go a lot faster because we all have a game plan.

How long do you take to track basics?

In the last few years I've developed a new approach to tracking. What I do now is split in half whatever tracking time we have available and track everything in the first half. Then we sit down and listen and decide what we want to retrack. I find that to be really productive.

For a long time I would track one song after the other until they were all done and then build on that. Now I try to give myself and the band an opportunity to revisit every song once we've tracked everything because even with a young and inexperienced band, after five days in the studio, they start to feel like it's their own space. They're totally down with how it sounds and they're comfortable with the headphones. Once you get to that stage where everyone is settled into the studio, I find that a band can do their best work and can usually do a good take in ten minutes.

So for me, the second half of tracking is really important because it's so often at that point that we all listen and go, "Oh, that one can be better," or "Let's do that one with a different snare drum," or "That bass guitar worked really well in that tune. Let's try it on this one."

It was a bit of a breakthrough when I realized that I could do it that way. Bands love it, and I love it too because we realize that what we've recorded is not so precious. That second half is when they can really start to deliver. We end up keeping some of the stuff from the first round of tracking, but a lot of it just gets done again.

As a result I changed from struggling to do a track a day to encouraging the band to do two or three tracks a day.

How do you manage the budget? Do you get the money and pay it out yourself?

Sometimes, but other times the label will be billed directly. That's how it works on the bigger budget projects I work on, which I'm happy with, actually. We'll go through rounds of spreadsheets where we'll tweak everything, but everyone can see how the budget is being spent. I'm happy with it because then I don't have the responsibility of dealing with the larger sums of money. I pick up my advance from the record company and that's it.

It's become very important now to get things done on time and on budget, which wasn't the case when I started. That's one of the reasons why I feel I've grown and developed so much (besides musically and psychologically), because purely administratively it's so important to deliver. I think that's now one of my skills—to deliver on that commitment. I think people appreciate that, especially these days.

Do you engineer your productions?

I do a mixture. If I'm doing a tracking session, I always hire an engineer and an assistant because I find that it's too much to deal with everything and get it all right. Obviously, I'm a producer with an engineering background, so I will not hesitate to go move a mic or something if necessary, but basically I want someone to run all that stuff so I can concentrate all my energy on the band and their performance and sound. Quite often, I might be in the studio with the band wearing headphones rather than in the control room.

I like old-fashioned tracking sessions where all of the band plays together and I try to do that as much as I can. As budgets continue to decrease, we might have to start making the kind of records where instruments are recorded one at a time again, because we won't be able to afford the large studios like we did in the '80s, but as far as I can, I love having the band play all together and I try to do that so that I get a real performance out of everyone. I'd rather have everyone commit to a performance rather than replacing everything but the drums later.

I can't stress enough that this is all budget-dependent. Quite often in the overdub phase I might just have an assistant or I might even do parts of the overdub phase alone depending on how much work I feel there is to do and the allocation of the budget.

Do you have any techniques for getting the best performance out of musicians?

I try to build a safe atmosphere, a focused atmosphere, a creative atmosphere, and one where the technology is always functioning so things are not overly complicated. I don't enter into clever manipulations of the artist to get them to perform. I just try to be open and let them do their thing, and that seems to work really well.

A lot of it for me is no-nonsense facilitation of the technology side so everything is as seamless as possible and the band can just record with no undue waiting or tech frustrations. I think that's really important. Also, it's developing an atmosphere of trust so people feel that it's okay to make a mistake and we all feel safe with each other.

I really find I have to enjoy the time in the studio anymore. It's really important to me. If I'm enjoying it, I'm not stressed. If I'm enjoying it, there's a really good chance that the artist is enjoying it too.

Do you use a mixer or do you mix your productions yourself?
On some records that I produce, we (the band, the record company, and myself) decide that someone else is going to mix it and that's great. I'm very happy for other people to mix it, but if I have the choice as a producer, I'll mix it because I enjoy it and it's part of my skill set. I feel that I can realize the vision of the artist easier if I do it myself.

While I find having an engineer for tracking and for overdubs useful if the budget will support it, I just find that when it comes to mixing there's a direct interface between me and the music, so I just do it myself unless we have a plan to get someone else in.

How long does it take you to mix?
A song a day, leave it up overnight, spend a couple of hours tweaking in the morning, and move on. I make sure that we have a bit of time at the end so we can revisit the tracks, and that seems to work well. We don't have time to get bored and there's usually lots to do. That's one way of working.

When I mix in the box (which I really like doing because everyone wants total recall these days), it's hard to say how long it takes because I try to get good rough mixes on everything, then I just keep revisiting the tracks until they're done. I love it because as a mixer, I'm not one of these geniuses who hits a bull's-eye every time. Sometimes my first mix will be good, but very often the mix really comes to life when I revisit it.

How do you choose a mastering engineer or facility?
I'm flexible. I'm very happy to suggest mastering engineers but very often it's a record company decision and I just go with that. It's not

worth me making a fuss about. I don't make much of a fuss about anything any longer. *[Laughs.]*

What's the best piece of advice you ever received?
Never forget the importance of the demo or the song.

MARK PLATI

Based in New York City, the versatile Mark Plati learned production the old-fashioned way, starting first as a musician and songwriter, and then later as an engineer. With a long list of diverse credits that range from a host of eclectic unsigned acts to David Bowie, The Cure, Robbie Williams, and Natalie Imbruglia, among many others, Mark has an "open-mind" studio philosophy that has kept him consistently on the cutting edge of modern music production.

How did you become a producer?
It was a natural progression from my beginnings as a musician in grade school. After high school I became attracted to the recordmaking process, and I began engineering and mixing in college while playing in cover bands. It was only natural to combine the two. After being in enough engineering or mixing situations, you sort of naturally make the transition after a while.

What was your first production project?
My first production was with a band from Dallas called Daughter Judy. I went to Dallas to be an intern in a couple of recording stu-

dios and on a 48-track remote truck. In exchange for my free labor, I'd assist and learn from the in-house and freelance engineers. Also, I could have all the studio downtime I could eat, so I produced and engineered an EP for this band in exchange for being able to crash on their couch for a few months. I actually listened to it last week and it doesn't sound too far off from a lot of what I've done since, for better or worse.

Where did you learn the most about production? A particular project? A mentor?

I learned a lot from watching everyone I came in contact with—producers, engineers, artists, gophers, mixers, musicians, assistants, etc. Again, for better or worse—sometimes watching the tiny (or huge) mistakes of others is the best teacher.

I suppose the biggest leap came when I began working for producer/remixer Arthur Baker at his Shakedown Sound studios in NYC in 1987. It was a combination of trial by fire and a 24-7 schedule—total, relentless immersion into the craft in an area of music where I had very little experience. It was an amazing time. I witnessed a slew of production and mixing ideas and techniques there, and I got to work with a wide variety of material as well as people. Many notable artists, producers, engineers, and musicians passed through those doors. I learned a lot there, much of which I still practice. I also witnessed plenty that I'd never repeat.

What attracts you to an artist?

An artist is somebody that has something to say, and lives and breathes what they do. They're on a journey. When I sense that, I know I want to be a part of it.

What do you see that's common between new acts that you produce?

They are more knowledgeable about the industry (or what's left of it) as well as the mechanics/technicalities of record making, given the laptop revolution and miniaturization of the recording process.

Anything and everything is ultimately useful, so it's no surprise that some of their Garage Band ideas can make it to the final mix. On the downside, all of that computer tinkering can lead to less accomplished musical chops—practice time gets sacrificed for laptop time, since there are only so many hours in the day.

What are the budgets that you're working with like these days?
Tiny! A lot less than they used to be . . . the '90s are indeed over. A number of projects are now funded by management or third-party investors, with the aim to own masters and then license them however they can—TV, films, ads, ringtones, etc. If I didn't have my own space—which I can discount accordingly—a lot of projects wouldn't happen. That would have been unheard of a decade ago.

Has your deal significantly changed with the budgets?
Yes, because people are figuring out new and unique ways to compensate me aside from the traditional advance against royalties. I still do a fair chunk of work in the traditional manner, but the shift continues to grow toward a new model.

Do you have a preproduction process?
I think preproduction is the most important phase of a record. It sets the tone for everything, mostly deciding crucial things like song selection, structures, tempos, getting the gear up to snuff, and figuring each other out on a musical and personal level.

How long do you like to have for preproduction?
A week is great, but realistically at least a few days before recording begins, provided there's a lot of discussion over email with MP3s. Different projects require different degrees of preparation or rehearsal.

Do you have any tricks that you use during preproduction to get to know the artists better?
I don't think that I really have anything in the line of tricks. All I usually do is reveal myself to the artist in the sense that I'm as obsessed with turning over every rock in search of answers as they are. They kind of get that pretty straight off the bat, and that's usually enough of an icebreaker. Really, it's just about revealing my love of the process, and my irreverence for pretty much everything else.

Do you have a secret for keeping everyone in the studio happy?
I think it's down to empathy, as in, "What would I want the producer to be doing if I was the artist?" and going from there. It's not really much of a secret if you picture yourself riding shotgun as opposed to driving, and not wanting some sort of total nutjob behind the wheel.

I make sure everyone feels like they've had a chance for their voice to be heard and their musical ideas to be pursued, even if it's not my cup of tea. It's a subjective process and I'm the first to admit I don't know everything and I can't tell if even the strangest, least obvious idea might lead us somewhere until we go there. You don't know until you try it. That seems to be the only absolute.

Do you have any diplomatic secrets?
Knowing when to say something—timing really is everything. Also, maybe more importantly, knowing when to keep my mouth shut.

What do you look for in an engineer?
I usually engineer a lot of what I do, though over the last few years I've been in the habit of having an engineer for major tracking sessions so I can concentrate on the bigger picture and not watch the meters and listen for rogue noises.

I don't really have any specific criteria other than making sure an engineer is a good personality match and his process, like mine, is mostly invisible. It's cool to have somebody I'm not that familiar with, to see what they add and what gear they use, so I can continue to add to my own bag of tricks.

How long do your sessions normally last?
Anywhere from 10 to 12 hours a day. It's tricky to say, as every project is different depending on the level of skill of the players, how many songs we're doing, what sort of sonic makeup we're looking for, and the amount of searching we'll need to do. I'd say it takes around three to four weeks to complete an album, on average.

Do you have any tricks for getting the best performances out of musicians?
Not really—it's pretty much all common sense stuff. One advantage to being a musician is knowing what it feels like to be at the other end of the red light, so I get it.

I keep my end of it as invisible as possible. Make sure they can hear themselves well—decent headphones can make or break everything. Be mindful of the arc—that there will be a period of acclimation and feeling the way through a song, and then they'll crack it. But, record everything, as one never knows if a first take will be a magic interpretation, or a warmup will yield a happy accident. Memory is cheap, so there's no reason not to hit that "3" button.

Do you have any tricks for getting the best performances out of singers?
Make sure they sleep enough and stay in good spirits. Don't save all the vocals for the end—that always creates a pile of stress. Again, catch the arc. This whole thing is like surfing—when you feel the wave coming, make sure you're on it.

Do you use a mixer other than the engineer you used for recording?
I generally mix everything I do unless there is a predetermined idea to have the project go through another set of ears at the end. I tend to have an idea of where I want a project to go musically and sonically, and a lot of that can be mix-dependent.

How many alternative mixes do you do?
Aside from the usual suspects—more vocal versions, playback tracks—I do tons of stems so I can make any sort of edit or remix later without having to do a full-on recall, if I can help it.

How do you choose a mastering engineer or facility?
I've been really happy with Sterling Sound the last several years—Greg Calbi, UE Nastasi, George Marino. Between the three of them, I can get whatever I need.

What's the best piece of advice you ever received?
When I was an intern in Dallas, for one week I assisted an engineer named Larry Wallace. Larry was the first hotdog engineer I'd ever worked with. He was totally passionate about his craft and traveled around the country freelancing. He'd use duct tape and spit to make a tape machine work. He'd stand on his head to keep the session going forward if he had to. He said, "If you can make a career between these two speakers, count yourself lucky." And I do.

CARMEN RIZZO

Two-time Grammy nominee, electronic musician, and underground darling Carmen Rizzo has parlayed his technical and computer acumen into numerous credits as a producer, mixer, remixer, musician, and cowriter for a wide range of influential artists including Seal, Coldplay, Alanis Morissette, Paul Oakenfold, BT, Tiesto, Jem, Esthero, Ryuichi Sakamoto, Cirque du Soleil, KD Lang, and Pete Townshend of The Who. Based in Los Angeles, Carmen knows the electronic music realm as well as anyone and was kind enough to impart his considerable insight about the world of production.

What was your first production job?
I was fortunate in that Jamie Cohen, who was a very influential A&R person in the '80s and '90s, gave me a chance to make the first non-new age record for Private Music with Kristen Vigard. Kristin was this wonderful singer who was very well-known in the local L.A. music scene. I will never forget Jamie because he took a chance on me and really gave me my first shot. I think at that point he was a risk-taker, so he gave me a chance and I passed the test.

One of the reasons that I don't participate in the pop world is that you always write and strive for a hit, and back then you did it even more than now. Kristen and I made this record with all local musicians that nobody had really heard of at the time, like the guys from the Red Hot Chili Peppers, Fishbone, N'Dea Davenport from Brand New Heavies, Amp Fiddler, and Bronx-Style Bob. The Peppers had a record deal and so did Fishbone, but they were just bubbling under. They were all friends of Kristen's. It was a fantastic record and critically acclaimed and that's what helped me become a producer. It was not only a record that I feel was ahead of its time because of the unusual instrumentation we used, but it also allowed me to become familiar with a lot of local musicians who went on to become quite successful. That spawned a lot of other things and allowed me to be known as a "local underground darling," as somebody called me.

What did you learn specifically from that project?

When you're a new producer, there's something that you have but can never get back and that's being fearless. That's one of the reasons that I don't participate in pop music or listen to those records because too many people refuse to be fearless.

By fearless you mean . . . ?

Too many producers are too cautious in the steps they take because they want a hit so badly. In any genre of music, when you hear a new record that sounds fresh and new and daring, there's an element of being fearless of the consequences by the producer.

When I made that first record, I didn't know or care about a hit. I was working with great musicians and trying techniques that were new to me and kind of fresh at the time. That's when I learned how to be fearless and just make good music and good records.

You insinuated that you lost that after that first record.

I wouldn't say that I lost that, because I still pride myself in making that kind of record. I try to be fearless and I try not to chase hits and I try not to follow people, but it would be a lie to say that we're not all influenced by someone.

I think that this is a great market for young producers who haven't done this before. They have an equal if not better shot than most established producers. Anybody can have success today very quickly, where before you couldn't accomplish that.

Unfortunately, most established producers today are so scared and lost that they're trying to manufacture success and not taking chances. Not everyone, of course, but a lot of them. It's discouraging because you can hear it in the music. That's why a lot of these records sound the same.

Did you have a mentor?

I did. My mentor was Susan Rogers, who got her chops doing all the engineering for Prince. She dated a dear friend of mine named John Saccittii, who was a tech at Westlake (where I got my start). I was a huge Prince fan and Susan was kind enough to sort of take me under her wing. I consider her a mentor early in my career. Later, when I was lucky enough to engineer and mix for Trevor Horn, he became a mentor as well. I learned an awful lot from him on how to make records.

What did you learn?

What I took from all those years working with Trevor was that the magic happened in the recording, not in the mixing. During that period in time, everyone held to the myth that it all happened in the mix. You hire a big mixer and a big studio, and you spend 15 to 20 hours mixing all day.

With Trevor, the assistant engineers would often mix the records and they would just throw the faders up. It all had to do with the charm, the time put into recording, and the technology. I was fortunate to work with Trevor because I was technically savvy as well as having chops as an engineer and as a programmer. So I was extremely at ease with technology like Euphonix, Syclavier, and Fairlight, and samplers and drum machines.

In all the things that we did, the instrumentation was how Trevor wanted to hear it while we were recording it. We would edit and manipulate and assemble the master in a way that was exactly how Trevor wanted to hear it, so when it came down to mixing, they were easy mixes and they would just throw the faders up. That's really what I learned.

He was way ahead of his time sonically and production-wise with those impeccable-sounding records. People will be studying those records for years to come. He always takes chances and seems to always make the right decisions. I was honored to be part of that team for a short while.

I didn't realize that you got your start at Westlake (Recording Studios).
Yeah, I grew up in the Bay Area and went to the College of Recording
Arts for one year. I was probably the least likely to succeed. *[Laughs.]*
I didn't have clue. I moved to Los Angeles when I was 19 and didn't
know a soul, and through a friend of a friend of a friend, I got a job at
Westlake Studios. I was the janitor in the morning, a runner during
the day, and then I would just hang out for free at night learning from
the techs, the engineers, and the musicians. I didn't have girlfriends or
dates, I just devoted my life to the studio until I learned what I needed
to and met enough people.

Eventually I became a second engineer there for a short time and
then I worked around L.A. for a while. I was friends with Wendy and
Lisa (from Prince's band) and got to engineer for them and I think I
must've met Jamie (Cohen) through them, and that started the next
phase of my career.

What attracts you to an artist that you want to work with?
I want an artist that sounds fresh to me. I will tell an artist, "If you
want to make something that's daring, then I'm your guy," but I'm also
the first person to tell an artist, "I'm the wrong guy for you," if they
want a direction that doesn't feel comfortable to me.

The artist also has to be a good singer, because I refuse to work
with a one that's bad. That's why I don't do certain types of music, because it's too easy to just get some mall girl who looks the part and just
phones it in. It could be anybody singing and that's just not my style.
I'm also interested in working with artists that like what I do. What I
don't like is when the artist is the producer.

***What are the budgets like these days on the projects you're work-
ing on?***
The budgets are lower and they're not going back up. Once you get
someone for a discounted rate, that's it. That's why we're all in survival
mode. I'm lucky because I do a lot of things. I'm an artist, I do some
film work. I'm not a one-trick pony, so I survive.

I'm finding that the budgets are healthier from third parties, like
when a new artist has their family fund their project, or they're a
trust baby, or they have an investor. I don't do many label projects
anymore. I do a lot of eclectic indie records and those budgets are
always small.

Also people are constructing records in different ways. Artists are bringing in a producer towards the end to help with vocals or just the mixing, so it's not like it used to be where you did a record from scratch.

How has that impacted your deal?
I don't care about points anymore. I want to get paid up front because the problem is that nobody sells records anymore. If I get an artist that wants to give me 5 or 6 points, I just tell him that I don't want any points, because how are you going to track the sales and get your money afterwards, and is he really going to sell any in the first place? Probably not, so I want cash up front.

I also demand 50 percent before we start. You have to now, because it's way too common, especially in this business climate, that the project never sees the light of day. They run out of money or something unforeseen happens and you never see a dime. I've had to threaten not to work until I got paid a couple of times and I have no problem with that.

What's your preproduction like?
It's intense and goes pretty deep, because most of it happens in the control room. Most of my records are technically savvy and they evolve in the control room in terms of programming. It's hard to say how long it takes, since you're recording and mixing as you go these days.

Do you do any prep work with the artist just to get to know them and find out their influences?
Sure. I'll sit down with the artist and have them play me their songs stripped down. Then I want to get educated as to what they like and don't like about what I do and about who they're listening to. I want an artist to tell me,"I really love what you did on this record but I really don't like what you did on this one." Then I can say either, "I had nothing to did with that, " or "That's too bad, because that's what I was looking to do." *[Laughs.]*

I don't want to be the artist. This is about them. Their name goes on it. I'm only a tool or vehicle for them.

Are you managing the budget? Do you get the entire budget and pay all the bills?
That's usually how it happens, although I don't often like that. I actu-

ally would prefer if they paid them directly so I have nothing to do with it, but often it comes to me and I pay it out.

Do you have a secret for keeping people happy in the studio?
Humility can never be underestimated. I also think it's important to not talk music 24-7 in the studio just to keeps things loose.

How long do your sessions normally last?
I'm an early riser because I have kids at home, so I like to start early and end early. I've got to be winding down by 11 p.m. so I can leave the studio by midnight. You don't need to work really long hours these days because you can accomplish a lot more with technology that helps with your decision making.

Do you have any tricks for getting the best performance out of a musician or vocalist?
I wouldn't say that there's a trick other than making them confident and making them believe in themselves. I also like to record low-stress demos with people and keep the performances because some inexperienced singers get scared when they think it's the real thing. It's too much pressure.

How long do your mixes take?
I mix as I go so my mixes are easy, but I try to do no more than a song a day.

Do you do alternative mixes?
Not any more because it's so easy to recall stuff if you're mixing in the box. My standard now is just a vocal mix and an instrumental.

How about mastering?
I don't take great value in mastering because I'm very confident about how things sound coming out of my room. That being said, I work a lot with Chris Bellman at Grundman Mastering and more recently Dale Becker at Bernie Becker Mastering. They're both very good so it's just really a cost thing, as Grundman is sometimes outside of my price range on some small-budget projects.

Unfortunately, there are so many mastering guys that think that just because they can buy the gear that they have to use it on your mix, and often, you don't. You want a mastering engineer to be able to tell you, "You know, it doesn't need much." There's a lot of engineers that swear by their mastering guy because he saves their mixes, but I've never had a record where I said, "It came together in mastering."

What's the best piece of advice you've ever received?
It came from Leeds Levy, who ran Chrysalis Publishing when I signed there. I was fortunate to have two cowrites on the big Seal record (*Seal II*) that went on to sell about 10 million units. When it came to my publishing company credit on the CD, it was called Povy Lu and he said, "Why did you do that? If you had named it 'Carmen Rizzo Music,' your name would've been on 10 million CDs." I said, "You are so right!" Since then I've changed my publishing name to Carmen Rizzo Music because you have to brand your name. That was the best advice I ever got.

STONEBRIDGE

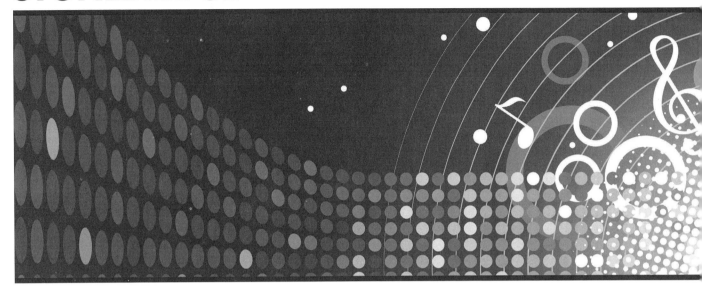

StoneBridge got his start running the Swedish DJ/remix group SweMix, which eventually led to remixes that became worldwide hits, including "Me and My Imagination" by Sophie Ellis-Bextor, "Talkin' 2 Myself" by Ayumi Hamasaki, and "Gimme More" by Britney Spears. His remix of Ne-Yo's track "Closer" was nominated for a Grammy Award. In 2012 he received the prestigious BMI Songwriter of the Year award for his contribution to Jason Derulo's "Don't Wanna Go Home."

Stone also has a weekly show on Sirius XM/BPM called *#bpm-Mix*, and tours worldwide as a DJ with recent shows in Las Vegas, New York, Sydney, Jakarta, Stockholm, and Dubai.

I read that you got started DJing at a party.
That's correct. It was my sister's graduation party and my dad saw the budget for a real DJ (a staggering $50) and said, "No, that's not going to happen. Stone, you play."

I was sort of a disco boy at the time. I was out in clubs and buying 12 inches, so I called a friend who had a mixer and two SL1200s [turntables] and I caught the bug from that one gig and never looked back.

Where you a musician before that?

Absolutely. I started on the flute, as all Swedes do, but that was boring so I switched to guitar. My family had a piano and it was always a family thing to play instruments.

That explains the musicality in what you do.

I learned early on that if you have a vocal, it has to carry the song. Sometimes you have a flat melody (we call them "flatliners") and then you have to come up with a riff or a chord progression that will make that flatliner sound very interesting. If the song isn't going anywhere, I can feel it in my whole body and I need to change it so it moves musically.

When you collaborate with someone, does it right from the beginning of the song?

There are basically three kinds of collaborations. The one I did with Crystal was in the studio in Stockholm where I had to rent a weighted keyboard for Rasmus Farber, which was a big drag. Crystal was blown away, though. She said, "I haven't seen real instruments in a studio for 15 years." She loved it because her dad was a jazz musician.

The guy (Farber) played some chord progressions, she was humming along, and I was thinking about the drums. He played it into Logic and I made a quick beat, then added a bridge later. I'm tempted to say that's the best way to do it, but not always. It takes a lot to come up with a knockout melody and the lyrics in one session like that.

Most of the time you create a track then send it on to the collaborator. Then we come to method three, which is that you take a remix that you did recently and you mute the vocals. You send it to a writer who comes up with the top line, then you sort of remix the top line. You take away everything from the remix and start over, because when you remix a lot that's how you approach it. You get the accapella line and build a song around it. These are the three methods for me.

How did you get into remixing?

We were ten Stockholm DJs that met in a record store and became SweMix. There were these two American record companies, Disconet and Hot Tracks, that did a subscription-based vinyl service every month with remixes of big tracks. Then there was the English one, DMC.

The problem with the English one was that they did medleys. No DJ in the world would put on a 25-minute medley of pop songs. What am I going to do when it's playing? The American ones had remixes of individual tracks, but it was a lot of freestyle at the time. It wasn't all house music, it was kind of random.

We decided that we needed to start a DJ service and we did. It was completely bootleg and we got busted with the first release. A rights organization called us and said, "Hey guys, what are you doing? You need clearance for this, please." [Laughs.]

Miraculously we managed to get one pretty big independent label that had licenses for Sugar Hill Records and stuff like that so we had some cool material to work with in the beginning. Gradually we got major support so by around 1986 so we could do Prince or Madonna or whatever was big at the time.

We were doing these simple remixes on a Tascam 4-track, with the mix on tracks 1 and 2, some silly samples on the other tracks, a re-edit and maybe a drum intro. As money came in we bought a 24-track Studer and a big console and things got serious.

Then some rappers started to come by and we'd make a beat for them, and then the labels started to take notice. One of them was Champion Records in the U.K., who contacted us and wanted us to do a few things for them.

I wanted to do international remixes so I asked if they had any old shit in the basement that I could remix. They said, "We have this song by Robin Stone, "Show Me Love." I thought, "That's meant to be. I'm StoneBridge, she's Robin Stone."

I did a mix and in typical English fashion I got an "It's all right but . . ." and there was a whole list of things that they wanted changed. I got really angry and had a gig to go to, so I went in the studio and cranked it out in like four hours. I switched the bass from preset #16 to #17 (an organ), added two chords in the chorus and a distorted Yamaha TX81Z for that thing in the beginning, and that was it.

I turned it in and all they they said was it was "Alright." Nine months later it was a top 5 record in the U.K. and a year later a top 5 in the U.S.. I said, "Why didn't you tell me, guys?" They said, "Because your remix fee would get higher." [Laughs.] I had no idea. I kept on getting hit up from these guys from New York and I had no idea why.

How long does it take you to do a remix?
It depends on the state of the parts. We used to call them parts— now it's called stems. Usually they're very processed through a mas-

tering chain. You get 9 or 10 stems and line them all up and that's the record.

I usually mute them all except for the vocal and start creating the drums. Then I play a few things, then un-mute tracks from the original. My theory is that the vibe of the record will be in these parts, so I like to use bits and pieces of them. Sometimes I just reverse something or use one chord, but I like to include pieces from the original to give it some identity.

The fastest it can take is probably two days. Trouble mixes, when it's in a major key where you want it to sound cool but it's way too cheerful, can take up to a week.

So it's easier for you to do a remix in a minor key?

With EDM I've noticed that it's a lot of major keys now, although sometimes it's only one bass note per bar so you can't really tell if it's major or minor. The major can really lift a song. We all know that the really strong songs have a mix of minor and major. You can get that really surprising effect where you go, "Oh, that's big."

If you got a song in a major key, would you decide to remix it in a minor?

There are a lot of tricks that you can do. A D# major against a C minor thing works. Sometimes you can get a wonderful tension with a major guitar part against a minor environment. Or you make it a little jazzy. Everything goes in jazz, doesn't it? [Laughs.]

How did you learn to mix?

It was a long painful journey. In the beginning we were five guys with a studio, so you either had to finish or you had to take Polaroids of the console settings. We also had these sheets to fill out, but it never matched up.

One day I noticed that I was only using two channels on the desk and the volume control. Everything else was in the box. That's when the mixing really started for me. I learned that headroom really mattered, and then I realized that kick drums have a key. A lot of guys miss on this. They have a massive kick drum sound in the key of B, but the track is in a different key, so it's completely incompatible and the bottom end gets really messy.

As house became more and more heavy, the bass and kick had to be more incorporated and be part of the same group, so to speak. If the bass and kick are good then half the battle is won. If they don't work, then you can work the song for years but it will never end up working.

What would you do to tune the kick with the track? Would you try another sample or key an oscillator?
The easy way now is with Nicky Romero's Kick plug-in, which has everything you need in one window. You select the transient and the body sounds and you just tune it.

Normally it's two kicks, though. One for the click and one for the meat, and the one with the long decay has to be in tune. I have the keys marked for all my kicks. I might try to use one in a different key but usually it's best if the kick is in the same key as the song. If you sidechain it with the bass, the whole bottom end becomes one big harmonious force.

Would you consider that a signature of what you do?
It's always been my trademark how my bass lines work with the chords of the songs, I think. It's hard to pinpoint exactly, but it's definitely in the mix as well as the playing.

How do you approach effects like reverb and delay? I notice that you tend to use reverb on a lot of your mixes these days.
It's the Universal Audio Lexicon 224 with the Vocal Thickening Plate preset and it's just the best. It's not very heavy to begin with, although you can filter out the bass so it doesn't get too muddy. I use it for vocals and some of the keyboards on almost every mix.

I also use the Logic Tape Delay, which I think is the best as well. It's kind of gritty and dirty, which is a good flavor. You need a little something in there to make it work.

Sometimes I create a room for percussion, but only if I want to highlight them. Sometimes I use a little of a flanger on random things to glue things together as well.

What are you using for monitors?
I'm using NS-10s for basic vocal and keyboard levels. Also, it's a good test for the low end. If you don't hear the bass on NS-10s, you will never hear it on anything else. My main monitors are Mackie HR-824s, the old ones that are built in America and not in China. I don't

believe in subs so it's important for me to have something that can deliver the low end, and these do for some reason. I have a Cranesong Avocet as a monitor controller.

I also use the SpectraFoo analyzer. It's expensive but it's worth every penny. Once you've looked at it for about a month you can see what everything sounds like, and you can see what's wrong with a mix immediately. Immediately you can see holes in a mix. I can't live without it.

What's the best piece of business advice?

I never give away a master. A lot of young guys don't understand what a master is, but it's your pension. Be very careful with your masters and your publishing and get some advice before you sign anything, especially in this digital age. If you're sloppy you can let labels collect your royalties that you should be getting. License records, don't give them away. In the dance industry you can license for five years, and at the end of your career you can control a catalog that can really be worth some money.

Find out more about StoneBridge at Stoneyboymusic.com.

GLOSSARY

0 dB full scale: The highest level that can be recorded in the digital domain. Recording beyond 0 dBFS results in severe distortion.

A&R: An abbreviation for *artist and repertoire*. A talent scout at a record label.

advance: A portion of expected royalties or fees paid before the royalties or fees are due, usually paid upon signing a contract and completion of the project.

airplay: When a song is played on the radio.

articulations: The way a note or phrase is played or sung.

art: A creative endeavor that you do for your own personal satisfaction.

attack: The first part of a sound or phrase.

automation: A system that memorizes and then plays back the position of all faders and mutes on a console.

Auto-Tune: A hardware device or plug-in used to adjust the pitch of a vocalist.

basics: See **basic tracks**.

basic tracks: Recording the rhythm section for a record, which may include all the instruments of the band, but may be only the drums depending upon the project.

baby band: A newly signed band that hasn't released a record.

bit rate: The transmission rate of a digital system.

book rate: The advertised rate of a recording studio or rental.

bpm: Beats per minute; the measure of tempo.

bridge: An interlude that connects two parts of a song, building a harmonic connection between those parts.

bottom: Bass frequencies, the lower end of the audio spectrum. See also **low end**.

boutique gear: High-quality, hand-built musical or audio gear with a limited production run.

build: Usually a one- or two-bar section of a song where the volume builds from soft to loud.

buy-out: A production situation where you only get paid for your initial work and nothing thereafter.

chorus (in a song): The refrain of the song following each verse that usually contains the hook.

chorus (electronic effect): A type of signal processor where a detuned copy is mixed with the original signal, which creates a fatter sound.

click: A metronome feed to the headphones to help the musicians play at the correct tempo (see Chapter 8).

clip: To overload and cause distortion.

clipping: When the input electronics overload because the audio level is too high.

competitive level: A mix level that is as loud as your competitor's mix.

contractor: The person in charge of hiring musicians for a union session. Occasionally non-union dates use non-union contractors.

converters: The analog to digital and digital to analog convertors connected to a digital audio workstation.

cross-collateralization: Royalties from one agreement used to cover the losses or advances of another agreement.

cue mix: The headphone mix sent to the musicians that differs from the one that the producer and engineer are listening to (see Chapter 8).

D/A: Digital to analog converter. This device converts the digital ones and zeroes back into an analog waveform.

DAW: Digital Audio Workstation.

delay: A type of signal processor that produces distinct repeats (echoes) of a signal.

digital overs: The point beyond "0" on a digital processor where the red "over" indicator lights, indicating a digital overload.

double: To play or sing a track a second time. The inconsistencies between tracks make the part sound bigger.

downbeat: A session's official start time.

feel: The groove of a song and how it feels to play or listen to it.

flanging: The process of mixing a copy of the signal with the original signal, but gradually and randomly slowing down the copy to cause the sound to "whoosh" as if it were in a wind tunnel. This was originally done by holding a finger against a tape flange (the metal part that holds the tape on the reel), hence the name.

groove: The pulse of the song and how the instruments dynamically breathe with it. Or, the part of a vinyl record that contains the mechanical information that is transferred to electronic information by the stylus.

guide vocal: See **scratch vocal**.

humbucker: A guitar pickup that uses two coils in reversed polarity to eliminate outside noise and interference (they "buck the hum"). Humbucking pickups have much higher gain than single-coil pickups.

hypercompression: Using too much buss compression during mixing or too much limiting during mastering in an effort to make the recording louder. Essentially leaves no dynamics and makes the track sound lifeless.

jingle: Any form of music used for an advertising spot on any media.

intermittent: Where the audio cuts in and out or crackles. Guitar cables are frequently intermittent.

intonation: The accuracy of tuning anywhere along the neck of a stringed instrument like a guitar or bass. Also applies to brass, woodwinds, and piano.

iso booth: Isolation booth. An isolated section of the studio designed to decrease or eliminate sound leakage.

ISRC code: An international standard code for uniquely identifying sound recordings and music video recordings. An ISRC code identifies a particular recording, not the song itself; therefore different recordings, edits, and remixes of the same song will each have their own ISRC code.

leakage: Sound from a distant instrument "bleeding" into a mic pointed at another instrument. Acoustic spill from a sound source other than the one intended for pickup.

Leslie: A speaker cabinet primarily used with organs that features rotating speakers.

lockout: A booking in a studio where you only get charged for 12 hours, but no one else can use the studio for the other 12 so all your gear and the gear in the control room can remain set up.

lossy compression: A digital file compression format that cannot recover all of its original data from the compressed version. Supposedly some of what is normally recorded before compression is imperceptible, with the louder sounds masking the softer ones. As a result, some data can be eliminated since it's not heard anyway. This selective approach, determined by extensive psychoacoustic research, is the basis for "lossy" compression. MP3 and AAC are lossy compression schemes.

look ahead limiter: A mastering limiter that delays the audio signal a small amount (about 2 milliseconds or so) so that the limiter can anticipate the peaks of a soundwave in such a way that it catches the peak before it gets by.

low end: The lower end of the audio spectrum, or bass frequencies usually below 200 Hz.

master: A final version of a recording that is destined for distribution.

mastering: The process of turning a collection of songs into a record by making them sound like they belong together in tone, volume, and timing (spacing between songs).

Mellotron: A keyboard popular in the 1960s that used tapes of recorded orchestral instruments to generate its sounds.

multiband compressor: A compressor that is able to individually compress different frequency bands as a means of having more control over the compression process.

Music 1.0: The first generation of the music business, where the product was vinyl records, the artist has no contact directly with the record buyer, radio was the primary source of promotion, the record labels were run by record people, and records were bought from retail stores.

Music 1.5: The second generation of the music business, where the product was primarily CDs, labels were owned and run by large conglomerates, MTV caused the labels to shift from artist development to image development, radio was still the major source of promotion, and CDs were purchased from retail stores.

Music 2.0: The third generation of the music business that signaled the beginning of digital music. Piracy ran rampant due to P2P networks, but the industry took little notice as CD sales were still strong from radio promotion.

Music 2.5: The fourth generation of the music business, where digital music became monetized thanks to iTunes and later, others like Amazon MP3. CD sales dive, the music industry contracts, and retail stores close.

Music 3.0: The fifth generation of the music business, where the artist could communicate, interact, market, and sell directly to the fan. Record labels, radio, and television become mostly irrelevant and single songs are purchased instead of albums.

Music 3.5: The sixth generation of the music business where YouTube and other online video platforms become the new radio, and the digital side of the business begins to slowly morph from one of downloads to streaming.

Music 4.0: The seventh generation of the music business where streaming becomes the preferred music delivery method for the consumer, which makes it profitable on a wide scale and increases revenue for artists, songwriters, publishers, and labels.

native resolution: The sample rate and bit depth of a distribution container. For example, the native resolution of a CD is 44.1 kHz and 16 bits. The native resolution in film work is 48kHz and 24 bits.

outboard gear: Hardware devices like compressors, reverbs, and effects boxes that are not built into a console and usually reside in an equipment rack in the control room.

out of phase: When the polarity of two channels (it could be the left and right channel of a stereo program) are reversed, thereby causing the center of the program (like the vocal) to diminish in level. Electronically, when one cable is wired backwards from all the others.

outro: The section of a song after the last chorus until the end of the song.

overdub: To record along with previously recorded tracks.

pad: Long sustaining note or chord.

pan: Short for panorama. Indicates the left and right position of an instrument within the stereo field.

panning: Moving a sound across the stereo field.

points: A percentage of sales or other revenues.

pocket: In the "groove" (the rhythm) with the song.

power chords: Long sustaining distorted guitar chords.

prechorus: A section of a song between verse and chorus sections. Not found in every song.

preproduction: A process of familiarizing an ensemble with the songs and arrangements before recording it.

producer: The equivalent of a movie director, the producer has the ability to craft the songs of an artist or band technically, sonically, and musically.

punchy: A description for a quality of sound that infers good reproduction of dynamics with a strong impact. The term sometimes means emphasis in the 200 Hz and 5 kHz areas.

record: A generic term that's come to mean a recorded project released for distribution to the public. A record may be in the form of a CD, digital audio file, vinyl disc, cassette, or some distribution container not yet invented.

rehearsal: A practice or trial band performance.

release: The end of a sound or phrase.

rushed fill: A drum fill that wavers ahead of the beat.

scratch vocal: A temporary vocal recorded during basic tracking with the intention of replacing it later.

sequencing: Setting the order in which the songs will play on a CD or vinyl record.

single coil: A type of guitar pickup found primarily on Fender guitars.

spread: The time in between songs on a CD or vinyl record.

spec: A situation where no money paid upfront with the promise to be paid later if the production is used.

snare: A thin drum with springs or "strainers" underneath that create a "rattling" sound.

snare strainers: The string of springs on the bottom of the snare drum.

sympathetic vibrations: Vibrations, buzzes, and rattles that occur in drums other than the one that was struck.

track: A term sometimes used to mean a song. In recording, a separate musical performance that is recorded.

TV mix: A mix without the vocals so the artist can sing live to the backing tracks during a television appearance.

union date: A session governed by the by-laws of the union, including the pay scale.

tempo: The rate of speed at which a song is played.

vibe: The emotional atmosphere communicated to and felt by others.

voicing: The way the notes of a chord are distributed.

word length: The number of bits in a word. Word length is in groups of eight. The longer the word length, the better the dynamic range.

INDEX

0 dB full scale, 173, 188, 271

10cc, 11

12-string, 112

A&R, xv, 4, 6–7, 34, 174, 180, 185, 223, 229–230, 234, 257, 271

acoustic, xix–xx, 68, 89, 98, 112, 114, 119, 122, 133, 161–162, 176, 192, 222, 272

advance, 26, 34–36, 38, 40–41, 46, 50, 54, 96, 194, 206, 219, 246, 248, 253, 271

airplay, 8, 40, 271

Aitken, Matt, 5, 11, 201

Amazon MP3, 193, 273

American Dad, 152

amp, 70, 113, 133, 163, 213, 258

Ampeg, 114

amplifier, xix, 53, 70, 110, 113–114, 118, 136, 211

amps, 30, 47, 70, 101–102, 109, 112–113, 119–120

Anderson, Laurie, 12

Andrews Sisters, 6

Apple, xx, 37, 194–195

Archie Bell and the Drells, 10

Armstrong, Louis, 6

arrangement, 6, 10, 26, 29, 42, 60–65, 68–72, 87–89, 91, 123, 169, 171, 205, 207, 209, 220, 228, 231, 246–247, 274

articulations, 81, 271

artist, xv–xvi, xviii, 4, 7, 9, 16–23, 25–27, 33, 35–41, 43–46, 48, 51, 56, 59, 70, 87–89, 99–100, 104, 125, 130–133, 143, 148, 153–155, 157–158, 168, 171–172, 177, 180, 184–186, 189, 194, 197, 200–201, 205–207, 209, 218–223, 228–231, 234–235, 239, 243–246, 248–249, 252–253, 260–261, 271, 273–274

artist development, 230, 273

artists, xiv, xvi, 4–6, 8, 10–11, 19–20,

26, 28–29, 34, 38–39, 44–45, 56, 59, 87, 99–100, 107, 130, 132–133, 145, 154, 158–159, 170, 173–174, 188, 195, 201, 206, 224, 228–230, 235–236, 244–246, 252–253, 257, 260–261, 273

Atkins, Chet, 7, 112

attack, 76–78, 81–83, 93, 117, 152, 175, 202, 208, 210, 271

automation, 170, 176, 180, 271

Auto-Tune, 139, 170, 271

Aviom, 118–119

baby band, 23, 40, 47, 271

background vocals, 7, 12, 27–29, 46, 60, 63–64, 66–68, 93, 129–130, 136, 151–153, 179–180

basics, 20, 86, 89, 96–97, 100–101, 103–104, 125, 134, 247, 271

bass guitar, 27, 29, 63–69, 76, 80–81, 84–85, 104, 109, 114, 120, 129, 133, 139, 144, 150, 152, 163, 171–172, 180, 222–223, 236, 247, 268, 272

Beastie Boys, 12

Beatles, xix, 4–5, 8–9, 13, 17, 34, 135, 159–160, 218

bands, xiii–xiv, 10, 20, 29, 45, 56, 59, 69, 73, 75–76, 82, 89–90, 96, 107, 119, 158, 160, 230, 243, 247, 251, 273

banjo, 7, 67–68

basic tracks, 27–29, 101, 103–104, 118, 123, 129, 134, 209, 271

Bennett, Tony, 7

Benson, George, 8

Berry, Chuck, 7

big ears, 184

bit rate, 97, 271

Blige, Mary J., 11–12

blues, xiv, 6–7, 40, 61, 92–93, 111, 157, 210

Bob Marley and the Wailers, 10

book rate, 271
Boss, 114
boutique gear, 116, 271
Bowie, David, xvii, xix, 12, 251
Boyz II Men, 11
bpm, 82–84, 201, 265, 271
Bradley, Owen, 7
bridge, 61–62, 64, 67, 69, 74, 82, 85, 130, 207, 210, 266, 271
Bright, Mark, xvi, 123, 137, 217–225
Brown, James, 80
Brown, Tony, 5, 11
Buggles, 11
build, 77, 82, 172, 177, 207, 213, 271
buy-out, 271
Byles, Junior, 10
Byrd, Charlie, 8

cartage, 46–51, 53, 55, 107–108
cross-collateralization, 272
cue, 16, 26, 118, 123, 272
cue mix, 118, 272
cymbals, 64, 163
cables, 109, 133, 272
Carey, Mariah, 11
Cash, Johnny, 4, 7, 12
cassette, xiii, 174, 274
CD, 34–36, 39, 44, 46, 49, 97, 153, 174, 182, 186–189, 191–194, 198, 206, 263, 273–274
cello, 53
Charles, Ray, 8
Cher, 11, 34, 170
Chess, Leonard, 7
Chiccarelli, Joe, 107, 227–234
chorus (electronic effect), 113–114, 150, 169, 271
chorus (in a song), 60–64, 66–69, 74–75, 77, 82, 84, 90, 130, 147, 153, 161, 179–180, 199–200, 207–208, 210, 267, 271, 273–274
Clapton, Eric, xvi, 113, 235
click, 83–84, 120–122, 124, 193, 209–210, 269, 271
clip, 271
clipping, 125, 271
Clooney, Rosemary, 7
Coldplay, xvi, 257
competitive level, 173, 188, 271
composers, 3–4, 200

compression, xx, 8, 174, 182, 188, 192, 272–273
compressor, 174, 192, 223, 273
Conga, 120
contractor, 54–55, 271

Danelectro, 112, 114
Davis, Miles, 9
DAW, 12, 30, 82, 84, 97–98, 102, 120, 124, 141, 148, 168, 176, 178–179, 183, 186, 189, 214, 272
delay, xx, 119–120, 148, 169, 212, 269, 272
demo, 25, 52–53, 91–92, 104, 108, 160, 182, 250
Devo, xvi, 12, 243
Diamond, Neil, 12
drum, xviii, xx, 11, 67–69, 80–81, 89, 95, 104, 106–109, 116–118, 122, 150, 152, 163, 201–202, 209, 238, 247, 259, 267–268, 274
Diddley, Bo, 7
digital music, 37, 52, 273
digital overs, 173, 188, 192, 272
DigiTech, 114
Dixon, Willie, xiv, 7
DJ, xvii, 13, 18, 20–21, 265–267
Doobie Brothers, 10, 122
double, 40, 46, 48, 50, 65–66, 130, 136, 223, 272
downbeat, 54–55, 80, 105, 109, 120, 124–125, 150, 208, 210, 272
Dozier, Lamont, 9
Dr. Dre, 5, 12, 202
Dr. Luke, 200
Dresel, Bernie, 108
Drifters, 8
Drum Doctor, 117
drummers, 83, 107–108, 116, 120–121
dub fee, 53
Dunbar, Sly, 238
Dylan, Bob, 8
dynamics, 61–64, 66–67, 73–78, 83, 93, 174, 189–190, 192, 200–201, 207–208, 272, 274

Eagles, 60, 70, 81
Earle, Steve, 11
Echoplex, 114
EDM, 13, 197–199, 201, 203, 268

Electro-Harmonix, 114
electronic dance music, 12–13, 67
engineer, xiii, xvi–xvii, xix–xx, 16–18, 20, 22, 29, 31, 45–51, 83, 95–96, 101–102, 105–106, 117–118, 136–137, 143, 147, 149, 153–154, 167–168, 173–176, 178, 182, 184–188, 190–191, 195, 197–198, 206, 208, 217–219, 221, 224, 228, 234, 240, 243–244, 248–249, 251, 254–255, 259–260, 263, 272
Eno, Brian, 12, 132–133
Epiphone, 112
Epworth, Paul, 19
EQ, xx, 174, 182, 185–186, 190

Faccone, Benny, 171
Feiten, Buzz, 85
Feldman, Richard, xvi, 235–241
Fender, 65, 70, 109–110, 112–115, 136, 211, 274
Fender Precision Bass, 114
Ferry, Bryan, 11
fiddle, 7, 12, 67–68, 223, 244
fills, 62, 64–68, 72, 189
Fitzgerald, Ella, 6
Fitzpatrick, Frank, 151
flanging, 169, 272
fund, 35–36, 46, 54–56, 260
Foo Fighters, 61, 68, 107
Four Tops, 9, 80
Frankie Goes to Hollywood, 11
Franklin, Aretha, 8
frequency range, 71–72, 168
Funk Brothers, 9

Gabler, Milt, 6
Gamble, Kenny, 10
Garfield, Ross, 107
Gaye, Marvin, 9, 172
getting paid, 40, 42, 46, 205
Getz, Stan, 8
Gibson, 112, 114
gig, 26, 41, 55, 108, 119, 144, 197, 265, 267
Gill, Vince, 11
Green Day, 172
groove, 12, 76–83, 90, 93, 120, 122–123, 126, 141, 150–151, 171–172, 201, 209–210, 213, 239, 272, 274

Guess Who, 61
Guetta, David, 5, 13
guide vocal, 96, 104, 123, 272
guitar, xiv, xix, 8, 12, 27, 29–30, 46, 60–66, 68–71, 76, 80–81, 84–85, 87–88, 101, 104, 109, 112–113, 119–120, 129–130, 133, 136, 139, 150, 152, 161, 163, 171–172, 175, 180, 208, 211, 213, 222–223, 236, 247, 266, 268, 272, 274

Hammond, 50, 65, 96, 109, 115, 124, 237
Hampton, Lionel, 6
Hancock, Herbie, 8
harmony, 16, 32, 63, 68, 130, 136, 152–153
harp, 53
headphone mix, 118, 146, 148, 212, 222, 272
heads, 116, 118–119, 209
Hear Technologies, iv, 119
Heptones, 10
hi-hat, 63–64, 104
Hill, Faith, 12, 60
hip-hop, 12, 153, 172, 176, 197, 199, 201, 203
Hiwatt, 113
Hofner, 114
Hohner, 115
Holland-Dozier-Holland, 5, 9
Holland, Brian, 9
Holland, Eddie, 9
home studio, xviii, 44–46, 49, 55, 91, 95, 97–98, 161, 163, 183, 220, 231
horn, xix, 29, 46, 49, 54–55, 60, 84–85, 96, 109, 121, 125, 129, 133
Horn, Trevor, 11, 259
Hubbard, Freddie, 8
Huff, Dann, 5, 12
Huff, Leon, 10
humbucker, 70, 112, 272
humbucking, 112, 272
hypercompression, 174, 188–190, 272

Impulse Records, 8
in the box, 30, 98, 176, 178, 232–233, 249, 262, 268
intermittent, 272
intonation, 84, 209, 272

iso booth, 272
ISRC code, 272
iTunes, xiv, xx, 37, 193–196, 273

Jackson, Janet, 11
Jacksons, 10
Jam and Lewis, 11
Jam, Jimmy, 11
Jamerson, James, 80
jingle, 26, 53, 55, 155, 272
Johns, Glyn, 20
Jones, Gareth, xvi, 243–250
Jones, Quincy, 5, 10, 19, 151

keyboard, 27, 29–30, 46, 49, 53, 62, 81,
    101, 104, 109, 115, 125, 129–130,
    180, 213, 220, 266, 269, 273
Kiss, 60, 153
Kravitz, Lenny, 61, 70
Kudu Records, 8

LaBelle, Patti, 10
Laine, Frankie, 7
leader, xv, 16, 46, 48–50, 53–54,
    143–144
leakage, 104, 119–120, 122–124, 164,
    169, 272
Led Zeppelin, 8, 81
Lee, Soo-Man, 200
Leslie, 115, 237, 272
Lewis, Jerry Lee, 4, 7
Lewis, Terry, 11
limiter, 173–174, 188, 192, 273
limiting, 165, 188, 192, 272
lockout, 105–106, 272
look ahead limiter, 173, 273
loop, 20, 199, 202
Los Angeles, xiii, xvii, 55, 107, 222,
    257, 260
lossy compression, 188, 272
Loveless, Patty, 11
Lovett, Lyle, 11
Ludwig, 109, 116, 198
Lynyrd Skynyrd, 60, 82

Macero, Teo, 9
manager, 4, 16, 21, 47, 56, 100, 185, 234
Mars, Bruno, 60, 66
Marshall, 70, 109, 113, 136, 211
Martha and the Vandellas, 9

Martin, George, 4–5, 9, 17, 34, 218
Martin, Max, 5, 13, 17, 200
master, xix, 25, 46, 52, 137, 173–175,
    182, 184–186, 190–192, 195–197,
    200, 213–214, 236, 240–241, 259,
    270, 273
mastering, xviii–xx, 16, 27–28, 30, 44,
    46–47, 49–50, 173–175, 181–191,
    193–195, 197–199, 206, 214, 224–
    225, 234, 241, 249, 255, 262–263,
    272–273
Mathis, Johnny, 7
Mavericks, 11
McBride, Martina, 12
McEntire, Reba, xvi, 11, 123, 217, 220,
    224
McLaren, Malcolm, 11
Meek, Joe, 4, 8
Mellotron, 109, 111, 115, 273
Melrose, Lester, 3, 6
Metallica, 12, 189
metronome, 120, 122, 271
Michael, George, 8
microphone, xvii, 30, 47, 101, 134, 164,
    210
mics, xiii, 102, 105, 117, 120–121, 134,
    163, 169, 209
Miller, Mitch, 7
Mingus, Charles, 8
Minimoog, 109, 115
mix, xx, 30, 46, 49–50, 63, 67–68, 84,
    98, 118–121, 135–136, 146, 148,
    150, 165, 167–180, 184–188,
    191–192, 198–199, 202–203, 209,
    211–214, 222, 224, 232–234, 240–
    241, 249, 252, 255, 259, 262–263,
    267–272, 274
Moby, 5, 12
motion, 65–67
Motown, 5, 9, 80, 159–160, 199, 201
Musitronics, 114
MXR, 114
MP3, 70, 186, 188, 191–194, 253,
    272–273
MTV, 273
Muddy Waters, 7
multiband compression, 192, 273
Murvin, Junior, 10
Music 1.0, 273
Music 1.5, 273

Music 2.0, 273
Music 2.5, 273
Music 3.0, 273
Music 3.5, 273
Music 4.0, xvi, 23, 36, 235, 273
Music Man StingRay, 114

Nashville, xiii, 7, 54–55, 107, 217–218,
     222–223, 232
native resolution, 97, 273
Neve, 30, 47

O'Jays, 10
Octavia, 114
organ,   63–66, 96, 124, 237, 267, 272
out of phase,175, 273
outboard gear, 30, 105, 117, 178, 209,
     219, 273
outro, 60–62, 66, 68, 74, 82, 273
overdub, xiii, 17, 27–29, 31, 40, 42,
     45–51, 84, 91–93, 96, 98, 101,
     103–104, 106, 123–124, 129–131,
     133–136, 141, 149, 160, 163–164,
     211, 222–223, 228, 231, 236, 239,
     241, 248–249, 273
Oblique Strategies, 12, 132–133

P2P, 273
pad, 60, 65–68, 89, 273
Page, Patti, 7
panning, xx, 165, 169, 274
passion, xiv, 149, 151, 171, 212, 219
Paul Ill, xviii, 144
Paul, Billy, 10
Paul, Les, 70, 109, 112, 136, 211
pay scale, 52, 274
pedals, 109, 114, 116
Peer, Ralph, 3, 6
percussion, 27–29, 46, 66, 125, 133,
     172, 202, 237, 269
Perry, Katy, 13, 61
Perry, Lee "Scratch," 10
Perry, Linda, 17
Pet Shop Boys, 11
Petty, Tom, 12, 17, 107
Phillips, Sam, 4, 7
piano, 62, 64–67, 84, 98, 115, 150, 220,
     222, 266, 272
Pickett, Wilson, 8
pickups, 112, 272

piracy, 273
pitch, 114, 139, 149–151, 153, 212,
     240, 271
Plati, Mark, xvii, 251–255
plug-ins, 97, 117, 170, 174, 182, 198,
     223, 269, 271
pocket, 79–81, 83, 93, 147, 149–151,
     210, 212, 274
points, 34–35, 41, 50, 140, 145, 171,
     206, 214, 218–219, 261, 274
Police, The, 20, 80–81
power chords, 68, 70, 274
preamp, 30, 134, 136, 211, 223
prechorus, 62–63, 75, 274
preproduction, 26–29, 45, 64, 86–93,
     103, 207, 220, 228, 231, 238, 244,
     246–247, 253, 261, 274
Presley, Elvis, 4, 7
record stores, 11, 266
Red Hot Chili Peppers, 12, 17, 107,
     258
rehearsal, 26–27, 29, 46–47, 49–50, 78,
     86, 89–90, 92–93, 99, 144, 208,
     220, 228, 231, 245–246, 253, 274
Pro Tools, 97, 102, 140, 219, 237, 240
publisher, xvi, 47, 235, 273
punchy, 117, 274

R&B, 11, 101, 176, 178, 184, 200
Raitt, Bonnie, xvi, 235
Rascal Flatts, xvi, 12, 67–68, 217
Rawls, Lou, 10
Ray, Aaron, 199
rentals, 28, 30, 48, 50–51, 107, 206
reverb, xx, 8, 30, 84, 113, 120, 144, 148,
     165, 169–171, 175, 212–213, 224,
     269, 273
Rhodes, 65, 115
rhythm guitar, 63–65, 68–69, 71, 76,
     80, 129, 150, 172
rhythm section, 6, 10, 65, 71, 80–81,
     101, 103, 163, 199, 210, 213, 228,
     238–239, 271
Rickenbacker, 70, 112, 114
Rizzo, Carmen, xvi, 257–263
Robbins, Marty, 7
Rogers, Jimmy, 7
Romeo, Max, 10
Ronson, Mark, 60
royalty, 34, 36–38, 219–220, 246

royalties, 4, 33, 35, 39, 41, 246, 253, 270–272
Rubin, Rick, 11–12, 17, 107
rushed fill, 274

scratch vocal, 104, 119, 123–124, 272, 274
Seabrook, John, 200
Seal, xvi, 11, 257, 263
Seay, Ed, 149
sequencing, 9, 186–187, 214, 274
set up, 55, 90, 105, 178, 223–224, 244, 272
Sherwood, Adrian, 10
Shure, 134
signal chain, 117
Simple Minds, 11
Sinatra, Frank, 7
singers, 27, 46, 48–49, 51, 54, 93, 96, 118, 124, 148, 151–152, 211–212, 222, 239, 255, 262
singing, 77, 81, 104, 123, 136, 146–153, 161, 211, 220–221, 260
speaker cabinet, xix, 272
spec, xiv, 41–42, 44, 205, 274
Spector, Phil, 4–5, 8, 13, 19
spread, 119, 182, 186, 191, 274
Springfield, Dusty, 8
Springsteen, Bruce, 20, 107
standard session procedure, 139
Stock-Aitken-Waterman, 11
Stock, Mike, 11
StoneBridge, xvii, 265–270
Strait, George, 11
Stratocaster, 112
strings, xix, 10, 29, 70, 125, 129, 133, 163
Strobotuner, 84–85
single coil, 70, 272, 274
sitar, 112
snare, 61, 66, 80, 82, 106, 108–109, 116–117, 119, 140, 150, 203, 247, 274
snare strainers, 274
solos, 27, 29, 60, 129
songs, 4, 9, 15, 26–27, 29–30, 37, 39–43, 46, 59–62, 64, 66, 68–69, 75, 80, 82, 87–89, 91–93, 98, 103, 108, 127, 153, 159–160, 171, 173, 175, 178, 181–182, 184–187, 190–191, 193–195, 199–201, 205–207, 213–214, 217–218, 223, 225, 228, 230, 232, 236, 245, 254, 261, 266, 268–269, 273–274
songwriter, xvii, 8, 16, 19, 22, 25, 31–32, 39, 60, 62, 64–65, 157, 160, 197, 200–201, 218–219, 223–224, 251, 265, 273
Sony, 121, 241
studio musician, xviii, 16, 31, 44, 109, 125, 160
Sunnyland Slim, 7
Supraphonic, 116
Supremes, The, 9, 80
sweetening, 103
sympathetic vibrations, 117, 209, 274

Talking Heads, 12
Talmy, Shel, 8–9
tambourine, 64–65
Telecaster, 112
Templeman, Ted, 5, 10
tempo, 76–77, 82–84, 90, 93, 120, 122, 201, 210–211, 238, 253, 271, 274
Temptations, 9, 80
texture, 7, 169, 200, 224
toms, 117
Townshend, Pete, xvii, 257
tuner, 84–86, 117, 209–210
tuning, 84–85, 107–108, 116–117, 124, 135–136, 221, 272
TV mix, 180, 213, 224, 274

U2, 12, 60, 79, 132, 164
Underwood, Carrie, xvi, 123, 217, 219–220, 223
Uni-Vibe, 115
union, 16, 46, 48, 51–55, 222, 271, 274
union date, 53, 271, 274
Univox, 115
Urban, Keith, 12
Usher, 11, 13

Van Halen, 10
Vaughn, Stevie Ray, 60
vibe, 99, 104, 106, 122, 143, 209, 238, 268, 274
video, xviii, xx, 53, 97, 109, 185, 272–273
vintage gear, viii, 109–110

vinyl, 44, 88, 173, 175, 182, 185–188,
    191, 194, 198, 206, 266, 272–274
violin, 222–223
vocals, xiii–xx, 7, 12, 27–29, 46, 60,
    63–68, 71, 75, 81, 89, 93, 129–130,
    133–134, 136, 139–140, 149, 151–
    153, 164, 179–180, 211, 221–222,
    245, 255, 261, 266, 269, 274
voicing, 70, 274
voicings, 70
Vox, 70, 113–115

Waterman, Pete, 11, 201
Wexler, Jerry, 8
Williams, Pharrell, 19, 66
Winehouse, Amy, 172
word length, 274
Wurlitzer, 115
Wynonna, 11
Yearwood, Trisha, 11
Yes, 11, 107

ZZ Top, 61